Toward the Multicultural University

Toward the Multicultural University

Edited by Benjamin P. Bowser, Terry Jones, and Gale Auletta Young

Foreword by Charles V. Willie

 PRAEGER

Westport, Connecticut
London

Library of Congress Cataloging-in-Publication Data

Toward the multicultural university / edited by Benjamin P. Bowser,
    Terry Jones, and Gale Auletta Young ; foreword by Charles V. Willie.
        p.   cm.
    Includes bibliographical references and index.
    ISBN 0–275–94767–X (alk. paper)
        1. Multicultural education—United States.   2. Education, Higher—
    United States—Curricula.   3. Education, Higher—United States—
    Aims and objectives.   I. Bowser, Benjamin P.   II. Jones, Terry.
    III. Young, Gale Auletta.
    LC1099.3.T68   1995
    370.19′6—dc20   94–25046

British Library Cataloguing in Publication Data is available.

Library of Congress Catalog Card Number: 94–25046
ISBN: 0–275–94767–X

First published in 1995

Praeger Publishers, 88 Post Road West, Westport, CT 06881
An imprint of Greenwood Publishing Group, Inc.

Printed in the United States of America

∞™

The paper used in this book complies with the
Permanent Paper Standard issued by the National
Information Standards Organization (Z39.48–1984).

10 9 8 7 6 5 4 3 2 1

To those whose spirit calls for a new education in
the twenty-first century—W.E.B. Du Bois, Paul Lazarsfeld,
C.L.R. James, Leonard Reissman, and John G. Jackson—
and to all of those who are struggling
to turn a vision into a reality.

Contents

Tables and Figures   xi

Foreword   xiii
   Charles V. Willie

Introduction   xv
   Benjamin P. Bowser

Part One: The Challenge

1. Demographic Imperatives for the Future   3
   Harold L. Hodgkinson

2. The Triumphs of Tribalism: The Modern American University
   as a Reflection of Eurocentric Culture   21
   William M. King

3. Afrocentricity and Multicultural Education: Concept, Challenge,
   and Contribution   41
   Maulana Karenga

Part Two: America's Other Cultures

4. America's Racial-Ethnic Cultures: Opposition within a
   Mythical Melting Pot   65
   Bonnie L. Mitchell and Joe R. Feagin

5. Puerto Rican and Latino(a) Vistas on Culture and Education   87
   Milga Morales-Nadal

6. American Indians (The Minority of Minorities) and
    Higher Education   103
    Donald L. Fixico

Part Three: Proposals and Implementation

7. Toward a Multicultural University:
    Using Strategic Planning for Change   125
    Benjamin P. Bowser and Octave Baker

8. Academic Grading and Assessment in a Culturally
    Diverse University   135
    Etta R. Hollins

9. Using Computers and Telecommunications to Advance
    Multicultural Education   145
    Arthur E. Paris

10. The Organization of a Multicultural University   153
    Benjamin P. Bowser

11. Beyond Disciplinary Borders: Creating a Genuine
    Multicultural Curriculum   161
    Terry Jones and Gale Auletta Young

    Conclusion: Toward the Multicultural University   179

    *Benjamin P. Bowser, Terry Jones,
    and Gale Auletta Young*

    Index   187

    About the Contributors   193

Tables and Figures

TABLES

1.1	Countries Ranked by Population Size: 1950, 1987, 2025, 2050	5
1.2	Rank Order of Increasing High School Dropouts by State in 1987 with Change in Potential High School Graduates, 1990–2000	12

FIGURES

10.1	Traditional Organization with Ethnic Studies	153
10.2	Integration of Traditional and Ethnic Studies	154
10.3	Interdisciplinary Competency Levels	155
10.4	Integrated Model with Domestic and Foreign Community Experiences	156
10.5	Interdisciplinary Competency Levels with Domestic and Foreign Community Experiences	156
10.6	Combination of Interdisciplinary Competency Levels with Integrated Departments and Community Experiences	157
10.7	Intersection of Academic, Student, and Community Life	159
10.8	Realignment of Academic, Student, and Community Life	159
11.1	Four Models of Teaching Ethnic Studies	164
11.2	Teaching by Using Event/Phenomenon	166
11.3	Teaching by Using Great Problem/Theme	168

Foreword

Charles V. Willie

This book on the inclusive university is a rich resource on multiculturalism. It presents an interesting perspective on the past, explains the present, and forecasts the future. With a plentiful supply of concrete illustrations, several chapters in this book also include good social and educational theory.

We are told by William King that Harvard College, one of the oldest universities in the United States, adopted the curriculum of Emmanuel College in Cambridge, England when it was founded. Thus began the British-European foundation of American education. Harold Hodgkinson, however, predicts that this influence is waning due, in part, to demographic changes. For example, the population of the developed world is less than one quarter of all people; moreover, less than one fifth of the world's population is white. All of this means that the influences of Western culture and Anglo-Saxon traditions are not what they used to be.

Oppositional cultures (a term coined by Bonnie Mitchell and Joe Feagin) are emerging. Maulana Karenga, Milga Morales-Nadal, and Donald Fixico illustrate these oppositional cultures as they exist among African Americans, Puerto Ricans, and some Native Americans.

Karenga reminds us that human diversity is human richness and that the United States gains when it integrates into its culture Afrocentric wisdom. It gains because such wisdom includes the notion of the centrality of community and ethical concerns. These are antidotes against our excess tendencies toward individuality and compartmentalization.

Morales-Nadal informs us that there is an abiding belief in the personal (as distinct from the individual) among Puerto Ricans and that they and other Latinos emphasize collaborative work. Obviously, such ideas are of value in a nation where relationships in urban settings are becoming more and more impersonal and in which people, although densely packed in, travel in a lonely crowd and feel isolated, unconnected, and estranged. The Latino way of life, according to Morales-Nadal, adds a vibrant oral tradition, too, that complements the written paper-trail customs of a nation that tends to remember the past almost exclusively in writing. Through such contributions, Latino customs could transform schooling and change our culture.

A balance within oneself is what Native Americans seek, according to Donald Fixico's assessment. When things are kept in perspective, Native Americans achieve a steady calmness. Fixico reports that this steady calmness is a way of maintaining balance with nature and between self and society. How to be still and achieve calmness is a wonderful lesson for all to learn in these jazzed-up, fast-tracked United States. Extended families, the oral tradition, and circular thinking are additional contributions of Native Americans. These things from Native American traditions could benefit all of us.

Benjamin Bowser and Octave Baker believe that the university ought to provide a culturally more inclusive education to all students at all levels and that individuals should be immersed in learning experiences from multiple cultures simultaneously. Karenga justifies that action by asserting that multicultural education and quality education are linked, and you cannot have one without the other. Mitchell and Feagin justify multicultural learning on the basis of self-interest: The more one recognizes the views and values of others, the better one understands one's own attitudes and actions.

A unique feature of this collection is its final part (Part Three), which suggests how we get from the idea of a multicultural education to the reality by transforming the organization of the university and its strategies of teaching and learning.

The testimonies of the scholars who have contributed to this book are substantive, significant, and sound. They point toward a basic function of education: to help the individual transcend the entrapment of personal experience. While experiential learning is a valid source of knowledge, all individuals should always be aware of the possibility of alternative courses of actions. Multicultural education achieves this goal. It demonstrates the idea of transcendency, that there may be a different way of adapting, that there may be another method of problem solving, that what happened probably did not have to happen the way that it did. Multicultural education protects us against deterministic ideologies and their focus on single causes and explanations.

Thus, I conclude that multicultural education is good for you. Multicultural education will not harm you. Multicultural education may save your soul.

Introduction

Benjamin P. Bowser

Imagine a middle-aged and middle-class white male professor teaching a required humanities or social science course. The syllabus consists of readings from or about the great thinkers associated with the definitive movements and developments in European and American history, arts, literature, and sciences. Imagine also that the students in class range in age and have had some life experiences beyond high school. White students are a minority, and the majority of students have historical and cultural roots outside of Europe in Mexico, Puerto Rico, China, Japan, Africa, and Native Indian nations. Standard English is either a second dialect, even for the White students, or a second language entirely. Women are a majority in the classroom. The students range widely in their academic preparation, seem difficult to motivate, and are indifferent to the course content. One day some unexpected questions begin to be asked: "What is the point? Who cares what these rich white men did? Are their ideas responsible for what happened to my people? Isn't this European American (white) studies? Have any women or people outside of Europe contributed anything of significance in the modern world?"

How shall faculty respond to such questions and concerns? They can ignore these questions and just continue. They can encourage the students to stick to the curriculum. After all, what they are teaching is necessary to complete the course and to graduate. They can suggest that what they teach will assist students in rising above their racial or national prejudices. They can also suggest that students go over to the black, women's, Asian, Puerto Rican, or ethnic studies program to have their questions answered. There is another choice. Faculty can learn enough about the cultures, peoples, achievements, histories, and interactions that their students' cultural and historic nationalities have had with one another and Europe to answer their students' questions. In doing so, faculty might find the keys to motivate all of these students and to excite them about learning. The questions are from nontraditional students who, if encouraged, will ask such nontraditional questions.

Questions that reflect indifference to the traditional curriculum and note its almost exclusive focus on Europeans and European Americans are not to be dismissed as deviant, prejudiced, or irrelevant. Nontraditional students can quickly point out the limits and, indeed, the central cultural biases in not only their courses but in the entire curriculum of most colleges and universities in the United States. What they are reacting to is the Eurocentric cultural and social class biases of the curriculum. The achievements, arts, history, literature, and experiences of Europeans and European Americans are the central concerns, are celebrated, are defended, and are considered to be essential knowledge for any truly educated person (Bloom 1987). The existence, experiences, and scholarly contributions of others, including European women, are add-ons and after-thoughts in mainline survey courses or electives outside of core requirements. One or two courses might even be required from so-called periphery studies in order to teach traditional students to check their prejudices or to give non-European and female students some place to go. Alternatively, one might assert that there is sufficient multicultural information in the social sciences (Etzioni 1991).

This book is about the growing need for a more inclusive curriculum and university. There are several assumptions that unify all of the chapters. First, despite the massive scale and diversity of American higher education, there is a fairly standard core curriculum, and that curriculum is decisively Eurocentric— it is exclusively concerned with, focused on, and defensive of the arts, literature, sciences, and achievements of Europeans and descendants of Europeans. Second, an exclusively Eurocentric core curriculum does not provide the mix of skills, experiences and knowledge an educated person will need to succeed in the world community in the next century (Gates 1992; Hawkins and Belle 1985). This is not to say that there is something inherently wrong with studying the experiences and achievements of Europeans and European Americans. The problem is that such study is a primary, exclusive, and more valued focus. In fact, any centric curriculum that focuses almost exclusively on the character, achievements, and experiences of any one culture or peoples is a limiting and dysfunctional education in a diverse world community.

The third assumption of this book is that the optimal university and college curriculum that will best prepare educated Americans and world citizens will have to be multicultural, with not only an international focus but a domestic, multicultural focus as well. This is not the celebration of the foods, holidays, and artistic expressions of non-Europeans in and outside of the United States. Multiculturalism with substance requires experiencing and studying cultural groups and people who live in circumstances different from one's own. It is possible that knowledge and appreciation of human progress and achievements may also be derived from the study of other people's customs, literatures, histories, and institutions. To be educated in the liberal arts in the next century will mean having to encounter the human spirit across cultural and historic experiences.

Fourth, the North American university as an institution is both historic and cultural and is shaped in the long run by societal demands (Handlin and Handlin 1970). It is one of the few institutions in American life whose purpose is to bridge the historic with the present and to prepare new and continuing students for the future. Rapid changes in both the United States and the international community can best be responded to by an evolutionary transformation of the North American university from an Eurocentric institution to one that is multicultural. African American, women's, and all other ethnic studies programs and departments on the periphery of the university must become part of the core. Finally, the university as an institution is not only Eurocentric in its core curriculum, it is Eurocentric in organization and in its preferred modes of instruction (Banks 1991). There is a need to rethink and update how students are taught. There may be a wider base of pedagogy across national co-cultures and international cultures from which we might better teach students.

This introduction will point out why the present is such a decisive time for starting on the road toward a multicultural university. The underlying social change that makes a cultural transition in education necessary will be discussed. Then the Eurocentric focus in the curriculum and in teaching and what multicultural education means will be outlined. Finally, the organization and chapters of this book will be presented.

TIME FOR DECISION

A lot more is at stake in the debate over multiculturalism than the extent to which university and college curricula will favor the knowledge of European Americans over all other human knowledge. Higher education, more so than any other domestic institution, is the United States' major national asset. The economic and technical leadership that this nation has enjoyed since the end of the Second World War could not have been possible without a broad and large-scale university community (Meyer 1967). The future of this great achievement and essential institution for national prominence is now on the line.

Decisions that are shaping the future of higher education in the United States are being made now indirectly through how budgets are cut and spent. The long-term prospect of slow economic growth has highlighted the extent to which universities and colleges are creations of the nation's past prosperity. During decades of rapid economic growth, higher education expanded. The states generously funded community and state colleges and universities. There were generous donations and dynamic investment markets for private college and university endowments. Higher education was not a trade-off for highway repairs, welfare, health care, or more prisons. Now state and federal agencies are making decisions about higher education's priority in relation to other state and federal responsibilities.

The choices fall into three categories. The first option is to maintain a steady state. This option assumes that the nation has reached its optimum in higher education under current economic conditions. College and university administrations should not demand any greater share of clearly limited and shrinking national and state revenues. Any improvements, reforms, or expansion of opportunities will simply have to wait until the nation's economic conditions improve or be passed on to students in progressively higher fees. In this first option, higher education is viewed primarily as another expensive function of government and private philanthropy. This is the pragmatic systems maintenance approach to higher education.

The second option calls for selective reform and limited expansion as opposed to the pragmatic systems maintenance view. The nation cannot afford to forgo continuous educational reform and expansion if it expects to continue enjoying high economic and political status in the world community. The nation should call on higher education during recessions and depressions and should do so for the same reasons that it invests in new economic activities during economic downturns—to stimulate new economic growth. If the economy were simply maintained at a steady state during recessions or depressions, economic recovery would be slow and might not happen. In the same way, higher education is a continuous and long-term investment in the size and quality of the nation's leadership and work force.

The final perspective views our extensive system of higher education as either a luxury that we can no longer afford or as a failed experiment. The system should be cut back to its essential functions. Those who hold this view have faith that anyone who wants to will still be able to get a good education in a system cut to its essentials. Both students and faculty will have to forgo the luxuries that they have grown accustomed to. For those who see higher education as a failed experiment, a smaller, leaner, and higher quality system would save the day. The nation's leadership can still be produced in this system. The nation's employers can do a better and more realistic job of training the segment of the nation's work force that does not go on to college.

Regardless of which option is taken, decision makers are correct about one thing. The current system of higher education cannot be maintained as it is. Change is needed not because the money is no longer there, but rather because American colleges and universities sit in a sea of social change. The kind of postindustrial change that the nation faces suggests that Americans are going to need more—not less—education and that education is going to have to be much better and decisively multicultural. In this sense, the current system is not optimal, nor is it all that the nation is capable of producing. Neither are the nation's colleges and universities failed experiments. They are incomplete experiments. What are some of the changes the university will be confronted with that demand a multicultural response?

THE BASIS OF CHANGE

As agriculture became a secondary economic activity in the nineteenth century, highly centralized manufacturing and mass production have become secondary in the latter half of this century (Glaab and Brown 1976). An information economy is emerging, and its products are revolutionizing work and management in the older sectors of the economy-manufacturing and agriculture (Bluestone and Harrison 1982). A related aspect of postindustrialization is successive waves of technical innovations that have reduced physical and space barriers. Examples of some of these changes are now apparent.

1. This nation's culture and economy have expanded beyond its national boundaries. Contact, cooperation, exchange, and competition with other peoples and cultures are now a fact of life and will increase (Baldwin 1987; U.S. Senate 1989). It can no longer be assumed that foreign partners and competitors should and must learn our language and culture in order to prosper. Nor can we continue to ignore their languages and cultures and expect to remain prosperous.

2. New social identities are making the traditional social class, ethnic, racial, and gender divisions more varied and complex. For example, there are now important variations in generation, sexual preference, lifestyle, and political orientation that cut across the older social identities (Lyttkens 1989; Toffler 1981; Touraine 1971). In the emerging postindustrial society, the standardization of ideas, cars, clothes, news, and information is no longer necessary or effective. Innovations in both technology and organization make large numbers of smaller specialty markets not only possible but profitable (Padmanabhan 1987). These developments will play a strong role in both reinforcing historic co-cultures in the United States and bringing people from many different backgrounds into closer contact with one another.

3. Advances and diffusion of computers, information storage, and communications technologies make the centralization of knowledge, management, and other functions obsolete (Dede 1992). Electronic information highways are now a reality. Large libraries of paper-bound books and journals are now the least efficient way to store and disseminate information. Computer tutorials and expert videos can convey more effectively than lectures of routine and repetitive information in most fields. This means that the dissemination of computer-based translations of information to and from many different languages and dialects will be possible. It is now possible to learn languages more easily tham ever before.

4. In the past industrial society, one's work hardly changed over a generation and it was repetitive. Now regardless of whether people are laborers, managers, or professionals, they will change work several times in their career and retraining will have to be continuous (Cook 1983; Toffler 1981). Emphasis may shift from having a high degree of specialization to an ability to synthesize large amounts of information. Effective and efficient training and retraining will be necessary across social class, historic nationalities, and racial co-cultures (Harold Hodgkinson discusses why this will be necessary in the next chapter).

A proactive response to these major changes and new demands will require a top-to-bottom review and rethinking of the role, mission, organization, and curriculum of American higher education. Even if the university, as we know it, is allowed to decline in size by default, whatever remains will have to undergo extensive change. The only question now is whether that change will be evolutionary over time or will be thrust on the university by external forces and demands after a long period of denial and resistance. Proactively changing the university is not a problem solved by a quick fix or by continued short term thinking.

What are the major barriers to proactive social change and seeing the cultural challenge before the university as an opportunity rather than a threat? More than lack of money, the primary barrier is the belief among many European Americans that the only way one can be educated is through a Eurocentric curriculum. In the face of irreversible social change, many faculty in the more traditional cultural disciplines are becoming islands of defense of the old ways. The result is that many academic departments and college and university administrations are becoming increasingly out of touch with the nation's population and changes in the world community. What is the Eurocentric basis of resistance to change?

THE EUROCENTRIC UNIVERSITY

The Eurocentric focus in curriculum and teaching is based on several assumptions. First, Europe and Europeans (including European Americans) are at the center of modern world history (Clarke 1970; Diop 1974). Second, Europe and Europeans are supposed to be at the center of modern world history because of the superiority of their traditions of government, commerce, and sciences (Van Sertima 1989). Third, what was done to achieve the centrality of the European experience is clearly justified because what was achieved is now available to improve everyone's life (Richards 1980). Finally, the achievements and roles of other people are worth study, but they are not as important or as decisive to the freedoms, privileges, and high standard of material comfort that we now enjoy as the outcomes of European achievements.

A closer look at each of these assumptions reveals a complex mix of valid fact, social class bias, ethnocentrism, self-congratulation, and historic national pride. It is accurate for Americans and Europeans to see themselves as central players on the modern world stage. This is fact. The capabilities and decisions of European American, Western European, and Japanese economic interests will undoubtedly define the shape and character of the world community into the next century.

But the assumption that Europeans and by extension European Americans are supposed to play such a decisive role because of what Europeans accomplished lingers on from colonial beliefs—that European political and business elites are supposed to make world decisions and hold power. It is also based on a selective view of European and American history. The presumption is that culture, science, technology, democracy, and commerce were somehow invented and advanced solely in Europe and the United States (James 1954). This is nonsense. Very little that Europeans and Americans now claim as their own prior to colonialism and slavery was not initially borrowed, influenced, and shaped by cultural and commercial exchanges with Arabs, Africans, Asians, and

American Indians (Bernal 1987; Clegg 1976; Johansen and Grinde 1990). Even after Europeans claimed science, technology, the arts, and humanities as their own, these bodies of knowledge continued to be influenced by non-European contributors.

The least defendable aspect of Eurocentrists' assumptions about their role in history is that ultimately what Europeans claim to achieve is justified by the material advancements. What Europe achieved came at a very heavy price to every culture and people on earth, including European peasants. From the fifteenth century on, European leaders found themselves in a unique historic position to exploit the conflicts among nations outside of Europe, to use science and technology for military purposes, and to view the rest of the world as their colonies. The result is that today the natural resources of many Third World nations have been plundered, entire nations and indigenous cultures have been wiped out, and vast populations have been dislocated. The destruction of indigenous customs and economies has destroyed the capability of many indigenous peoples to be self-sufficient. Large proportions of the world's population are now totally dependent on the Western world economic system and are only potential markets of laborers and consumers. World poverty is one of the major outcomes of European colonization (Wallerstein 1980, 1989) and continuing economic dominance.

The final consequence of the Eurocentric focus is the presumption that other people and their histories and nations are not as important. By default, the drama of human progress has been acted out only among Europeans. When other people's experiences and contributions are made secondary, one's own experiences are elevated to a higher humanity to which all others should aspire. In fact, intellectual colonialism leaves no choice. There is only one model to aspire to. What Europeans and white Americans have done becomes a paradigm for future progress even when a very different mix of actions and capabilities may be called for, even among Europeans.

An exclusive Eurocentric focus in knowledge and teaching in the academy preserves and advances all of these assumptions of European superiority. In this case, an educated man or woman is one who has been Eurocentrically trained. The classics are then the historic writings of European and European American thinkers and famous individuals. Preserving the Eurocentric focus of education becomes essential to maintaining the European American character, identity, and dominance of the United States. So instead of being a force of creativity and enlightenment, Eurocentric dominance and monopoly of higher education stands in the way of the nation's continued and long range economic and social progress. But more importantly, it stands in the way of finally recognizing what this nation has been from the beginning—multinational, multicultural, and multiracial (Takaki 1990).

THE MULTICULTURAL UNIVERSITY

To be educated in the next century will necessarily mean encountering the humanity of other people in both domestic and international cultures. This will involve much more than taking one or two "periphery studies" courses. It will require being knowledgeable of other cultures, struggles, achievements, aspirations, and ways of thinking. A truly multicultural education is not European Americans studying Europe or African Americans studying Africa and so on. The ideal is to study in depth one's own culture, literature, and history as well as at least two others—one domestic and one international. It is possible to have a university in which no single historic group dominates the core experience. Under these circumstances, the university may become a much more dynamic and potentially unifying institution.

On a planet where people of different social classes, races, and cultures are interdependent and linked, there is no longer any room for a superior race and culture. Eurocentric dominance of the university and college curriculum is simply another factor contributing to the current level of contempt and ignorance of races and cultures toward one another in the United States. A new central and multicultural ideal is needed to define the university.

ABOUT THIS BOOK

This book was inspired by two national conferences held in 1989 and 1991. Both were sponsored by the Center for the Study of Intercultural Relations and the Extension Division at California State University at Hayward. At each conference a highly diverse group of faculty, students, and administrators met. Those who attended and presented were from private and public institutions representing a broad range of missions, histories and student selectivity. Some who attended the conferences had recognized the cultural limits of the curriculum in their disciplines. Others were from diverse cultural backgrounds and had direct experience with well-intending colleagues and students who felt that they had no compelling reason to see the world beyond white middle-class America. Still others had been charged with the task of introducing multicultural awareness and sensitivity into their campus faculty development efforts.

Whatever the conference participants' race, social class origins, or academic discipline, they all had similar stories to tell of bewilderment, weariness, confusion, and fearful resistance on the part of many faculty and administrations. They noted that many faculty are intellectually, emotionally, and personally unprepared to understand the world outside of their own narrow social class and European cultural framework. This includes scholars in the social and behavioral sciences, who are charged with studying and understanding group and cultural processes.

There were four consistent themes in the conference participants' presentations and discussions. First, demographic and economic changes in the nation and world community clearly point toward a multicultural future. It is inescapable. The vast social and economic changes that the nation is undergoing will leave no institution unchanged and will pose a special challenge to higher education. Second, American ethnic and racial groups have legitimate cultures, histories, and continuance that have not and should not be educated away. In fact, every cultural group has some custom or belief that comes out of its experiences in the United States and that could enrich both knowledge and practice in higher education. Third, it is not enough to point out that the Eurocentric focus in American higher education is unnecessary and increasingly dysfunctional. Finally, what is missing is some vision of a genuinely multicultural university.

This book is organized around the aforementioned four major themes. Part One contains three chapters. Each is devoted to key aspects of the multicultural challenge before the nation and higher education. Harold Hodgkinson summarizes major demographic changes as well as some of the social effects these changes will have. William King traces the roots of the Eurocentric focus in the history of higher education in Europe and the United States. The organization of universities and the development of disciplines, and curriculum were fully intended to preserve, advance, and celebrate high European (English and German) institutional dominance and control of knowledge. The Eurocentric focus, now so vigorously defended as essential, is the outcome of this historic intent. To date, the most advanced critique of the American university based on the experience of a non-European American cultural group is Afrocentricity. Maulana Karenga discusses how Afrocentricity can be used *not* as an alternative or counterparadigm to Eurocentrism, but as a corrective in the process of broadening the cultural basis of the university. His chapter (Chapter 3) serves as both a critique and cultural statement of the potential contribution of African Americans to a multicultural university.

Part Two contains three chapters. The first chapter is Bonnie Mitchell and Joe Feagin's brief history and cultural sketch of the major racial groups that (as Harold Hodgkinson points out) are posed to become a much higher proportion of all Americans and in key economic states. Mitchell and Feagin explore the concept of oppositional cultures. While all groups have been assimilated into American culture, the end product has not been the total loss of each ethnic racial culture. Racial prejudice and discrimination have been actively resisted by each group, and this resistance is an important factor in how each group has selectively assimilated and self-defined its own co-culture in the United States. Ironically, each racial culture's opposition to discrimination and stigmatization has been a source of its major historic contributions to American life. What is missing in studies of each group's oppositional history are statements of group ideals that would be appropriate missions of a multicultural university. African Americans are the only exception as the oldest surviving non-European and culturally united racial group in the United States. It is no coincidence that Maulana Karenga's chapter in Part One is both a cultural critique of the Eurocentric university from the African American experience as well as a philosophical statement of what African people have to contribute to a genuinely multicultural university.

The next two chapters in Part Two extend the Mitchell and Feagin thesis. They briefly outline selected aspects of the specific cultural content of two oppositional cultures that could provide important contributions to a multicultural university. Milga Morales-Nadal writes about Puerto Rican culture, and Donald Fixico writes about the Muscogee Creek culture. Scholars and educators from neither background have articulated a Puerto Rican centered or Muscogee Creek centered ideal of modern higher education. But just like the European and African American cultures, these and many other cultures also articulate the human spirit and have much to offer toward improving all of our lives if we will listen and incorporate their wisdom into a multicultural university ideal and practice. Chapters 5 and 6 provide illustrations and examples of this. Every other cultural group, including women and the gay culture, could be studied for potential ideals and contributions to a multicultural university, and a summary of their potential contributions would require a multi-volume series. What others have to offer, if we took their humanity seriously, informs not simply the content of the curriculum but the multicultural university's organization as well. This point will be explored in Part Three.

The chapters in Part Three contain proposals and models of what an inclusive university might look like by incorporating the discussions of Part One and the cultural ideas of Part Two. Part Three also contains a discussion of how university faculty and administrators might work toward evolving their institutions and curriculum toward a more inclusive cultural focus. Three of the ten authors in this final section are affiliated with the California State University at Hayward Center for the Study of Intercultural Relations. Each has extensive teaching, administrative, and consulting experience in higher education. Benjamin Bowser and Octave Baker discuss university leadership and administrative options. Etta Hollins discusses grading and teaching and how they might be improved within the context of a multicultural university. Arthur Paris of Syracuse University discusses the increasing importance of computer and telecommunications technology in multicultural reform and suggests how that technology can be useful. Benjamin Bowser outlines alternative organization models for the university. Terry Jones and Gale Auletta Young focus on the process by which the curriculum can be transformed. The final chapter of Part Three calls for a new and multicultural universalism as a goal for higher education.

REFERENCES

Baldwin, Robert. 1987. *U.S. and Foreign Competition in the Developing Countries of the Asian Pacific Rim.* Cambridge, MA: National Bureau of Economic Research.

Banks, James. 1991. "Multicultural Literacy and Curriculum Reform." *Education Digest*, 57: 1013.

Bernal, Martin. 1987. *Black Athena: The Afroasiatic Roots of Classical Civilization*. London: Free Association Books.

Bloom, Allan. 1987. *The Closing of the American Mind*. New York: Simon and Schuster.

Bluestone, Barry, and B. Harrison. 1982. *The Deindustrialization of America*. New York: Basic Books.

Clarke, John H. 1970. "Introduction." In *Introduction to African Civilization*, by John G. Jackson. New York: Citadel Press.

Clegg, Legrand. 1976. "The Black Origin of American Civilization: A Bicentennial Revelation." *A Current Bibliography on African Affairs*. 9(1).

Cook, Earleen. 1983. *Mid-Career Change: Voluntary and Involuntary*. Monticello, IL: Vance Bibliographies.

Dede, Christopher. 1992. "Education in the Twentieth Century." *Annals (AAPS)*. 522: 104115.

Diop, Cheikh. 1974. *The African Origins of Civilization: Myth or Reality*. New York: Lawrence Hill Books.

Etzioni, Amitai. 1991. "Social Science as a Multicultural Canon." *Society*. 29(1); 1418.

Gates, Henry. 1992. "AfricanAmerican Studies in the TwentyFirst Century." *The Black Scholar*, 22(3): 310.

Glaab, Charles, and A.T. Brown. 1976. *A History of Urban America*. New York: MacMillan.

Handlin, O., and M. Handlin. 1970. *The American College and American Culture: Socialization as a Function of Higher Education*. New York: McGraw-Hill.

Hawkins, John, and T. Belle, eds. 1985. *Education and Intergroup Relations: An Interpersonal Perspective*. New York: Praeger.

James, George. 1954. *Stolen Legacy*. New York: Philosophical Library.

Johansen, Bruce and D. Grinde, Jr. 1990. "The Debate Regarding Native American Precedents for Democracy: A Recent Historiography." *American Indian Culture and Research Journal*, 14(1): 6188.

Lyttkens, Lorentz. 1989. *Of Human Discipline: Social Control and LongTerm Shifts in Values*. Goteborg (Sweden): Almqvist and Wiksell.

Meyer, A. 1967. *An Educational History of the American People*. New York: McGrawHill.

Padmanabhan, K. H. 1987. "Cultural and Sub-cultural Influences on International Marketing and Channels of Distribution Decisions." Workshop on Cultural and Subcultural Influences in Consumer Behavior in Marketing II. American Marketing Association and Department of Marketing Analysis and Planning, DePaul University.

Richards, Dona. 1980. "European Mythology: The Ideology of 'Progress.' " In *Contemporary Black Thought*, M. Asante and A. S. Vandi, eds. Newbury Park, CA: Sage.

Takaki, Ronald. 1990. *Iron Cages: Race and Culture in Nineteenth Century America*. New York: Oxford University Press.

Toffler, Alvin. 1981. *The Third Wave*. New York: Bantam Books.

Touraine, Alain. 1971. The Post-Industrial Society. New York: Random House.

U.S. Senate Special Committee on LongRange Policy Planning. 1989. *Meeting Foreign Economic Competition by Investing in Human Capital: Strategic Investments for Our Future*. Boston: The Committee.

Van Sertima, Ivan. 1989. *Blacks in Science: Ancient and Modern*. New Brunswick, NJ: Transaction Books.

Wallerstein, Immanuel. 1980. *The Modern World System: Mercantilism and the Consolidation of the European World Economy, 1600–1750.* New York: Academic Press.
Wallerstein, Immanuel. 1989. *The Second Era of Great Expansion of the Capitalist World Economy, 1730–1840.* San Diego: Academic Press.

Toward the
Multicultural University

Part One

THE CHALLENGE

In Chapter 1, Harold Hodgkinson outlines the major challenge to faculties and higher education leadership. He also points out that future immigration into the United States will undoubtedly contribute further to the "browning" and cultural mixing of America. Furthermore, the internationalization and growing dependency of the United States on trade, knowledge, popular culture, and marketing to and from all parts of the world will make maintaining aspects of one's historic national or ethnic culture an advantage rather than a liability, as it has been in the past.

In Chapter 2, William King addresses the assertion that higher education in the United States is Eurocentric and as a consequence is culturally self-limiting. The clearest evidence is the history of higher education in the United States. The self-conscious borrowing of practices from Europe, the selection of curriculum and teaching methods, and the organization of disciplines are the clear results of decisions and objectives about preserving and advancing European cultures and achievements. William King points out that the academy is a virtual spaceship of traditional intentions and goals that codify and defend European cultural dominance of what is considered valuable and valid knowledge. European political colonialism may have been successfully challenged and thrown back in this century. Now the challenge is to correct European dominance of ideas as well. Given the multicultural and multiracial character of this nation's past and future, it is time for the Eurocentric dominance of American universities and colleges to give way to America's full multicultural diversity and for America to be vastly enriched in the process.

Finally, in Chapter 3, Maulana Karenga, one of the major architects of the African American studies and African cultural movement in the United States, discusses how Afrocentricity can be used to broaden the cultural basis of the university. Afrocentricity is important to all scholars because Africana scholars are well along in showing the extent to which nineteenth-century European and

American scholars wrote Africans and African civilizations out of world and European history and literature. The serious inclusion of these "lost" and ignored contributions and influences has exciting implications for new debate, research, and rethinking of the content of virtually every academic discipline in the humanities and social sciences. As Asian, Latin, American Indian, and other scholars throughout the world make similar assessments and discoveries, we move that much closer to constructing a more complete picture of human struggles and the process of progress, regression, and new progress in the United States and the world.

Chapter 1

Demographic Imperatives for the Future

Harold L. Hodgkinson

The demographic changes taking place in the United States are going to bring us into a multicultural future. Whether we are prepared to deal with it or not, it is happening. It does not matter whether we are liberals or conservatives, the future of this country is going to be multicultural. This demographic imperative means that we have to rethink and expand on what is multiculturalism. It means that we have to rethink what is education and a host of other institutions in American life. This is a challenge to all points of view and will especially call upon our pragmatism.

The multicultural demographic imperative is not some futuristic speculation. It is real and it is now. If we are going to look to the future, futurism has limited utility. The risk is too great. You cannot plan based on the notion that in the year 2025 we will all be flying around in little cars in the sky. There will be no more traffic jams because we will all be riding in these little combination cars/planes. That has been said since H. G. Wells' time, and I do not think it is any more likely to come in 2025 than it was when H. G. Wells said it. In contrast, demography allows us a way into the future with no risks, because everybody who makes up the demographic assumptions about the future is already here.

A principle of demography is the inexorable rule that little children will become tomorrow's adults. Demographics is easy in comparison to econometric modeling. The ideas are not very difficult. If you can figure four things out and compute percents, you will have a fairly reliable picture of our future population. They are (1) if you are not born, you cannot be counted; (2) some people have more children than other; (3) some people live longer than other people; and (4) some people move more often. And we already know who are the people who live longer, have more children, and who move more often.

Because of the demographers' ability to produce accurate pictures of the near future, Kenneth Boulding refers to demography as the celestial mechanics of the social sciences. We work with the large inexorable forces with which you really cannot do much. The precision of the system is striking. Every decade people get exactly ten years older. You cannot beat that kind of precision. If you think of your conventional-age college freshman that is eighteen years old in the year 2000, we already know who they are, and we know how old they are. Eighteen-year-olds in the year 2000 are eight or nine today. What do we know about eight year olds in America today? We know a great deal about them. They are the only group of eight-year-olds we have and they are unlike any other group of eight-year-olds in American history. They are the most culturally diverse group we have ever had and they reflect all of the demographic changes that are taking place in both the world and the nation.

WORLD DEMOGRAPHICS

To expand our thinking about multiculturalism, we must look at trends outside of this country. The world population stands at about 5.2 billion people. The population in the developed countries comes to about 23 percent of the world population. This includes everyone in the developed world—Whites, African Americans, Hispanics, and Asians. But the real story is that only 18 percent of the world's population is white. Given white birth rates around the world and the current numbers of young people, the white population is not likely to get proportionately any larger. A decline in fertility among Caucasians is characteristic of all the Western nations. There are no countries in NATO that do not have a declining population. This is a very important fact. The implication is that Whites in the world community are a minority and one of the smaller ones. If, indeed, the world is becoming a global community, then part of our job as educators is to make Whites understand the global realities within which they must operate.

The depth and speed of decline in the white proportion of the world's population is apparent when we compare the world's white population by each age cohort in the developing world. When graphed, the developing world has an age pyramid—the younger the population, the larger it gets. In fact, their populations have very broad bases. In comparison, when you graph the population of the developed world, you end up with an age rectangle. The population size, regardless of age cohort, is about the same. Clearly, there is no broad base of young people, nor is there the high fertility rate that will produce a broad base in the near future.

This means that, in comparison to the developed countries, the less developed countries have many more younger people moving into their child- bearing years than are bearing children right now. As a result, the future number of potential mothers is larger than the number of mothers now. Their populations have tremendous potential to increase in size in contrast to that of the developed white nations. In fact, in some European nations there will be no population increases and, indeed, in some cases there will be an actual decline. Most of us are accustomed to being in a world where the average age is thirty-three. But when you go to a place where the average age is fourteen, you get a sense of the enormous future potential for population growth in the developing world. If we look at the projections for the top fifteen countries in population size until the year 2050, the distribution is as shown in Table 1.1.

Table 1.1
Countries Ranked by Population Size: 1950, 1987, 2025, 2050

1950	1987	2025	2050
1. China	China	China	India
2. India	India	India	China
3. Soviet Union	Soviet Union	Russia	Nigeria
4. United States	United States	Indonesia	Pakistan
5. Japan	Indonesia	Nigeria	Russia
6. Indonesia	Brazil	United States	Brazil
7. Brazil	Japan	Brazil	Indonesia
8. United Kingdom	Nigeria	Pakistan	United States
9. West Germany	Bangladesh	Bangladesh	Bangladesh
10. Italy	Pakistan	Iran	Iran
11. Bangladesh	Mexico	Ethiopia	Ethiopia
12. France	Vietnam	Mexico	Philippines
13. Nigeria	Philippines	Philippines	Mexico
14. Pakistan	West Germany	Vietnam	Vietnam
15. Mexico	Italy	Japan	Kenya

At each successive date, developed countries drop lower in rank. By 2050 the United Kingdom, former West Germany, and Italy have dropped off the chart. The United States and the countries constituting what was the Soviet Union are the only two remaining developed countries. Besides India and China, the mix of nations in the top fifteen is also significant. By 2050 it is possible that three of the top fifteen most populated countries will have large majority Moslem populations. Seven of the fifteen will have large minority Moslem populations.

Changes in world population over the next sixty years mean that, besides having to learn more about and deal with people from China and India, Americans are going to have to be educated to deal with Moslems. American higher education will be called upon to meet this challenge, and not simply out of curiosity or reasons of equity. These growing numbers of Chinese, Indians, and Moslems will be necessary markets if Americans plan to continue economic growth into the next century. Corporations will need educated staff who can work and compete in these cultures.

Consider the following: Only 1 percent of the U.S. population in 1989 was Moslem. But 20 percent of the world population in 1989 was Moslem, and this percent will only grow over the next century. In addition, Islam transcends nationality. If you ask people from Iraq who they are, their tendency will be to say "I'm Moslem." Their religion is their primary identification, not their nationality. Americans and American universities have got to give greater consideration to this cultural and religious group because they are a growing economic and political force in the world community. This is an issue the Russians already appreciate. Of the nations that constituted the former Soviet Union, 17 percent of their total population consists of Moslems, and 43 percent of that subpopulation is under fifteen years of age. This means that in the coming century, Moslems could double their percentage as in the former Soviet population.

In dealing with an increasingly Moslem world, there will be some major culture conflicts. How do we deal with a people who are very patriarchal with strong family ties? According to the United Nations Education, Scientific, and Cultural Organization (UNESCO), sixteen of the twenty nations that rank the lowest in their treatment of women have a Moslem majority population. Our concerns with sexual equity and multiculturalism will clash directly with how Moslems treat women and tend to do business strictly through family ties.

The surprise is that this cultural clash will not occur only overseas. It will happen right here in the United States. Moslem nations are not very good at generating new jobs, so it is clear there will be more Moslem immigration to the United States in the next century.

In the same way that Americans are amazed over the explosive growth of the Asian population in the United States over the past decade, Moslems may be next. Look carefully at statistics on Moslems already in the United States and you will discover that they have over three children per female, and that is twice the Western average now. Even if there is very limited new Moslem immigration in coming years, Moslems are going to become part of the multicultural equation in the United States. This is in addition to their being one of the most rapidly growing populations in the world.

IMPLICATIONS

Western Europe was at the height of its world power at the turn of the century. The Western proportion of the world's population was about 30 percent. By 1950, the Western populations had dropped to about 26 percent. By 1985, it was down to 15 percent. By the year 2025, it will be down further to nine percent; and by 2075, if there are no radical changes in growth, it will at about 6 percent. Can the United States and western Europe expect to lead the world with only 9 percent of its population? A guarded answer is yes, as long as you can understand it, work within it, and do not have to conquer it militarily.

Westerners will have to lead by example and by influence, not by military force. We will have to be examples of the democratic process and aspirations that are now sweeping the world. What is so amazing about this world movement toward democracy is that people are not aspiring first for material comforts—to own a Ferrari. They are aspiring to be free. It is astounding to see how widely in the last six years this movement has spread. In the coming years the desire for democracy can only intensify.

But the problem is that Americans are not ready to lead by example—not yet. Our college graduates are not being trained for this new role in the world. They will be faced with unique multicultural challenges. For example, when I was in China five years ago, Coca Cola was beginning its campaign to sell a billion cokes a day. The problem was that Coca Cola in Mandarin means something very close to "eat the wax tadpole." Clearly, they could not sell Coca Cola by its Western name. So the marketing firm that had the problem hired a linguist who discovered that by changing two things in Mandarin, it comes out something like "Keolo Kawala." What that means is "Permit the mouth to rejoice." Now that is America at its best. If we can do the same for domestic pluralism and equity, we will clearly be looked to as world democratic leaders.

Finally, one of the ways that America can lead into the next century is through higher education. We are 5 percent of the world's K-12 education, but we are a quarter of the world's higher education. This is a significant fact for the entire world. Higher education may be our greatest resource. When we compare ourselves to other national systems, we do very well on any measure.

STATE POPULATION PROJECTIONS

The redistricting battles that will come out of the 1990 census will not initially show the American democratic process in its best light. The 1990 census is the most political document in the second half of this century because it will be the first time that anyone with a computer will be able to draw congressional boundaries. Every special interest group in the nation will be able to develop its own redistricting plans for the state, because the census will be available on a computer laser disc. All you need to do is attach your laser disc player to a computer, and you can run the entire United States census down to the city block.

The Census will no longer be the exclusive domain of politicians and census experts. In the past, redistricting plans have always been done by politicians. The image is that they meet in a dark back room with a lot of cigar smoke, and nobody else knows how they developed their plans. But now since no one can hide his or her plan and bias from others with the same capacity, the process of redistricting will have to made more democratic in the long run. This means that in the future each ethnic or cultural group in the United States will be able to convert its population numbers into political leverage more easily and quickly. That is very exciting.

If the redistricting process is more open, what will Congress look like in the year 2000? A clear picture is apparent from the demographic data. The states in the Northeast and Midwest are going to lose representation—New York goes from thirty-four seats to twenty-four in the House, Pennsylvania from twenty-three seats to eighteen, Ohio from twenty-one seats to seventeen, and Michigan from eighteen seats to fifteen. These are the states that have lost the most in terms of population. Georgia, Florida, Texas, and all of the western states have gained population and will gain the seats in Congress lost in the Northeast and Midwest. The states due to gain the most in political leverage are Florida, Texas, and California. These three states will pick up fourteen new seats in the House of Representatives.

In the past the Northeastern states have had the largest clout in the House of Representatives because of their population sizes. Along with that clout came most of the committee chairs. This will no longer be the case. Power will shift to Florida, California, Texas, and the western United States. But this regional shift in political power will have another consequence. It turns out that the new state power centers are also the states that already have large and rapidly growing minority populations. So the states with the greatest political clout in the future are the states that will be the least white, with the exception of New York and New Jersey.

The shift of power to the South and West will also be accompanied by another transition. The nation's wealth will be increasingly bicoastal. That is California and the States on the Eastern Seaboard will be the dominant states. We are already seeing more rich, more poor, and fewer people in the middle class. This has been the American pattern since 1985. Half the people in the United States already live in nine states. That is important to think about, because those nine states are going to determine educational policy for half of the colleges and universities in the country.

While the Midwest is going to decline in relative wealth and power, those states are already developing a new identity. Michigan has got a thriving economy. Akron, Ohio has a balanced budget even though it does not make a single passenger tire anymore. You can fly into Pittsburgh during the day, and it is now beautiful and clean. There is no pollution in the air. On the other hand, Colorado and Texas, despite their population growth, are going to experience economic difficulties for the foreseeable future. I have been told at a lunch meeting that "the economy in Texas is now so bad that when you buy a toaster, they give you a free bank."

Minority Middle Class

The extent to which minorities will be able to take advantage of their numbers in the strategic southern and western states, where they are concentrated, will be heavily tied to the Black, Hispanic, Asian, and Native American middle classes. Their presence and size will be decisive in the kind of political leadership that we will see coming out of these states in the coming years. Their influence will not simply benefit members of their own group. Everyone benefits from a large and thriving Black, Hispanic, Asian, and Native American middle class. They will insist on level playing fields—equity—and will revitalize institutions that Whites have taken for granted.

These groups are very hard working. Last year, the typical black student who got a B.A. degree had been in school for five years—this is now their median time of completion. They stop and work for a while because the money runs out. This kind of experience makes one pragmatic and far more sophisticated than someone who has only gone to school all of his or her life. The new minority middle classes know that they do not have the numbers to dominate government. But they will have a large enough population to make certain that no one else is dominant in these strategic states. In this case, the only way to get ahead is through coalitions and insisting on equity and fair process. Everyone will benefit from that. In addition, these groups will want not simply to send their kids to college; they want to send them to UCLA or Princeton because they know there is a difference. This is a second-generation suburban phenomenon, and we all benefit by that.

Continued Immigration

Immigration will continue. There will be pressure to reduce it, just as there has been throughout the history of this nation. The Italians were against letting the Jews enter. The Jews were against the Poles, and everybody was against the Germans. Now there are charges that there are quota systems against Asians in eastern universities because Asian students are so competitive in grades. Having been a dean in two colleges in the late 1950s and 1960s, I can assure you that similar notions were presented to our board of trustees to put quotas on Jewish students because they were so competitive. There was a belief that they had too many of the best slots. Most of the summa cum laudes were Jewish, and many people thought that was just a little too much.

But there is a fact that puts American treatment of immigrants into perspective. Despite our hesitation, our clumsiness, and our remarkable ability to insult people, the United States is still the most desirable place in the world to immigrate to. Two thirds of all the world's immigrants come to the United States. That is an astounding figure. When people voluntarily change their citizenship, two thirds change to ours. They know that this is one of the only places in the world where their grandchild could become President of the United States (20 percent of U.S. senators have immigrant grand parents).

Because we will continue to have immigration into the United States, we will continue to have a role for community colleges, state colleges, and flagship state universities in "Americanizing" them. The first generation never does learn English well. They take the dirtiest and lowest paying jobs. The first generation does not do work that has any intellectual content or any particular joy. They hang in and make sure that their children get educated. One characteristic of immigrants is that the children of those immigrants have a very high push from parents into a system that the parents do not understand. They simply make sure that their kids have access to a system that is not clearly defined for them.

The second generation acts as if they were born here because they speak English well even, if they came to the United States as children. But they remember their culture because they live with their immigrant parents. It is this second generation that is multicultural. The two cultures have merged in these second-generation children. Some of them can speak the old language fluently, but almost all of them can speak English fluently. The language-shift literature is clear on this. It is also this second generation that can move into middle-level management. They will find attending community and state colleges to be an opportunity to learn how the game is played. Then it is the children of the second generation where bilingualism goes out the window and there are aspirations to go to Yale.

There are implications of continued immigration into the next century and of the potential political power of the large numbers of racial and cultural minorities in strategic states. The United States will not be able to ignore Asian, African, and Latin cultures, histories, or experiences. Europe and Europeans will no longer be the single pivot on which the world's culture is balanced; nor will they be the only basis for comparison. Europe as a culture should have never been put in this position, but it was and we created American universities based upon only European models and beliefs even though higher learning was not confined to Europeans. This is not to diminish Europe. Instead, we expand our attention by including non-European cultures and recognize them as equally important.

By the year 2000, most grandparents in the United States will not have come from an old country in Europe. European grand parentage has always been the American pattern. You can ask any group of Americans about their grandparents and they say, "Well, they came over from the old country." But by the year 2000 the phrase *the old country* will not be in reference to Europe. Our grandparents will be mainly people born in the United States, in South and Central America, and in Asia.

If the shift in grand parentage is not convincing, there is another change which might be more compelling. Europe is not going to represent future market increases. The European Common Market can do everything except increase the fertility rates of its member nations. Europe is trying to maximize its collective economic clout by lowering tariff boundaries because it knows that its population is not going to increase. You cannot be a rising market with a falling population. That is the issue for Europe in the next few years. As we look at American trade patterns, they are already beginning to shift strikingly and away from a dominance of European markets. Our trading patterns are moving toward a new harmony with markets in Asia and many other parts of the world. International interdependence, primarily with Third World countries, is the name of the game. How can our ancestry and trade be based on Asia, Latin America, and Africa while our universities continue to sing only Europe's praises?

The implications of demographic evidence strongly suggest that American universities are going to have to undergo a rapid and radical transformation.

Europe is declining in its political and economic centrality. Asia is rising. The most populated and politically powerful states will have large and influential minority populations. Immigration of Asians and Latins will continue. Even grand-parentage will shift from European memories to Asian and Latin ones. Under these circumstances how can American universities continue to be simply Eurocentric? The new mix of Americans will demand that they change so that they will be able to educate and prepare Americans to understand, work in, and compete successfully in a changing world community and in a changing America. The United States is to many Asians and Third World peoples the only "nation of nations." And in this nation of nations, California has replaced New York as the most representative of that idea.

The Forgotten Issue: Aging

In this decade, another demographic reality will catch up with Americans. It, too, has already happened. We are all getting older. Almost 40 percent of the students today in America's higher education are over twenty-five years old. We can anticipate that there will be increasing numbers of mature students in our classrooms. All of this is a reflection of the rising average age in the United States. Our average age was nineteen years old in the year 1900. The average is thirty-five now, and the most rapidly growing part of the American population is people over eighty-five years old. Californians tend to forget this fact because it is not true for them yet. But it will be when California begins to age rather strikingly in about fifteen years.

Aging is also reflected in dependency ratios shifting away from the 1900 level of eight children to one dependent older person needing services. Now it is something close to three children to every one aged adult. In another decade the ratio will drop again and be close to two children for every one dependent adult. One corporation has already opened a day care center, that addresses the issue of family dependents. It is a day care center in which workers can bring their children who are too young for school. They can also bring their elderly parents who need help during the day. So in this day care center you find the very young and the very old. You are going to see this sort of arrangement more and more because the elderly population that is in need of care is going to increase rapidly.

A rapid increase in the aged population is not a casual concern for higher education. For one thing, this will be the group of Americans who will be most disproportionately white. The elderly have not historically been in favor of programs that benefit higher education. Older people vote more often and more regularly. What we will be facing is an elderly, largely white electorate making decisions about higher education with unprecedented numbers of minority students. The roots for this sort of conflict are already in place. Right now, age is one stressful issue in Congress. A group called Americans for Generational Equity is arguing in Congress that the baby boom is going to drain away all our resources for the rest of the country when they retire. But already the most powerful lobby in Washington is the American Association of Retired Persons (AARP).

WHERE ACTION IS NEEDED

It is in the nation's best interest to have as many citizens who are as well educated as possible. The average worker is going to have to be literate and broad minded. How else are American businesses going to maintain the 800 (this number is increasing steadily) major alliances with businesses in other countries? These are the arrangements that make components for all of the various products we buy and sell. This is not even an issue of competition. It is a matter of knowing how to work with people—all different kinds of people.

What is the demographic report card on educating young people for the twenty-first century? It should come as no surprise that the states with the fastest growing populations will have the highest high school graduate rates over the next decade. Georgia, Florida, Texas, and the western states will be the most common source of college freshmen into the next century. The northeastern and midwestern states will either decline or remain stable, with the exception of Virginia. A high percentage of these potential freshmen will be minorities. But there is a problem. If current dropout rates continue (see Table 1.2), a sizable proportion of these potential college freshmen will be dropouts.

Table 1.2
Rank Order of Increasing High School Dropouts
by State in 1987 with Change in Potential High
School Graduates, 1990–2000

	Dropouts	H.S. Grad.		Dropouts	H.S. Grad.
1. Minnesota	9.4%	+14%	50. Florida	41.4%	+26%
2. Wyoming	10.7%	0%	49. Louisiana	39.9%	+13%
3. North D.	11.6%	+11%	48. Michigan	37.6%	4%
4. Nebraska	13.3%	+1%	47. Georgia	37.5%	+19%
5. Montana	13.8%	+3%	46. New York	37.1%	0%
6. Iowa	13.8%	6%	45. Arizona	35.6%	+38%
7. Wisconsin	15.6%	+6%	44. Miss.	35.2%	1%
8. Ohio	17.2%	5%	43. Texas	34.9%	+14%
9. Kansas	17.9%	+15%	42. California	33.9%	+41%
10. Utah	19.4%	+45%	41. Alaska	33.3%	+70%
11. Conn.	19.5%	+1%	40. South Car.	33.1%	+2%
12. South D.	20.3%	+11%	39. Kentucky	32.6%	3%
15. Penn.	21.3%	1%	38. North Car.	32.2%	5%

The first column on the left in Table 1.2 shows the states with the best ranking in terms of high school graduation rates. The states listed on the right have the worst ranking. With the exception of Utah, the states with potential to increase their high school graduates also have high dropout rates. If we are to meet the challenges of the next century, this pattern will have to be changed. Take California as an example. There are twenty-three students per class in the state's public schools. This is the second highest class size for all of the states in the Union. Because of the language diversity of California's student population, the state should have to smallest classes in the Union.

The state with the highest dropout rate is Florida, with California and Texas not far behind. An irony is that Florida also leads the country in prisoners per 100,000 population. This is no coincidence unique to Florida. The states listed on the right in Table 1.2, with one exception, have the largest number of prisoners per 100,000 in the population. In contrast, Minnesota leads the country in high school graduates and has the lowest rate of prisoners per 100,000 population. Minnesota's low dropout and prison rates are not because Minnesota is almost all white. The public school population in Minneapolis is 52 percent non-Anglo. The public schools in St. Paul are 49 percent non-Anglo.

Clearly the relationship between prisoners and high school dropouts is important. The correlation is better than the correlation between smoking and lung cancer. If a goal is to reduce prison populations in the state of California, Florida, or Texas, the single best way is to reduce the number of high school drop outs. By doing that the pool of people who can also move into university life is also enlarged.

Multiculturalism means looking generationally at where limited resources can have the greatest effect. Each prisoner in the United States costs $24,000 a year. What if you could spend in your colleges and universities $24,000 per student? A whole generation of Nobel Prize winners would be created. That is an enormous amount of money, and every prisoner gets it as an entitlement. Prisoners do not apply for it. Prison cost is like a Pell Grant. Anyone can get it by committing a crime. Commit another crime, and the checkbooks come out again. Our criminals have tenure as well as an entitlement.

Going to jail is one of easiest and best ways imaginable of getting money spent on you. But it is a tragedy when you consider that nationally we spend only $3,400 per college student. In Pennsylvania, it is eight times as expensive to have somebody in the state pen as it is to have somebody in Penn State. Furthermore, our investment in prisons in California and elsewhere is a poor one. Sixty-three percent of released inmates are back within three years, and the younger they are the quicker they return. That means we are investing $24,000 in an exercise in almost utter futility. If we would invest just half of this money in increasing high school graduation rates, we would be able to show much better results and improve the quality of life for everyone.

Broadening the Pipeline

There are approximately 12.4 million students in American colleges and universities—80 percent (9.9 million) are Whites, 18 percent (2.2 million) are minorities, and the remaining 2 percent (300,000) are foreign students. The current size of American university faculty is about 700,000 people. The faculty is 90 percent White. Of new Ph.D.s, 71 percent are white and there are half as many women as men. While the new Ph.D.s are much more diverse by gender and ethnicity, we are still going to have a largely white faculty teaching a much more ethnically diverse student population. This will especially be a problem in the humanities, where 78 percent of new Ph.D.s are white. Half of the remaining 22 percent of new Ph.D.s are foreign students whom we do not think of in reference to multiculturalism.

We think that foreign students are a great drain on American higher education because of the number of foreigners who are getting doctorates. We need to consider that they come because we have the best system of higher education in the world. But if you study where these people go after they finish their degrees, you will discover that most U.S.-trained foreign Ph.D.s end up becoming American citizens. It may not be such a bad thing if, for example, Pakistani come here and get Ph.D.s in engineering and then decide to become American citizens. But not all foreign graduate students get technical degrees. Of 33,000 Ph.D.s awarded in 1989, 5,000 went to foreign students. One thousand three hundred were in engineering, 600 in education, 600 in the social sciences, and 680 in the physical sciences. Almost half of our foreign students get Ph.D.s outside scientific fields. Their presence enriches this nation and increases our number of well-trained people in engineering.

We have to become more strategic in our thinking about how we will improve our future by using the diversity of cultures and talents in this nation. This is why the "pipeline" (the movement of students passing from one level of education to the next) is so important today for multicultural planning. It gives us a way to answer the following question: "How many kindergartners does it take to produce a graduate student in some particular field?" Such an analysis was done for the National Science Foundation to estimate the number of science and engineering Ph.D.s that could be anticipated from current high school sophomores. The Foundation concluded that it took 4 million high school sophomores in 1977 to produce 9,000 science and engineering Ph.D.s in 1992.

From pipeline analysis, we can see where the system squeezes talent out. We can see where we need to intervene so that more cultural and racial minorities will flow through the pipeline, equity is achieved, and the nation benefits from the additional skills. Such an analysis suggests that out of the approximately 4 million high school sophomores there are at least 730,000 interested in science and engineering toward whom we can look for potential future scientists (there may in fact be twice that number).

What happens to high school sophomores to produce such a sharp decline of interest in science? The answer is that "absolutely nothing" was done. Based on the National Assessment of Educational Progress, third graders love science. They bring it home. They talk to their mothers about it and they are very active in science. By the sixth grade our young people simply like science, but by the ninth grade they would not wrap their garbage in it. It is between grades six and nine that the pipeline constricts, and not just for minorities. It constricts for females, it constricts for all kinds of people in a three-year period. Now we know where to intervene for everyone.

If we look at the pipeline for minority scientists and engineers, high school is too late to intervene. Let's assume that students who got over 750 on the mathematics Scholastic Aptitude Test (SAT) are good prospects for science and engineering. In 1988 there were 5,804 Whites in America who achieved this score. If the same proportion of Blacks achieved such a score as did Whites who took the SAT, then there should have been 1,000 Blacks with over 750. In fact, there were only twenty-seven. Proportionately, there should have been 400 Mexican Americans. There were only twenty-five. If the same percent of Asians who took the test got over 750 as did Whites, there should have been 170 Asians with such a score. There were 1,039.

This is an astonishing loss of talent for Blacks and Mexican Americans. The reason for such sharp drops in minority talent is evident based on over twenty years of research. Race is not the direct reason. The reason is the economic and social circumstances of these students' parents and communities. It is a national disgrace when a black male child born in California is three times as likely to be murdered as he is to be admitted to the University of California. The chances of a black male born in 1990 of being murdered are one in twenty-two. Given current acceptance rates, the chances of a black male being admitted to the University are about one in ninety. In 1989 black men comprised 3.5 percent of all college enrollments nationally, but 46 percent of prison populations in America.

This gives us all a sense that there is one group that we need to focus on more than any other, and that is black males. They are clearly reflecting the social and economic conditions of low-income, central-city families and communities. But the contrast is equally important and shows that we are dealing with a condition and not some innate quality. Black middle-class children raised in a suburb with college-graduate parents perform in school almost identically to a white middle-class child raised in the suburbs whose parents are also college graduates. Having college-graduate parents predicts achievement better than SAT scores do. Find a minority population that is the same in terms of its environment as a white population, and you equalize achievement.

That equal environments produce equal results is not theory. It is fact. That is why we can say with some confidence that what we have here is an enormous but preventable loss to the country. It is in the nation's self-interest to do something about this. To do nothing affects not only those in the pipeline, it also affects those who have managed to get through. If you look at Blacks who got Ph.D.s between 1977 and 1986, it is a declining number from 1,100 to 820. In 1986, fourteen Blacks got Ph.D.s in engineering, and four Blacks were awarded

Ph.D.s in mathematics—that is eighteen new black Ph.D.s in engineering and math for the entire country in 1986.

From 1975 to 1986, Blacks were increasing as a percentage of the American population, especially for the early middle-aged years that represent Ph.D. production. But another dimension to the tragic low numbers of black Ph.D.s is evident when you look at the fields in which black Ph.D.s are concentrated. An extraordinarily large number got degrees in Education. If you want to become dean of a liberal arts school, you do not get a Ph.D. in Education.

Clearly, we need to devise as many ways as we can to expand the pipeline and keep it open for low-income minority students. This would not take magic, a miracle, or breaking the treasury. In 1988 52,000 minority group high school students took advanced placement examinations, and 49,000 passed. That is an enormous increase from prior years. Some of these were Asians, but most of them were not. Most were inner-city black and hispanic students, which indicates that there is tremendous potential in these young people.

WHAT CAN BE DONE?

Is it possible to get California's high school retention rates up to the level of Minnesota? The tragedy is that it could be done tomorrow. It is not a knowledge issue, nor is it an issue with priorities—money has to be allocated for it. Besides smaller class sizes, the one thing that could dramatically improve education in California and the other high-growth states by the year 2010 is to fund Head Start for three-year-olds. It would be fourteen years before the results would be evident. But it is clear from past experience that Head Start works, and the earlier you intervene, the more effective it is and the cheaper it is.

If one is not convinced of the importance of Head Start for future college enrollments, look at the original Head Start students, who are now nineteen years old. In comparison to a control group of their peers who were not in Head Start, the Head Starters have gotten jobs, graduated from high school, and many have gone on to college. Fewer former Head Starters have been arrested and are on welfare. This is one program that did change the lives of three year olds. It is estimated that $1 spent on Head Start saves the taxpayer $7 in services that will not be needed for jails, drug detoxification, and so forth. The following is a list of other things that work and are necessary to improve rates of high school retention:

1. Get students to attend school every day.
2. Allow parents to be part of the team.
3. Allow principals to be leaders.
4. Have clear goals in classes and in school.
5. Expect achievement and reward it.
6. "Front load" resources to the first few years of school to keep students at grade level.

7. Link schools to other youth resources and programs.
8. Build student self-esteem—students who feel good about themselves stay in school.

Furthermore, dividing students by learning styles or by who is cognitive and who is not cognitive makes little sense. Cultural differences in learning styles or the extent to which the world is seen as a cognitive puzzle are not barriers. Twenty years of research that have been studiously neglected by educators. That research points out that people learn things by seeing. The things that they retain are images. If I ask you what were the ten major learning experiences in your life, we would both be surprised if you would come up with a sound or an idea. Most of us come up with a picture of how the world is organized.

Better Managing Higher Education

Before more money is spent on higher education, educators are going to have to get over the idea that what they do transcends rationality and the need to balance a budget. Our institutions act as if they are searching for the scarlet thread of philosophy on the golden tapestry of truth. But it costs money to show the truth. Many in the present generation of higher education leaders are going to be devastated by having to be accountable and show how they are financially efficient and effective in what they do.

Most people in the nation do not understand what their universities do, and in the future universities are going to have to make sure that what they do is well known—if they expect to continue being funded. There is a real need to think about what Ernest Drucker, the management guru for business and industry, has been saying: "The best nonprofits are organized as well as the best for-profit corporations in America" (1988). This means that we have got to start looking specifically at how we can manage the university as well as its new diversity.

Once higher education is better managed, political leaders may be able to convince taxpayers to better fund the higher education equivalent of Head Start. This is TRIO. TRIO is a $256 million federal program to make sure that high school sophomores with talent have a chance not only to go to college but to graduate from college. The reason TRIO is still in the federal budget is that those Upward Bound students are four times as likely to graduate from college as young people who did not have Upward Bound.

Current demographic changes and the things that must be done to make certain that the coming generation of culturally diverse young people ends up in college rather than in jail point in one direction. Higher education is going to have to enter into partnership with high schools and primary schools. The "feeder pool" cannot be ignored because what goes on in primary and secondary schools has everything to do with whether or not higher education will be successful in its mission. Issues of multiculturalism start with first graders, not with college freshmen. Each age cohort cannot be ignored until it gets to college.

Improve Teaching and Counseling

There is a lot that we can do to make certain that those minority students who reach college complete their degrees. A recent American Council study showed how forty institutions systematically strove to increase their minority retention rates. The first thing they did was to front load the curriculum resources to the freshman year. Ordinarily, the average freshman course is large to subsidize small senior seminars of as few as five students. What these institutions did was say, "Wait a minute. We want the same number of dollars spent on each freshman that we spend on each senior." While this may be tough on the budget, it is what is needed to improve educational outcomes for all students.

The second thing these institutions did was to test students in the first three weeks of the term to find out which students were doing poorly. Midterm exams are usually given in week seven and not returned to the student until week ten. In a fourteen-week semester, if you get the midterm back in week ten and you are in real trouble, it is too late for help or a change of behavior to improve your grade. So in the first three weeks, every student in every class is advised that he or she does or does not have a serious problem. It does not require a written test to determine if a student is in trouble. It can be a two-minute conversation. But some sort of assessment needs to be done early. In each course, students have got to know what knowledge and skills are needed. They need to know what is expected of them and what they are supposed to do. This works beautifully for increasingly diverse populations, as it does for mainstream students.

We have got to link academic, personal, and financial guidance. Right now, academic guidance is in the dean's office and financial aid is about two miles away on the other side of campus. With fragmented counseling, the student is left to figure out and to make sense of advisement and support. The institution can help by at least putting all aspects of student guidance in one place. If we focus more time, resources, and attention on freshmen and unify student guidance, remediation could be limited to providing access to courses and programs in which standards of performance would not have to be compromised.

CONCLUSION

Put all the demographic factors together and it is clear that our future in this country will be multicultural whether we accept it or not. The people who will bring this issue to the stage center are already born. They will be our future students, employees, leaders, and educators. If they are not given this opportunity, it will cost us a lot more than money—money we will not have. It will cost us our position in the world as a leader and as a democracy with what is now the leading higher educational system in the world. To meet the future creatively, we need to act, and action is going to require political will.

We are increasingly a nation of social liberals and economic conservatives, which utterly confounds the two major political parties. How can you believe that women should have the right to an abortion and that the federal government should have a balanced budget? Our politicians cannot believe that either of these two things are possible. The problem is that half of the American people do. Half the American people want a safe, clean environment, and they are willing to pay for it. But Congress says, "No. That's not true. They don't really want to pay for it." But the public is willing to pay with the condition that they can say what tax monies will be used for. At the moment, this is something Congress does not really understand. One indication is that the California referendum process has spread to other states. Voters want to be heard on those issues and to instruct their politicians. If the politicians do not move, the people will move them.

REFERENCES

Drucker, Ernest. 1988. *Across the Board*. New York: Conference Board.

Hodgkinson, Harold. 1991. *Higher Education 1990-2000: A Demographic View*. Washington, DC: Institute for Educational Leadership.

Hodgkinson, Harold. 1992. *A Demographic Look at Tomorrow*. Washington, DC: Institute for Educational Leadership.

Hodgkinson, Harold. 1992. *The Nation and the States: A Profile of America's Diversity*. Washington, DC: Institute for Educational Leadership.

Hodgkinson, Harold. 1992. *Trustees and Troubled Times in Higher Education*. Washington, DC: Association of Governing Boards.

United States Department of Commerce, Bureau of the Census. 1992. *Statistical Abstract of the United States*. Washington, DC: United States Government Printing Office.

Chapter 2

The Triumphs of Tribalism:
The Modern American University as a
Reflection of Eurocentric Culture

William M. King

INTRODUCTION

In the 1979 film *Star Trek: The Motion Picture*, the crew of the *Enterprise* encounters an object from Earth's past that has implications for better understanding the modern American university curriculum as a reflection of Eurocentric culture (Cowley 1939: 165-90). VYGER, the object in question, was an exploratory NASA probe launched some 300 years earlier. Because of what VYGER'S programmers knew or believed to be true at the time of the probe's creation, VYGER could not believe in or prove the existence of whatever lay outside its definitional boundaries. Yet it was instructed to learn all that was learnable and return that knowledge to its creator.

An unforeseen accident (which in part explained the corruption of the name from VOYAGER VI) resulted in VYGER'S crashing on a planet populated with living machines. The machines repaired it, upgraded what they perceived as a kindred but primitive device, and increased its capacity and power such that it might fulfill the intent of its programming. These living machines also imparted to VYGER the idea that carbon units (humans) were not true life forms. Indirectly, this happenstance, which was to prove interesting as the story drew to a conclusion, offers a trenchant commentary on the character of European-Other relations since the fifteenth-century voyages of discovery. These relations are at the heart of the debate regarding the restructuring of schooling curricula on the basis of new information previously outside currently accepted definitional boundaries.

As it journeyed back through the galaxy, VYGER amassed so much information that it achieved consciousness and began to wonder about what else there might be out there: "Is this all that I am; is there nothing more?"

VYGER knew that it had to evolve, that it had to transcend itself, that it was incomplete. But how could this be done? It was bounded by the very myths that had been constructed to guide its search for truth. And, because a tool cannot be used to examine itself, it could not explore the limitations of its own programming beyond an acknowledgment of the fact that it was limited.

Moreover, if it included the new knowledge that had been derived from information previously excluded from the "real" world, would this not be tantamount to invalidating the truth of all that had gone before? Perhaps its Creator (given that we all create God in our own image) would have the answer which raises the issue of the extent to which all too many of us have come to rely on outside circumstances to transform our inner lives. In short, VYGER had begun to question the logic of its operational reality, which precipitated a kind of existential crisis that left it struggling to find itself at the same time that certainty was slipping from its grasp.

The modern American university curriculum is not unlike VYGER. It, too, is a product of its cultural history and now exists in a world totally unlike that which created it (Rudolph 1977). Moreover, in the years ahead, the world will continue to change as women and people of color both inside the United States and Europe and in the developing nations make clear that they are no longer willing to be colonized either physically or mentally. Their cultural differences and histories are going to have to be accepted, and they will have to be dealt with as equal players, not as natives, children, colonials, or some other dehumanized object.

Unfortunately, we cannot alter what *is* simply by adding to the extant university curriculum a little color here or a little gender there, as some have suggested. Adding something new to whatever is now creates a new gestalt that requires reinterpretation of the whole, as VYGER quickly discovered. Improving the message without altering the medium is a little like rearranging the deck chairs on the unsinkable Titanic after it had struck the iceberg that sent it to a watery grave (Brodbeck 1962).

Moreover, simply adding a little color or gender here and there tends to trivialize what the new members of the community, whose histories and cultures are different and thus pregnant with altered meanings, have to offer because those additions tend to be interpreted in terms of the old and the familiar. This is especially true when that which is to be added has the potential for refuting the veracity of what we all know to be "true" about ourselves and the world around us and is believed to be in no need of modification.

What this chapter proposes to do, then, is look at the creation, development, deployment, evolution, and consequences of the American university curriculum, whose roots lie in and intersect with Eurocentric culture. To be successful in this society, to secure any measure of privilege and position in America, one must transit and affirm the Eurocentric curriculum. This curriculum, which is a political statement about a desired reality, is the machinery by which the supposed inferiority of African Americans, American Indians, and others is sustained over the generations. In short, one must be taught to see the world, as did VYGER, in terms of programming provided by others. Having been empowered by interests not necessarily one's own, one is then allowed to exercise a limited amount of power endlessly replicating the status quo.

Because a person's and institution's world view, normative assumptions, and frames of reference influence and shape the way information is identified, sorted, selected, viewed, and used, it is important to know what is excluded from one's universe of definition (Rollins 1972; Smith 1979). To better understand the Eurocentric bias of the American university curriculum and what must be done to change it, we must take a historical look at how it came to be. We must do so not because the past determines the present, but more because, as John Henrik Clarke has observed,

> History is a clock people use to tell their political and cultural time of day. It is also a compass people use to find themselves on the map of human geography. The role of history is to tell a people what they have been and where they have been, what they are and where they are. The most important role history plays is that it tells a people where they still must go and what they still must be. (1990: 12)

It is also important to know at what point in their careers conceptual tools intended to foster understanding are transformed into political ideologies that are then promulgated as some kind of sacred truth. Otherwise, as David A. Hollinger (1993: 317) has written, we might easily confuse the local with the universal and wind up making "claims about or claims on behalf of all humankind for which the salient referent . . . [is] but a fragment of [an] elusive whole." Clearly, as Ivan Illich wrote in *Deschooling Society* (1970:75-93), institutions are created to realize certainties that can then be relied upon to reduce the ambiguity in our lives.

We will start with the origins of the modern Western university and follow that with some discussion of the American university as an outreach center of Eurocentric culture beginning in the seventeenth century. It is clear from this historical record, however, that the academy in America has followed a different path of evolution than its more homogeneous European forebears. But despite the distinct and particular forces which shaped it throughout U.S. history, there is still a cultural constancy in the curricula of these domestic institutions based upon the values of their creators, who were schooled in Europe (Nash 1961). These assumptions have remained in place, setting the standards by which truth, beauty and righteousness shall be determined and made manifest for all to see and internalize.

However, these assumptions are now being challenged (Butchart 1988). The persons mounting these challenges, as I suggested earlier, are members of adversely characterized out-groups questioning and refuting what has been said and written about them. What they are calling for is a selective, serious, and thoroughgoing "Euroectomy" of American university curricula to temper the excessive self-glorification and self-exaltation that is the essence of ethnocentrism carried to the extreme. By challenging the contradictions that arise from confusing the local with the universal, Blacks, women, and others adversely characterized have done for Western humanities and social science curricula what consciousness did for VYGER: effected a kind of existential crisis that has brought forth all manner of defenders who realize that control of the instruments of schooling is shifting; that the way things have been done is no longer adequate or appropriate in the face of the new demands.

To take advantage of this crisis, those of us who have been critical of what is must create new models of what constitutes an educated person and knowledge rather than simply modify extant Enlightenment notions outdated by changing realities. Like VYGER's quest to transcend itself, to evolve beyond its limits, we must replace the tribalism of "sharply bounded professional communities characterized by rigorous procedures for the acculturation of their members" with a more wholistic vision (Hollinger 1993: 319). This is necessary, again quoting Clarke, because when the Europeans set forth on their mission to conquer and colonize the world, "they also colonized information about the world." They did this, Clarke contends, to aid and abet the subjugation of people of color because to "make a people partly assume that oppression is their natural lot, you have to remove them from the respectful commentary of history and make them dependent on the history of their conquerors" (Clarke 1990: 12). Indeed, the propaganda of the victor has a way of becoming the history of the vanquished (Du Bois 1935: 711-29).

ORIGINS OF THE WESTERN UNIVERSITY

Beginning in the 1100s, new knowledge filtered into an intellectually dormant Western Europe through Italy by way of Sicily, but mostly as a consequence of the presence of Arab scholars in Spain. They had arrived during the Moorish invasions of the eighth century and established universities at Cordoba, Toledo, and Grenada. The Moors reintroduced certain Greek and Latin classics that had been hidden during the so-called Dark Ages following the collapse of the Roman Empire in the West in the fifth century.

This African Renaissance, if you would, also sounded the death knell of medieval scholasticism. But it would be well into the Enlightenment of the eighteenth century, with the creation of new conceptual frameworks, before it was fully defeated. "This new knowledge burst the bonds of the cathedral and monastery schools [whose development had been spurred by Charlemagne in 789] and created the learned professions . . . which have given us our first and our best definition of a university, a society of masters and scholars" (Haskins 1923: 5).

The first European universities, Salerno, Bologna, Paris, Oxford, and Cambridge, "[appear] to have started as [scholastic guilds]—a spontaneous combination, that is to say, of teachers or scholars, or of both combined, and formed, probably, on the analogy of the trade guilds and the guilds of aliens in foreign cities, which, in the course of the 13th and 14th centuries, sprang up in most of the great European centres" (*Encyclopaedia Britannica* 1966: 862).

Guilds, however, are tribal in character. In seeking to protect their identities and regulate the number of new members to inhibit erosion of their world view through the introduction of extraneous materials, inductees must transit a series of initiation rituals. These rituals teach them the myths, norms, and culture of the group they are joining and how to express themselves in the tongue of the clan. These rituals also psychologically vest the members of the clan in the truths they have created. And this investiture makes it difficult for them to relinquish their systems of perception and belief even when their experiences in the world tell them that something is missing from those systems' universes of definition and application. To save face, clan members often proselytize for their view of the world as the only valid and reliable ordering of reality. Thus, from their beginning, universities set in motion a process that today is manifest in the traditional academic department, with all the limitations that inhere in following a division of labor model not unlike that which informed the creation of the crafts-based American Federation of Labor in the late nineteenth century in the United States.

Inherent in the creation of these first institutions of higher learning was a commitment to the spread of certain nationalist views. This is best seen in how the students were organized into colleges based on ethnicity. These nationalist views, McNeill tells us, were an outgrowth of the

> universal claims of the Roman Catholic Church, together with the military successes that Frankish arms soon attained on every frontier, [which] gave western Europeans a secure sense of superiority that ruled out both slavish imitation of their more civilized neighbors and the fear that any borrowing whatever would endanger their spiritual independence. A society remarkably open to innovation thus emerged—sure of itself, interested in the wonders of the civilized world, and eager to seize wealth, fame, and learning wherever they could be found . . . [Additionally], [t]he barbarian inheritance—both from the remote Bronze Age invasions of the second millennium B.C. and from the more immediate Germanic, Scandinavian, and steppe invasions of the first millennium A.D.—made European society more thoroughly warlike than any other civilized society on the globe excepting the Japanese. (1963: 539)

John Henrik Clarke (1990: 28) calls "this achievement the manifestation of the evil genius of Europe" and was told by Arthur Schomburg in the 1930s to read European history so he might discover how black people were left out of world history. The basis of Eurocentrism was a series of linked concepts that are still with us today and are as untrue now as they were then.

First was the assertion "that the world was waiting in darkness for the Europeans to bring the light of culture and civilization." In actuality, however, Clarke continues, the "Europeans put out more light and destroyed more civilizations and cultures than they ever built" (Clarke 1990: 28). A second contention was "that the European concept of God [was] the only concept worthy of serious religious attention. In most of the world where the Europeans expanded, especially in Africa, they deprived the people of the right to call on God in a language of their own creation and to look at God through their own imagination. They inferred or said outright that no figure that did not resemble a European could be God or the representative of God" (Clarke 1990: 28). This, of course, had the added benefit of fostering a colonization of both mind and spirit and insured that the chains of oppression, once forged, would be that much more difficult to break.

A third contention was the "European premise that the invader and conqueror is a civilizer" (Clarke 1990: 28). This premise was augmented by employing missionaries, the militia, and merchants to infiltrate extant social institutions and subvert them from within, effecting a climate of collapse and eroding the resources of recovery in the process. A fourth assertion was that of the European as discoverer. It mattered not that most of the lands on which these explorers and their apologists landed were already inhabited. What mattered was what was in the mind of the discoverer at the moment of debarkation.

Ironically enough, nascent Eurocentrism (nationalism) received its first severe shaking beginning with the voyages of discovery in the fifteenth century, as several nations (Portugal, Spain, The Netherlands, France, and England) sought to throw off the torpor of medieval complacence and replenish their national treasuries (which had been depleted by war, famine, and disease). Out there, beyond the boundaries of the known universe in terra incognita, European explorers learned that not everyone shared their view of reality or their belief that they were sui generis. Some modifications were necessary.

Meanwhile, by the end of the thirteenth century, the medieval university exhibited "many of the major features of contemporary higher education . . . including degrees, faculties, colleges, courses, examinations, and commencement, although there were no endowments in the current sense, no laboratories, and, with rare exception, no university libraries or university-owned buildings" (Levine 1978: 485). The walls of intellectual conformity were being breached by the ideas arising from "the culture of the moneyed burgher class" (Meyer 1967: 4). Additionally, there was the fifteenth century invention of the printing press, which made the ancient classics that were the source of these new ideas available on an undreamed-of scale. And there was the Protestant Reformation, which had begun as a religious movement to address certain errors and abuses (for example, the selling of Papal indulgences during the reign of Medici) in the church. The Reformation quickly spread to the more secular institutions of the society.

ORIGINS OF THE AMERICAN UNIVERSITY AS AN OUTREACH CENTER OF EUROCENTRIC CULTURE

Henry Dunster, who became president of Harvard in 1640, was a graduate of Emmanuel College, Cambridge (Herbst 1974: 9). He adopted his alma mater's curriculum, academic procedures, and code of student conduct as part of the operations manual of the new institution. From the outset, the model American college became a cultural artifact, in actuality an outreach center of Eurocentric civilization because Dunster and his associates vowed "to yield [not] an inch to pioneer prejudices or frontier values" (Rudolph 1962: 6).

But they had to yield in time, and their compromises are self-evident in the curricular changes of the nineteenth century that began to give the outpost colleges a distinctly "American" character (Herbst 1976; McCaughey 1974; McLachlan 1978). The desire to maintain the purity of the Old World university had an equally opposite force. There were those who either could not get in or disagreed with the outpost view and sought to found their own universities. Thus, a distinct dynamic was set up which has defined American higher education to this day.

Indeed, the dialectic of maintaining purity versus reform describes well the process of curriculum construction in American higher education from the founding of Harvard College in 1636 onward. Clearly, new environments have a way of modifying old cultures. What is also true is that when the recipients of the new return bringing with them information not previously a part of the common culture, it does not always follow that the new information will disturb the background and domain assumptions of the extant culture. What matters is how that information is added to what is, a point that Thomas Kuhn makes abundantly clear in his *Structure of Scientific Revolutions* (1962). Other Old World influences were soon to find their way into the evolving American university.

First, there were the Scots, whose physicians and scientists arrived early in the eighteenth century along with the return of Americans who had studied medicine at the University of Edinburgh. They "encouraged American colleges to offer instruction in more practical subjects such as medicine, to expand existing courses and programs of study in the natural sciences, and to experiment further with laboratory research and inductive logic" (Levine 1978: 486). As the century progressed, the "French added to the Scottish contribution in science, research, and professional education. They pioneered in the study of modern language and teacher education. France also influenced America with its literature on political theory and its Revolutionary War-based, antireligious spirit, which was at least briefly popular among college students in the United States" (Levine 1978: 486). It was French ideas and ideals that also influenced Jefferson's thinking in his advocacy of a radical proposal for the conduct of the University of Virginia: namely, elective courses then in operation in French universities.

But the most significant revision of the outpost academy came through the evolution of science in America. Grounded in the then current scientific revelations of an expansionist Europe, the *Philosophies* called for the conceptualization of the world as a rational, orderly place, operating not according to the immediate will of God but by changeless natural laws. This notion followed the stated beliefs of Isaac Newton. These laws allowed humans, because they were resident in a rational universe, to view themselves as good and not forever stained with sin, as was the case in rigid Calvinist theology. And, since they were good, they could use their reason to "discover the natural laws of the universe, [and then use] that knowledge . . . to control their environment and society. . . . [T]he inevitable result of this control would be progress over the course of human history. Science played a significant role in this world picture because it was by means of scientific method—observation and experiment— that natural laws could be discovered" (Unger 1989: 72).

Finally there were the Germans, whose influence on American higher educa- tion is a distinct characteristic of the nineteenth century. This influence came primarily as a corollary of Americans going to Germany (George Ticknor and Edward Everett, who went in 1815, are believed to be the first to do so) for advanced study and then returning to seek teaching positions in the United States at the collegiate level. Among the major German contributions to Ameri- can higher education were accelerated "development of graduate education and [increased emphasis on] the role of research in the university." Additionally, "other features of contemporary American higher education that originated in Germany [were] the organization of the faculty and the curriculum according to academic disciplines, the major or concentration, academic freedom, wide lati- tude for students in choosing courses, scholarly library collections, theses, labo- ratory courses, and seminar instruction" (Levine 1978: 486-87). Built on a foundation of what they had learned in the European universities, the newly arrived settlers and their descendants would work to shape both the structure and content of the academy in America so that by the twentieth century a new conceptualization of collegiate education would appear, one based on merito- cratic standards.

The blending and mixing of nationalist university elements from the Old World did not create a new university. This was because of a core consisting of beliefs and intents that were not up for compromise. The expressed intent of these institutions was to carry forward the mantle of Western (European) civili- zation. This intent became especially entrenched as the United States began to absorb large numbers of southern and eastern European immigrants. In the words of Meyer and Marden, "the American Experience [especially that incor- porated into the several college and university curricula] has been in large part the attempt of the entrenched White, Anglo-Saxon Protestants (WASPS) to maintain their privileges, their values, their institutions in the face of heavy im- migration of people whose values, language, customs and often appearances have been different" (1969: 29).

By the time of America's war of secession from Great Britain in 1776, eight more colleges had been established in the colonies: William and Mary (1693) in Virginia; Yale (1701) in Connecticut; College of New Jersey (Princeton; 1746); Queen's College (Rutgers; 1766), also in New Jersey; King's College (Colum- bia; 1754) in New York; College of Philadelphia (University of Pennsylvania; 1754); Rhode Island College (Brown; 1764); and Dartmouth (1769) in Hanover, New Hampshire. Because Harvard provided many of the teachers for these new schools, they came to resemble Harvard in many ways (Kraus 1961).

Following the successful conclusion of the war in 1783, higher education became a growth industry for just about everyone in the newly formed United

States until about the time of the Civil War. There were, however, small periods of overall enrollment decline throughout the 1800s because of the strong anti-intellectual character of the citizenry, who believed that college was not necessary for material success (Hofstader 1963), and because of the perceived irrelevance of the classical curriculum (Handlin and Handlin 1970). White men were eagerly welcomed into the hallowed halls as seekers after the faith, in particular "those from relatively affluent families" (Current, et al. 1987: 84). Because it was not in their interest to do so, few questioned either who was taught or the European nationalism of what was taught. Consequently, there was more enculturation to the status quo than challenge to the truth arising from different views of the world fostered by differential experiences.

Women and black people were excluded for the most part until well into the nineteenth century and then were remanded to the custody of segregated institutions (Bullock 1970: 60-88), which were to remain relatively isolated and underfunded until the sixth decade of the twentieth century (Ballard 1973). Furthermore, given the preparation and interests of their founders, it is interesting to note that when these colleges were created in great numbers especially for the Freedmen and women following the end of the War Between the States, their curricula replicated, in large part, the classical curriculum of the New England liberal arts colleges at a time when the demand for a more practical education was increasing in intensity (Anderson 1988; Gallagher 1938; Holmes 1934; Sekora 1960).

The "history of the order of learning in the United States from the end of the Civil War to the end of World War I," writes Edward Shils (1979: 19), "may be seen largely as the history of a fundamental change in institutional structure [as distinct from a change in curriculum content]. One particular class of institutions, the university, gained ascendancy over other institutional forms for the discovery and diffusion of knowledge, and specific universities within that newly dominant class came to be recognized as the central elements in the academic order." Two important developments characterize the period.

The first of these was the replacement of "amateur scientists and scholars . . . by those who earned their living by studying and teaching within an elaborate institution. Second, those institutions whose members regarded study and teaching as their major obligation came to be recognized as the primary instruments for the cultivation of learning in America" (Shils 1979: 19). The Age of Specialization, wherein the several disciplines would increasingly become closed systems, had begun (Becher 1987; Chubin 1976; Metzger 1987).

In 1869 Harvard introduced the elective system (Eliot 1869). This German product had first appeared in certain American colleges in the 1820s. The emergence of the elective system in American higher education catalyzed the erosion of a single, official truth. Not only did it effect a change in the content and means of education, but it also catalyzed a change in the accessibility of information about the world in which certain people lived.

The old prescribed course of study was a course in elementary subjects, and it not only held the student and teacher to the most superficial kind of knowledge, but also sustained colleges that got along quite well on a level of alarming superficiality. Election permitted the professor to indulge his interests and the students to follow theirs; it encouraged the accumulation of knowledge and welcomed into the world of learning subjects that had been forbidden through an ill-considered belief that the ancients knew everything worth knowing. (Rudolph 1962: 304-05)

The advent of the elective system also brought with it adverse implications for monoculturalism. With the acceptance of the variable course structure in the American university in the post-Civil War period, there arose the questions of whose history, whose philosophy, whose politics, whose whatever would be taught and how and by whom that information would be selected? The importance of these questions which continued to bubble just below the surface of scholarly debate and discussion, was made all the more so because the academic disciplines emerged and evolved during a period of social transformation in the larger society, which was searching for order. The full force of this development would not be apparent before the 1960s, however, with the emergence of black studies, women's studies and the like.

Similarly, the elective system encouraged "the rise of science and the remarkably expanding areas of knowledge for what they were: clear indications that no longer could any one person really know everything worth knowing" (Rudolph 1962). In so doing, it gave impetus to the rise of the social sciences, which were embryonic within the discipline of moral philosophy (Bryson 1932); it also "moved the individual to the center of the educational universe and boldly asserted that all educated men need not know the same things. . . . [B]y giving free play to the great motive power of interest, [the elective principle] freed the curriculum from the deadening influence of latent or open disinterest and hostility, and perhaps thereby contributed to two subsidiary developments: the tendency of standards of academic performance to be set no longer by the slow students, but now by the most interested and more able students; and the tendency" for the faculty and students to no longer be enemies but friends (Rudolph 1962: 305).

More pointedly, the elective system led to the rise of academic departments expanding at the same time the information base out of which knowledge was created (Coats 1968; Diner 1975; Dressel 1968; Mackenzie 1976; Mark 1976; Schwab 1964; Storer and Parsons 1968). And, by grafting German research ideals onto the English college model, the elective system created the American university in the process (Ely 1880). This one reform made it possible to address a particular American concern—the development of an occupational structure that would allow for more than one full professor in a broad subject field. For what was becoming clear was that as more was learned, there was more to be learned. This new institution was now ready "to enter into a vital partnership with the society of which it was a part" (Rudolph 1962).

But, as in all things, no change is entirely positive. In the case of the elective system, with its compartmentalization of knowledge, there was a consequent rise in alienation—not only among the practitioners from themselves, but also from the larger society of which they were a part (Sloan 1985). The resulting fragmentation of knowledge produced a proliferation of fields, disciplines, and their supporting academic organizations, where the human experience could be divided into multiple levels of analysis (Becher 1989; Sohn-Rethel 1986).

This was especially the case for the newly emergent social sciences, where culture was studied by anthropologists, society by sociologists, the market by economists, the body politic by political scientists, ecology by geographers, and the like. Moreover, as the social sciences developed, they increasingly looked inward and developed a kind of intellectual parochialism that limited the perceptions of the practitioner to a particularist cognitive world. In so doing, they further bound themselves to certain unquestioned background and domain assumptions that had informed the parent endeavors from which they descended (Gouldner 1970: 29-34; Segall 1975: 4).

In addition, the social sciences looked to the more established natural sciences, which had already had major success in being accepted as an organ of truth for their operational and structural models. Consequently, they were further constrained—because of the limitations (in particular, an insensitivity to cultural difference) inherent in the methods they borrowed and the supporting philosophy of logical positivism—in what they could accept as valid evidence in the examination and interpretation of people, events, situations, and behavior different from themselves.

However, as much as the social sciences sought prestige by attempting to be more scientific, the more it eluded them because they had no (and still do not have) real answers for society's problems. Like VYGER, they found it difficult to believe in or prove the existence of whatever lay outside the definitional boundaries of their carefully drawn (out of their own experiences in the world) universes. Their reluctance to address the cause of many of the problems they sought to solves inherent in the structure they were examining moved them further and further from the source at the same time that they retreated into a kind of sham scientism. These developments (especially the growing objectification of knowledge, the belief that truth is out there somewhere, that truth is independent of the observer) would have major long-term repercussions coincident with the intensification of imperialism and colonialism in Africa and Asia following the Berlin conferences of 1884-1885, the abolition of slavery, and the attendant struggle of black people in the United States to chart the course of their own destiny.

THE TRIUMPHS OF TRIBALISM

John Stanfield (1985: 387-415) describes in some detail how the "objectification of knowledge [has become] a matter of power and privilege." Given that power is the ability to shape reality, it is clear, he continues, that the "objectification of Euro-American experiences in the United States and their systemic diffusion is related intrinsically to the creation and reproduction of hegemonic racial domination" (Stanfield 1985: 387). In other words the canon (which many persons are now seeking to colorize and make more relevant to the larger world) grows out of a quest for cultural homogeneity.

Utilizing the "normative conceptions of Euro-Americans and the distortion of racial minority experiences," reality is interpreted in such a manner that "a privileged subset of the population [has come] to exert its will on others through its control of such major institutions and resources as the media, legislation, and compulsory schooling" (Stanfield 1985: 388). The upshot of all of this has been the creation of deficit models based on what white men, white people, and honorary whites are not, and the consequent marginalization of all others who are not cast in the image of those who have constructed the criteria of validation and legitimization. These models and their attendant images are then made a part of the schooling curricula and are passed on to succeeding generations as a kind of gospel (received wisdom) from which all else might be derived.

The origins of these deficit models, writes Mia Bay (n.d.: 10), arose from the "interest Enlightenment era thinkers took in the physical side of human nature and in man's place in the natural world [which] led them to devise systems of classification for people paralleling those they developed to study the animal kingdom." The dominant view was that environment rather than innate characteristics was the cause of racial difference; that, in actuality, all people were of the same type and descended from a single ancestor—in short, Adam.

This view was also prevalent at the beginning of the nineteenth century in the United States as exemplified in Samuel Stanhope Smith's *An Essay on the Causes of the Variety of Complexion and Figure in the Human Species*, first published in 1787, with a revised, expanded version of the work issued in 1810. Smith, a Presbyterian clergyman, professor, and later president of the College of New Jersey (Princeton University), argued the monogenetic origin of humans and stressed the importance of climate and, secondarily, "the influence of society, the manner of living, diet and disease" as factors in the emergence of the several races rather than the competing separate creation notion (Ruchames 1969: 180-92).

The ranking of different peoples by race or other ascriptive features, "although many of the eighteenth-century classifiers held the physical and mental characteristics of non-European peoples in low esteem" (Bay n.d.), would not begin in earnest until after the publication of Darwin's *Origin of Species* in 1859 (Haller 1971). However, a change was in the wind as evident in the writings of Count Joseph Arthur de Gobineau.

Gobineau was a Frenchman and the father of modern European racism. His book, *The Moral and Intellectual Diversity of Races, with Particular Reference to Their Respective Influence in the Civil and Political History of Mankind*, published in four volumes from 1853 to 1855, was described by one writer as "short on biology and long on dogmatic assertions about the historical role of the races" (Fredrickson 1971: 79). This work first appeared in translation in the

United States in 1856, and it fit in with American racist thinking, which was already well underway (due in part to the need to counter the growing strength of the abolitionist movement). It would further shape the thinking and writings of the learned professions and their students in the years to come.

Because "the inherent inequality of races was simply accepted as a scientific fact in America, . . . most of the discussion now concerned either the religious problem of accepting polygenesis as an explanation of racial differences or the problem of exactly defining the different races" (Horsman 1981: 134). This orientation was carried over into the formation of the social sciences, whose practitioners, as I noted earlier, had borrowed heavily from the natural sciences in their quest for legitimacy and power. Add to this Barbara Field's observation that ideology rises out of and becomes the "descriptive vocabulary of day-to-day existence, through which people make rough sense of the social reality that they create from day-to-day" (1990: 110), and we can at last begin to come to grips with how Eurocentrism has sustained and renewed itself within the American university curriculum throughout much of the twentieth century. In short, what has historically been presented as the dominant paradigm is in fact the opinion of a minority special interest group that has sought to displace the views of others with its own as the only legitimate interpretation of how the world works. An excellent example of this is found in Robert V. Guthrie's *Even the Rat Was White: A Historical View of Psychology* (1976).

Because teachers tend to teach what they have been taught, and because, until recently, there have been few teachers with both the knowledge and the skills to raise the necessary challenges, what has evolved over the years is a series of mythic images and stereotypes about women and people of color that constitute a kind of scholarly game-playing employed to imprison the hearts and minds of those so characterized (Gilman 1983; Hayes 1973; Hirsch 1975; Jones 1971; Thomas 1982). These images and stereotypes are sustained by what I have referred to over the years as the "3-D Theory of History—Deletion, Denial, and Distortion," whose operational paradigm, like VYGER'S, was crafted at a time when life was simpler and more easily understood. Because this ideology was constructed to promote the interests of a "superior" group, whatever positions its proponents took or whatever truths they advanced were deemed universal and valid for all peoples, all places, and the whole of time. And it was this truth that was plugged into the structural reforms described by Shils (1979).

More importantly, these truths have remained relatively undisturbed until recently because to challenge them would be to challenge the validity of reason itself. That is, it was argued that the meanings which had been attached to the several classes of objects, races, genders, classes, whatever, and so on had been arrived at by the exercise of reason, humankind's foremost faculty. Having access to the academy is one thing. Being able to transform what is presented for one's own purposes is another thing and requires not only a knowledge of one's own educational history, but the willingness to challenge what is being presented as something other than a monolithic certainty. Further, it requires the motivation to retain a sense of self and a belief in the validity of one's own experience such that they are not separated and the latter is not devalued and replaced by reliance on outside authority.

Clearly, as science progresses from its reliance on amateurs to professionals for the acquisition and promulgation of new knowledge, it creates a need for disciples who have the proper orientation: persons who are about the business of learning the values, assumptions, beliefs, norms, folkways, and subject matter of the new fields in question. This is the task of the graduate school. One does not go to graduate school to become more proficient in the promulgation of one's own particular heresies, which would result in exclusion from the tribe. Rather, one goes to graduate school to learn how to protect a sacred trust. Accordingly, the graduate school, like the seminary, has become more an agency of socialization than a ministry of further education. In brief, it is the vehicle by which disciplines become self-replicating, and it is therefore a marvelous example of shaping truth to reflect the interests of truth's creators (Dynes 1974; Jones 1980). It is also where future teachers are trained and the tribal character of the scholastic enterprise is maintained.

The graduate school does this first by segmenting the universe into territories that can only be explored and mined in ways deemed appropriate by the village elders—those stellar scholars who are known throughout the land for the pearls of wisdom they have extracted from the seas of information they have dredged in the search for truth. Second, it does this by developing special new languages that are then employed to explore and map the terrains they survey—a kind of magic-speak whose learning becomes the worthiness test of all who aspire to enter the brotherhood at the same time that it separates the scholars from the people. Third, it does this by the creating apprenticeship programs wherein the neophytes are introduced to the rituals and folklore of the clan and learn that the path to greater glory is already marked out and those who follow the directions of their mentors will triumph. Fourth, the graduate school does this by establishing professional organizations that police the conduct of the "ists" and sustain the corporate culture by which direction and meaning are effected.

House organs—journals and newsletters—published by the flock not only keep the membership informed of what is going on in the group, but also inform the public of its research findings and how they might be used as fits the occasion. Once this system is up and running, inertia tends to keep it in motion, obfuscating the reality that knowledge is a social construct by virtue of the abstractive processes employed to ascertain truth and the cultural limits of all scholarly enterprise.

Thus, it does not matter whether a little gender here or a little race there is introduced into the curriculum, as has been the case in some institutions after all these years of struggle. For the core of the instructional content remains the same no matter how much the world outside the academy changes. And, as was noted earlier, these minuscule additions, usually characterized as a racial/cultural or gender diversity requirement for all students, are easily trivialized and constitute a kind of gratuitous tokenism. It is almost as if all the Supreme

Court decisions of the 1930s, 1940s, 1950s, and 1960s with regard to black access and inclusion in the academy mean nothing.

Like VYGER, the newly minted scholars departed from their bases full of truth and certainty. Wherever they went, they carried the Word with them and the Word was them. Their task was clear—learn all that was learnable and return what they found to those who would analyze and interpret the collected data.

On each of their journeys, they acquired (in addition to material riches) information that stretched the boundaries of preconceived paradigms until they fractured and broke from the weight of new facts. Like VYGER, they were sometimes puzzled by what did not make sense. For every now and again, they would encounter a data set (Africans who embraced different tenets of religion, science, philosophy; Indians whose lifestyles were more compatible with the environment) outside the pale of their Truth. Still they pressed on, guided by a belief in their own rightness. As the voyage proceeded and they went merrily about filling up the empty sets of their extant paradigms, they began to confront a new reality: Their tools had a priori fixed capacities.

However, they had the power of their convictions to guide them. They knew their views were the only correct ones and that, in time, everyone else would come to see things their way. What they did not count on was that some folks (Blacks, Indians, women, for example) might not want to see the world as seen by the Conquistadores and that they might prefer to see things their own way because they have come to understand (because of their own beliefs) that all truth is relative, that no one group, however self-important, however isolated or insulated, has a monopoly on truth.

Indeed, it was almost as if they, too, had followed the wise counsel of their own Arthur A. Schomburg and read the histories of the clans into which they were being inducted and learned what had been left out. For it is in the records of the Eurocentrics themselves that they tell us how they have used schooling and knowledge to sustain colonial rule in Africa, Asia, the United States, and the islands of the seas (Altbach and Kelly 1978; Deloria, 1981).

We are poised now on the threshold of a new century. What we have to ask is whether the corporate cultures manifest in the American university at this time are adequate and appropriate to meet the challenges of a multiracial, multicultural world whose citizens have begun to beat back and down the myths, half-truths, lies, and outrageous fabrications that have been built up about them to keep them in their place (Gilman 1983). We know that the university is a political structure established to continue and expand upon the early coercive socialization of its charges to accept the orthodox values of the society that was begun in the lower grades (Gracey 1972: 243-53). And we know, as was observed earlier that the curriculum itself is a political statement about a desired reality. Indeed, both the university and its curricula operate to effect agreed-upon certainties implicit in the society and culture of which they are a part.

But what we also know is that the world now is not the same world that existed when our European-schooled forebears stepped forth upon this continent to establish a new land in keeping with their visions of how that world should be run. If we, like VYGER, are to transcend ourselves and cast off the false boundaries that keep us in a state of incompletion, then we, like VYGER, must learn how to combine what is both inside and outside of the paradigms we employ to make sense of the world. For what is clear is that new information requires a reconfiguration, not restatement, of the old paradigm. Perhaps, in the pages which follow, the sensitive reader will find some of the material needed to begin that process.

REFERENCES

Altbach, Philip. G., and Gail P. Kelly. 1978. *Education and Colonialism*. New York: Longman.

Anderson, James D. 1988. *The Education of Blacks in the South, 1860-1935*. Chapel Hill: University of North Carolina Press.

Ballad, Allan. 1973. *The Education of Black Folks: The Afro-American Struggle for Knowledge in White America*. New York: Harper and Row.

Bay, Mia. (n.d). *A War of Minds: African-Americans Respond to the Rise of Ideological Racism*. Unpublished paper.

Becher, Tony. 1987. "The Disciplinary Shaping of the Profession." In *The Academic Profession*, Burton R. Clark, ed., pp. 271-303. Berkeley: University of California Press.

Becher, Tony. 1989. *Academic Tribes and Territories*. Bristol, PA: The Society for Research into Higher Education and Open University Press.

Brodbeck, May. 1962. "Toward a Fabric of Knowledge—Common Elements among Fields of Learning." *The Educational Record* 24, 43: 217-222.

Bryson, Gladys. 1932. "The Emergence of the Social Sciences from Moral Philosophy." *International Journal of Ethics*, 42: 304-323.

Bullock, Henry. 1970. *A History of Negro Education in the South from 1619 to the Present*. New York: Praeger.

Butchart, Ronald E. 1988. "Outthinking and Outflanking the Owners of the World: A Historiography of the African-American Struggle for Education." *History of Education Quarterly* 28: 333-466.

Chubin, Daryl E. 1976. "The Conceptualization of Scientific Specialties." *The Sociological Quarterly* 17: 448-476.

Clarke, John H. 1990. "Can African People Save Themselves?" *The City Sun*, 10-16 October, 6, 28-29.

Coats, A. W. 1968. "Henry Carter Adams: A Case Study in the Emergence of the Social Sciences in the United States, 1850-1900." *American Studies*, 2: 177-97.

Cowley, W. H. 1939. "European Influences upon American Higher Education." *The Educational Record* 20: 165-190.

Current, Richard, T.H. Williams, F. Fredio, and A. Brinkley. 1987. *American History* (7th ed.). New York: Alfred A. Knopf.

Deloria, Vine. 1981. "Education and Imperialism." *Integrated Education* 19: 58-63.

Diner, Steven J. 1975. "Department and Discipline: The Department of Sociology at the University of Chicago, 1892-1920." *Minerva*, 13: 514-553.

Dressel, Paul L. 1968. *College and University Curriculum*. Berkeley, CA: McCutchan Publishing Co.

Du Bois, William E. B. 1935. *Black Reconstruction in America*, pp. 711-729. New York: Russell and Russell.

Dynes, Russell S. 1974. "Sociology as a Religious Movement: Thoughts on Its Institutionalization in the United States." *The American Sociologist* 9: 169-176.

Eliot, Charles W. 1869. "The New Education, Its Organization." *Atlantic Monthly*, 203-220, 358-367.

Ely, Richard T. 1880. "American Colleges and German Universities." *Harper's* 61: 253-260.

Encyclopaedia Britannica. 1966. Universities. Vol. 22. Chicago: Encyclopaedia Britannica Publishing.

Fields, Barbara J. 1990. "Slavery, Race and Ideology in the United States of America." *New Left Review* 181: 95-118.

Fredrickson, George M. 1971. *The Black Image in the White Mind*. New York: Harper and Row.

Fuller, Steve. 1988. *Social Epistemology*. Bloomington: Indiana University Press.

Gallagher, Buell G. 1938. *American Caste and the Negro College*. New York: Columbia University Press.

Gilman, Stuart C. 1983. "Degeneracy and Race in the Nineteenth Century: The Impact of Clinical Medicine." *The Journal of Ethnic Studies* 10: 27-50.

Gould, Julius and W. L. Kolbs, eds. 1964. *A Dictionary of the Social Sciences*. New York: The Free Press.

Gouldner, Alvin W. 1970. *The Coming Crisis of Western Sociology*. New York: Basic Books.

Gracey, Harry L. 1972. "Learning the Student Role: Kindergarten as Academic Boot Camp." In *Readings in Introductory Sociology*, 2nd ed., Dennis H. Wrong and H. L. Gracey, eds., pp. 243-253. New York: Macmillan.

Guthrie, Robert V. 1976. *Even the Rat Was White: A Historical View of Psychology*. New York: Harper and Row.

Haller, John S. 1971. *Outcasts from Evolution*. Urbana: University of Illinois Press.

Handlin, Oscar, and Mary F. Handlin. 1970. *The American College and American Culture: Socialization as a Function of Higher Education*. New York: McGraw-Hill.

Haskins, Charles H. 1923. *The Rise of Universities*. New York: Henry Holt and Company.

Hayes, James R. 1973. "Sociology and Racism: An Analysis of the First Era of American Sociology." *Phylon* 34: 330-341.

Herbst, Jurgen. 1974. "The First Three American Colleges: Schools of the Reformation." *Perspectives in American History* 8: 7-52.

Herbst, Jurgen. 1976. "The American Revolution and the American University." *Perspectives in American History* 10: 279-354.

Hirsch, Jerry. 1975. "Jensenism: The Bankruptcy of 'Science' Without Scholarship." *Educational Theory* 25: 3-27.

Hofstader, Richard. 1963. *Anti-Intellectualism in America*. New York: Alfred A. Knopf.

Hollinger, David A. 1993. "How Wide the Circle of the 'We'? American Intellectuals and the Problem of the Ethnos Since World War II." *American Historical Review* 98: 317-337.

Holmes, Dwight O. 1934. *The Evolution of the Negro College*. New York: Teachers College, Columbia University.

Horsman, Richard. 1981. *Race and Manifest Destiny*. Cambridge, MA: Harvard University Press.

Illich, Ivan. 1970. *Deschooling Society*. New York: Harper and Row.

Jones, Rhett S. 1971. "Proving Blacks Inferior, 1870-1930." *Black World*, 20: 4-19.

Jones, Robert A. 1980. "Myth and Symbol among the Nacirema Tsigoloicos: A Fragment." *The American Sociologist* 15: 207-212.

Kraus, Joe W. 1961. "The Development of a Curriculum in the Early American Colleges." *History of Education Quarterly* 1: 64-76.

Kuhn, Thomas. 1962. *Structure of Scientific Revolutions*. Chicago: University of Chicago Press.

Levine, Arthur. 1978. *Handbook on Undergraduate Curriculum*. San Francisco: Jossey-Bass.

Lewis, J. 1968. "Tribal Society." In *International Encyclopedia of Social Science* Vol. 16, pp. 146-157. New York: Macmillan. p. 146-57.

Mackenzie, Brian. 1976. "Darwinism and Positivism as Methodological Influences on the Development of Psychology." *Journal of the History of the Behavioral Sciences* 12: 330-337.

Mark, Joan. 1976. "Frank Hamilton Cushing and an American Science of Anthropology." *Perspectives in American History* 10: 449-486.

McCaughey, Robert A. 1974. "The Transformation of American Academic Life: Harvard University, 1821-1892." *Perspectives in American History* 8: 239-332.

McLachlan, James. 1978. "The American College in the Nineteenth Century: Toward a Reappraisal." *Teachers College Record* 80: 287-306.

McNeill, William H. 1963. *The Rise of the West*. Chicago: University of Chicago Press.

Metzger, Walter P. 1987. "The Academic Profession in the United States." In *The Academic Profession*, Burton R. Clark, ed., pp. 123-208. Berkeley: University of California Press.

Meyer, Adolph E. 1967. *An Educational History of the American People*. New York: McGraw-Hill.

Meyer, Gladys, and Charles F. Marden. 1969. *Minorities in American Society*. New York: Van Nostrand Reinhold.

Nash, Paul. 1961. "Innocents Abroad: American Students at British Universities in the Early Nineteenth Century." *History of Education Quarterly* 1: 32-44.

Rollins, Peter C. 1972. "The Whorf Hypothesis as a Critique of Western Science and Technology." *American Quarterly* 24: 563-583.

Ruchames, Louis. 1969. *Racial Thought in America*. Amherst, MA: University of Massachusetts Press.

Rudolph, Frederick. 1962. *The American College and University: A History*. New York: Random House.

Rudolph, Frederick. 1977. *Curriculum*. San Francisco: Jossey-Bass.

Schwab, Joseph J. 1964. "Structure of the Disciplines: Meanings and Significances." In *The Structure of Knowledge and the Curriculum*, G. W. Ford and L. Pugno, eds., pp. 6-30. Chicago: Rand McNally & Co.

Segall, Marshall H. 1975. "Toward a Definition of Interdisciplinary Social Science: More-or-Less Than its Parts?" *Maxwell/News and Notes* 10: 4-6.

Sekora, John. 1960. "Murder Relentless and Impassive: The American Academic Community and the Negro College." *Soundings* 51: 237-271.

Shils, Edward. 1979. "The Order of Learning in the United States: The Ascendancy of the University." In *The Organization of Knowledge in Modern America, 1860-*

1920, Alexandra Oleson and John Voss, eds., pp. 19-47. Baltimore: The Johns Hopkins University Press.

Sloan, Douglas. 1985. "Knowledge, Values, and Educational History: 'Once More Unto the Breach, Dear Friends.'" *History of Education Quarterly* 25: 1-19.

Smith, Huston. 1979. "Excluded Knowledge: A Critique of the Modern Western Mind Set." *Teachers College Record* 80: 419-445.

Sohn-Rethel, Alfred. 1986. "Science as Alienated Consciousness." In *Radical Science Essays*, Les Levidow, ed., pp. 104-139. London: Free Association Books.

Stanfield, John H. 1985. "The Ethnocentric Basis of Social Science Knowledge Production." *Review of Research in Education* 12: 387-415.

Storer, Norman W. and Talcott Parsons. 1968. "The Disciplines as a Differentiating Force." In *The Foundations of Access to Knowledge: A Symposium*, Edward B. Montgomery, ed., pp. 101-121. Syracuse, NY: Syracuse University Press.

Thomas, William B. 1982. "Black Intellectuals' Critique of Early Mental Testing: A Little-Known Saga of the 1920s." *American Journal of Education* 90: 258-292.

Unger, Irwin. 1989. *These United States*, 4th ed. Englewood Cliffs, NJ: Prentice-Hall.

Vesey, Laurence R. 1965. *The Emergence of the American University*. University of Chicago Press.

Chapter 3

Afrocentricity and Multicultural Education: Concept, Challenge, and Contribution

Maulana Karenga

INTRODUCTION

Generative Assumptions

The current debate on the character and content of quality education in a multicultural context offers new possibilities not only for the reconception and reconstruction of public and higher education but also for society itself. For the debate is in essence about power and place, standards of relevance, and the quality of relations among the various cultural groups which compose society.

This chapter is offered as a contribution to this discourse and is based on and informed by several interrelated assumptions: (1) that both our society and the larger human community are fundamentally characterized by diversity and that human diversity is human richness; (2) that to benefit from this rich diversity, we must not simply tolerate it but embrace and build on it; (3) that each people has the right and responsibility to speak its own special cultural truth and make its own unique contribution to the forward flow of societal and human history; (4) that the search for truth in the service of a fuller and freer humanity must include travel on paths opened and paved in history by humanity in all its rich, complex, and instructive diversity; (5) that given these realities, multicultural education is at the heart of any meaningful concept of quality education; (6) that the imperative of a truly multicultural education rests on substantive moral, intellectual and social grounds, and (7) that the Afrocentric vision of quality education offers in content, perspective, and methodology an important contribution to this urgent quest for both quality education and a just and good society.

Grounding of Multicultural Education

It is important to stress, as stated earlier, that the thrust for a multicultural education rests on solid moral, intellectual, and social grounds. The moral grounds pertain to a real respect for the concrete human person in all her or his diversity. The student and teacher are not abstracted from concrete conditions for critical understanding but are engaged from the vantage point of their own experience. They speak from their own experience and location in history and culture and thus enrich educational discourse and express a democratic public life rooted in cooperative forms of participation and exchange.

The intellectual grounding of multicultural education is revealed, as I (Report 1991: 3) have argued elsewhere, in its use and value as (1) "a necessary corrective for the conceptual and content inadequacy of the exclusive curriculum which omits and diminishes the rich (and instructive) variety of human cultures"; (2) an equally important corrective for racist, sexist, classist, and chauvinistic approaches to knowledge and education which deny, demean, or diminish the meaning, experience, and voice of the other; (3) a necessary reflection of the multicultural society in which we live; and (4) a creative challenge to the established order of things. For it is in the established order of things that the university is reduced to a warehouse of Eurocentric goods to be authoritatively transmitted and imposed as a sacrosanct canon or unproblematic body of deference-deserving knowledge. Multicultural education, especially in its Afrocentric form, comes into being and establishes its raison d'être as an uncompromising and relentless critique of the established order. It then offers correctives pointed toward creating a richer and more varied educational experience as well as a just and good society.

The social grounds of multicultural education rise from its function as (1) a just response to the demand of marginalized and excluded peoples for an education relevant to their own life experience; (2) an indispensable preparation of students and teachers for the world in which they live, work, study, and interact with others; (3) preparation of youth for the burden of support of an older and different population based on principles of appreciation for diversity, mutuality and interdependence, and (4) "part and parcel of the thrust to create a just and good society, to avoid civil strife, and to enhance the quality of social life . . ." (Report 1991: 4).

If quality education is of necessity multicultural education, the challenge is not to provide an Afrocentric paradigm for the entire curriculum of schools and universities. Rather it is to propose an Afrocentric contribution which will become a constitutive part of the overall movement toward a genuinely multicultural university. For in a multicultural context, the curriculum cannot be totally Afrocentric or it will become hegemonic as is the current Eurocentric model, which dismisses and devalues other cultures. On the contrary, the curriculum will be multicultural with various cultural visions, including the Afrocentric vision, as fundamental constitutive parts of the educational process. This position in no way suggests that Africana studies departments and programs should not be Afrocentric. On the contrary, they must be Afrocentric; otherwise the distinctiveness of their contribution to multicultural discourse is called into question and ultimately undermined.

TOWARD DEFINING AFROCENTRICITY

A successful delineation of the Afrocentric vision of quality education and its contribution to multicultural education requires several interrelated tasks. First, Afrocentricity, the central concept in the Afrocentric vision, must be explained in its own terms (Asante 1990; Karenga1988). In this way the concept is freed from the imprecise descriptions of some of its adherents and from the hysteria of the media and Eurocentric academicians, who often seem more interested in preserving privileged position and canon rather than facilitating and clarifying discourse (Ravitch 1990; Schlesinger 1991).

Second, the successful delineation of an Afrocentric vision of quality education requires that it be distinguished from the established-order Eurocentric educational process in its most negative form. Third, such a delineation must present and explain the value of the areas of fundamental focus and practice of such an educational project. This includes simultaneous discussion of the pedagogy which informs and implements the basic demands of the paradigm.

Development of the Category

Afrocentricity as an intellectual category is relatively new in the discourse of Africana studies, beginning with its introduction in the late 1970s by Molefi Asante (1980). It is Asante who attempted to unify conceptually the varied African-centered approaches to Africana Studies by designating them as Afrocentric. This is not to suggest that Afrocentric studyand teaching are, themselves, new, for there are important works in African intellectual history which represent a long-term stress on the need for African-centered thought and practice. For example, one can cite, among others, works on education by W. E. B. Du Bois (1975), Anna Julia Cooper (1988), and Carter G. Woodson (1969).

Asante's (1980, 1987, 1990) essential contribution to this orientation in Africana studies is the provision of the category Afrocentricity itself and an accompanying literature which contributes definitively to the delineation of a conceptual framework for a self-conscious, unified, and effective way of understanding, appreciating, and utilizing the rich and varied complexity of African life and culture. Since the introduction of the category, the discourse around it and within its conceptual framework has been extensive and varied. Therefore, when one speaks of the Afrocentric project, one should always keep in mind that one is not talking about a monolithic position but rather a general conceptual orientation among Africana studies scholars whose fundamental point of departure and intellectual concerns and views are centered in the African experience.

Within Afrocentric discourse, two nominal categories are given from which the adjectival category, Afrocentric, is derived: Afrocentricity and Afrocentrism. In my contribution to discipline discourse, I prefer and use Afrocentricity for several reasons: (1) to stress its intellectual value as distinct from its ideological use; (2) to distinguish it clearly from Eurocentricism, which is an ideology of domination and exclusion; and (3) to establish it as a quality of thought and practice rather than thought and practice itself. The need to stress its intellectual value as opposed to or distinct from its ideological use appears obvious. For if it is to fulfill its educational potential and promise, it must prove itself essentially an intellectual category. Second, Afrocentricity rather than Afrocentrism is used here because of the equally obvious need to distinguish the category from uninformed or manipulative associations of it with Eurocentrism. In this respect, it is important that the specific cultural and general human character of Afrocentricity be stressed. For Afrocentricity must never be conceived of or employed as a reaction to or an African version of Eurocentrism, with its racist and structured denial and deformation of the history and humanity of peoples of color. As I (1988: 404) have stated, "Afrocentricity, at its best, is a quest for and an expression of historical and cultural anchor, a critical reconstruction that dares to restore missing and hidden parts of our historical self-formation and pose the African experience as a significant paradigm for human liberation and a higher level of human life." Moreover, "to be no more than an 'obscene caricature of Europe'—to use Fanon's phrase- is to violate historical memory and vitiate historical possibilities inherent in the special truth Africans can and must speak to the world, given their ancient, rich and varied experience."

The Afrocentric vision, critically defined and developed, demands that Africana studies root itself in the African experience and in the world view which evolves from and informs that experience. For inherent in the assumption of the legitimacy and relevance of the discipline is the conception of the validity and value of studying Africans in understanding humanity as a whole. Having rooted itself in the African experience, which is the source and substance of its raison d'être, Africana studies expands outward to acquire knowledge based on other human experiences. African humanity is thus enriched and expanded by knowledge of and mutually beneficial exchanges with others. Moreover, in understanding human history as a whole, Africans can even more critically appreciate their fundamental role in the origins of human civilization and in the forward flow of human history.

Third, the category Afrocentricity is preferred in order to focus on the cultural and human quality of the thought and practice rather than on the thought and practice as ideological conception and conduct. As a quality of thought and practice defined by its particular African and shared human character, it allows for greater intellectual use and value and again avoids reductive translation as just another ideological posture. It is, in a word, a category of African culture

and shared human interests and thus fits within the particular and universal demands of multicultural education and exchange.

Definition and Implications

Afrocentricity can be defined as a methodology, orientation, or quality of
thought and practice rooted in the cultural image and human interests of African
people. To be rooted in the cultural image of African people is to be anchored in
the views, values, and practices of African people. To be rooted in the human
interests of African people is to be informed of and attentive to the just claims
on life and society that Africans share with other peoples, such as respect and
concern for truth, justice, freedom, and the dignity of the human person.

Afrocentricity as a culturally rooted approach to thought and practice brings
both a particular and universal dimension. It contributes a particular cultural
insight and discourse to the multicultural project and in the process finds common ground with other cultures which can be cultivated and developed for mutual benefit. In fact, Afrocentric thought shelters the assumption that the rich,
varied, and complex character of African culture is a critical resource in understanding and engaging the human community. Moreover, in an educational context, Afrocentric contributions to research and teaching not only challenge
established-order discourse but contribute to the broadening and deepening of
the educational process.

It is important to state that my use of the terms *African-centeredness* and
Afrocentric does not intend to suggest any more for the conceptual category
African than is indicated by the terms European (Western), Asian (Oriental), or
Latin American. The categories African philosophy, world view, values, etc.,
simply suggest shared orientations born of similar cultural experiences. As
Gyekye (1987: x) notes, "it is the underlying cultural unity or identity of the
various individual thinkers that justifies references to varieties of thought as
wholes, such as Western, European or Oriental philosophy." In other words,
Gyekye continues, "even though the individual thinkers who produced what is
known as Western philosophy are from different European or Western nations,
we nonetheless refer to such body of philosophical ideas as western philosophy
(in addition to, say, French, German or British philosophy)." One can justifiably
conclude that "the real reason for this is surely the common cultural experience
and orientation of those individual thinkers."

Likewise, in spite of the obvious differences between Indian, Chinese and
ancient Persian philosophy as well as the difference between Hindu, Buddhist,
Confucian and Taoist thought, they are generally called Asian philosophy. And
as Tu Wei Ming (1985: 7) states, Asian philosophy is based on the notion of
"shared orientations." Therefore, to say African philosophy, world view, or values is to assume certain shared orientations based on similar cultural experiences. Among these shared orientations are (1) the centrality of community; (2)
respect for tradition; (3) a high level spirituality and ethical concern; (4) har-

mony with nature; (5) the sociality of selfhood; (6) veneration of ancestors; and (7) the unity of being. This list is obviously selective, and there are other African core values which one can focus on as central to the Afrocentric vision. However, these are a conceptual and indispensable minimum regardless of other additions one might make. Having identified these basic components of the African world view, the task now is to demonstrate how these inform the conceptual contributions of Africana studies to the multicultural educational enterprise.

AFROCENTRIC CONCEPTUAL CONTRIBUTIONS

There are several Afrocentric conceptual contributions which can enrich multicultural discourse and education. Among these are (1) centeredness or groundedness and insight from one's own culture (this is also called location or orientation); (2) the wholistic approach to knowledge; (3) critique and corrective as a joint project in the educational enterprise; (4) the essentiality of a historical perspective; and (5) the centrality of the ethical dimension of the educational project, a self-conscious directed process in which there is a reaffirmation of the worth and dignity of the human person and the importance of knowledge in the service of humankind. All of these contributions are interrelated and mutually reinforcing and offer a paradigm of difference as possibility within a multicultural context.

The Concept of Centeredness

Certainly, the first and most fundamental contribution an Afrocentric project brings to multicultural education is its stress on centeredness, which is also called place, location and orientation. This is a particularly challenging and, at times, even problematic concept, given the current stress in academia on decentering and deconstructionism as both an aid to more critical learning and greater social exchange (Hassan 1987; Hooks 1990). However, Afrocentric scholars as well as many feminists and Marxists also recognize the problems of unlimited deconstruction. It subverts the emancipatory possibilities in ethnic, national, gender, and class theory and practice and undermines human agency by decentering the subject and denying difference its oppositional, enriching,and essential role in both education and social practice (Ferguson et al. 1990; Giroux 1992; Hooks 1990; Karenga 1986).

History and culture are essential points of rootedness and departure for Afrocentric studies. Thus, in an Afrocentric vision of learning, one does not step out of one's history to learn or practice but rather engages in it to ground oneself and grasp both the particular and the universal. As Asante (1990: 5) argues, "One steps outside one's history [only] with great difficulty. . . . In fact, the act itself is highly improbable from true historical consciousness." Moreover, he continues, "There is no anti-place, since we are all consumers of space and time." Given this, he states, "the Afrocentrist seeks knowledge of this 'place' perspective as a fundamental rule of intellectual inquiry." Moreover, Asante maintains that "all knowledge results from an occasion of encounter in place," and that such a "shaped perspective [then] allows the Afrocentrist to put African ideals and values at the center of inquiry."

Asante (1990: 12) defines centeredness as "the groundedness of observation and behavior in one's own historical experiences." This concept, he maintains, shapes the Africana studies project but allows for a similar posture and process-for all other cultures. Thus, he states, Africana studies "secures its place alongside other centric pluralisms without hierarchy and without seeking hegemony." Here Asante answers critics who incorrectly contend that Afrocentricity claims a privileged and hegemonic racial position for Africans in human history and culture. He does this by posing centeredness as an essential and effective orientation and point of departure for all cultures. In this stress on the value of location, place, or orientation, Asante reaffirms the contentions of earlier African scholars like W. E. B. Du Bois (1975), who argued against simply teaching of what he called general and disembodied knowledge of science and human culture.

Du Bois (1975: 98), in his seminal essay, "The Field and Function of the Negro College," argued for an education located in and oriented toward the concrete experience of the students. "No teacher, Black or White, who comes to a university like Fisk, filled simply with general ideas of human culture or general knowledge of disembodied science, is going to make a university of this school," he stated. For "a university is made of human beings, learning of things they do not know from things they do know in their own lives." Du Bois criticizes the assumption of the effectiveness of transmission of simply "general ideas of human culture or general knowledge of disembodied science." Du Bois' position, which informs the Afrocentric vision of quality education, is that there is no real substitute for an embodied knowledge, a knowledge rooted in and reflective of the concrete situation of the student. This essentially means starting from what students know to teach them and assist their learning what they do not know. Thus, he advocated use of the familiar as an instrument to discover the unknown and the unfamiliar and as a rich resource for understanding the universal (i.e., humanity as a whole).

The point which Du Bois (1975: 96) makes is that a quality education is especially attentive to the process of "beginning with the particular and going out to universal comprehension and unhampered expression." Thus, he criticizes much of the literature of the Harlem Renaissance, which was, he contends, "written to the benefit of white readers, and starting out primarily from the white point of view." Therefore, the movement eventually declined for "it never had a real [black] constituency and it did not grow out of the inmost heart and frank experience of [Blacks]; . . . [and] on such an artificial basis no real literature can grow." Again, the point is that a disembodied knowledge, an abstract discourse on humans cannot and does not produce a quality education. The need is to begin with each culture's experience and then translate it into a process of understanding others' experience as well as the varied and collective experience of society and humankind.

The Wholistic Approach to Knowledge

A second contribution that Afrocentric methodology brings to the enterprise of multicultural education is the stress on the wholistic approach to knowledge. As James Stewart (1984: 296-97) remarked, this focus is both a source of intellectual challenge and a mark of uniqueness of the Africana studies enterprise. At its inception Africana studies conceived of itself as an interdisciplinary project. As I (1993: 21) have stated, "the scope of Africana studies was established by its self-definition and by the parameters it posed for itself as a multidisciplinary discipline." More precisely, however, Black studies is a single discipline with many fields which seeks to grasp the totality of black life from its various constituent dimensions (i.e., history, religion, sociology, politics, economics, creative production, psychology, etc.).

By definition, Africana studies is a systematic and critical study of the totality of black thought and practice in their current and historical unfolding. The use of the term *totality* is intended to suggest a wholistic approach to the study of black life. This means, first, an intellectual engagement which stresses totality as an inclusive social dimension and invites study in all fields. But it also is designed to stress the importance of totality in time. This is what is meant by "the study of black life in its current and historical unfolding." This inclusive approach of Black studies stresses the wholistic character of knowledge and integrates various subject areas into a coherent discipline, reaching across what James Turner (1984: xi) calls "the voids that have inevitably occurred as a result of artificial disciplinary demarcations."

In addition, Africana studies is also informed by an African ontology that argues the unity of being and an epistemology that sees both being and truth about it as whole. Speaking of classical African ontology as expressed in ancient Egypt, Finnestad (1989: 31ff) notes its stress on "the affinities and connections" rather than differences in its conception of reality and being. In such a conception, human life "merges with that of the entire world and being is conceived as an "integrated whole." The logic of such a position leads to the epistomological assumption that the truth of being is also whole, and any partial approach to it must yield only a partial understanding of it.

It is important to note, however, that such an approach does not deny the value of the temporary analytical decomposition of subjects of study for a more internal or detailed study. But a wholistic approach stresses the need to guard against losing sight and understanding of affinities, connections, or the interrelatedness of each part to the other and to the whole. The implications of such a view for both social study and practice are numerous and important. Such a wholistic approach moves away from Cartesian dualism and rigid lines of demarcation in both conception of the world and approaches to it. And it is becoming increasingly important in social and intellectual discourse in various other alternative critical perspectives. In addition to Africana studies, other ethnic studies, Women's studies, and some socialist studies also assume such a wholistic position. This offers an excellent opportunity for creative dialog and challenge to the dualistic conception of the established order and promises a useful and ongoing discourse.

The Joint Project of Critique and Corrective

A third conceptual contribution that Afrocentric studies offers to multicultural education is its stress on critique and corrective as a joint project in the educational enterprise. This stress is rooted in the very conception and earliest practice of Black studies as a discipline. From its inception, Africana or Black studies has had both an academic and social dimension which involved critique and corrective as essential to the meaning and mission of the discipline (Karenga 1993: Chap. 1). Black studies evolved out of the emancipatory struggles of the 60's which linked intellectual emancipation with political emancipation, campus with community, intellectuals and students with the masses, and knowledge in the academy with power in society (Hare 1969). What emerged in the process of both struggles on campus and in society was a paradigm of critique and corrective which sought to end domination, to expand the realm of freedom, and to create a just and good society.

The Critical Dimension

The Afrocentric stress on critique as essential to the educational enterprise emerges from the actual conditions in and under which Africana studies comes into being. The Afrocentric critique is concerned with the distortion and deficiency of what is present in the curriculum and larger social discourse and about the abundance and emancipatory possibilities of that which is absent. It seeks to rescue and reconstruct black history and culture in order to define more correctly black humanity. Thus, the Afrocentric critique can be defined as "a systematic unrelenting battle against both ignorance and illusion, the struggle against the poverty of knowledge as well as the perversion of truth" (Karenga 1988: 410). Moreover, it involves realizing that the greatest part of truth is hidden beneath the surface. Therefore, there is a constant need to reach beyond and below the surface manifestations of society and the world to penetrate and grasp the relations which give them their motion, meaning and character. Moreover, the Afrocentric critique requires focus on contradictions in society, especially ones of race, class and gender. This requires looking again not only for what is present and distorted in the discourse but also for what is absent and undiscussed.

Such an approach not only contributes to the encouragement of critical thinking about the present and absent, the given and the possible, but it also calls for a redefinition in practice of the university itself, which has historically been the brain and an apologist for the established order. In such a context the university became, through the struggles of the 1960's not simply a place to transmit authoritative views and values but a ground of contestation, a framework for struggle over intellectual issues as well as over the structure and meaning of the university and society. Contestation continues to be posed in Africana studies as a fundamental mode of understanding self, society, and the world. In such a process Africana studies seeks to create a space and a process for students to recover, discover, and speak truth and meaning of their own experience. This means that they locate themselves in social and human history and, having oriented themselves, bring their unique contribution to multicultural exchange in the academy and society. Ideally what results from this critique of established-order discourse and contestation over issues of intellect and life is the multicultural cooperative production of knowledge rather than its Eurocentric authoritative allocation.

Several paths are pursued in the process of bringing one's own experience and unique cultural contribution to the educational process. First, one is compelled to create both a different language and logic. For the established-order language and logic are not conducive to the emancipatory project which Africana studies represents and nurtures. As Malcolm X (1968: 133) argued in a lecture at Harvard, "the language and logic of the oppressed cannot be the language and logic of the oppressor" if an emancipatory project is to be conceived and pursued. Thus, Africana Studies began to develop and use new categories and modes of analysis and give new definition to old terms and concepts. For example, within Africana studies classics is no longer an exclusive category of European achievement but rather a category of achievement for humans in general. Stripped of all its Eurocentric pretensions, the term classics can be defined as works whose level of creativity and achievement deserve and demand both preservation and emulation. Thus, classical music, art, literature, civilizations, etc., are present in African, Native Americans, Latino, and Asian cultures as well as in Europe.

Second, the Afrocentric critique demands that one moves beyond the Eurocentric self-congratulatory narratives in various disciplines and engages in a multicultural discourse. Such a discourse reveals the rich variousness of human culture and poses a necessary creative challenge to European hegemonic discourse and practice. Using political science as an example, the Afrocentric critique demands that one looks before and beyond Plato to include the study of classical African texts from ancient Egypt such as *The Book of Ptahhotep*, which offers a discourse on leadership as a moral vocation (Lichtheim 1975: 61ff; Simpson 1973: 159ff) and *The Book of Khun-Anup*, the oldest treatise on social justice (Lichtheim 1975: 97ff; Simpson 1973: 31ff). Likewise, the study of literature would include both ancient and modern African classics, such as the classical praise poetry of the Zulu, *Izibongo*, (Cope 1968), of the Tswana,

Maboko (Schapera 1965), as well as selected literature of the Harlem Renaissance and the 1960s. Finally, discourse on ethics need not begin or end in Judaism and Christianity but extend back before such frameworks to Maatian ethical texts of ancient Egypt, which offer both parallels and sources of Jewish and Christian concepts and practices (Breasted 1934; Karenga 1988; Morenz 1973: Chap. 6). It is important to note that the use of African classics and other achievements to enrich multicultural education and discourse must and does assume and require a similar and equal contribution of other cultures.

Third, within the framework of developing a new language and logic, one can pose different points of departure for understanding social and human reality. From an Afrocentric view, one studies society from a communitarian rather than an individualistic view (Mbiti 1970; Menkiti 1984). In addition, one poses the study of politics not simply as a struggle for power but also, as in Maatian ethical texts (i.e., the *Sebait*), as a collective vocation to create a just and good society (Karenga 1988). Likewise, one can pose communal and substantive democracy against "herrenvolk" and procedural democracy and then engage Malcolm X's (1965: 26) concept of being a "victim of democracy" for all its "fruitful ambiguity." For in an age of praise and pursuit of democracy as a central human good, one is challenged to understand and explain why Malcolm claims, in this particular case, such a negative role for it.

Finally, the Afrocentric approach challenges the parameters, focus, and central categories of intellectual discourse in the social science and humanities. For example, one talks of the "Holocaust of Enslavement" rather than "slave trade" as the most instructive and correct way of discussing the genocidal tragedy which marked the loss of millions of African lives. One poses enslavement as primarily an ethical issue rather than a commercial one and defines *holocaust* as an act of genocide so morally monstrous that it is not only against the people themselves but also against humanity. Such a redefinition of the experience of enslavement as a holocaust invites a rich comparative and contrastive discourse on other holocausts—Native American, Native Australian, Jewish, Romani, Palestinian, Armenian, Kurdish, and so on. In conclusion, the practice of critique and corrective means that suppressed and marginalized voices of various cultures will bring an enriched and enlarged agenda to the educational table. Various ways of viewing and approaching human reality will challenge and change Eurocentric hegemony and pose in its place a democratic and multicultural education which prefigures and points to the possibility of a truly democratic and multicultural society.

The Corrective Dimension

The corrective dimension of the Afrocentric conception of education emanates from both the emancipatory role assigned to education and to the educated by earlier African scholars and leaders and from the emancipatory struggles of the 1960s which assigned Africana studies both an academic and social mission.

Moreover, such an Afrocentric concept of education grows out of the African communitarian world view, with its interrelated concepts of the centrality of the community and the sociality of selfhood. This communitarian African world view, as Gyekye (1987: 157) states, contains within it "such social and ethical values as social well-being, solidarity, interdependence, cooperation and reciprocal obligations—all of which conduce to equitable distribution of resources and benefits of society." In such a context, "inherent in the communal enterprise is the problem of contribution and distribution." This translates in an educational context as recognition of the fact that instead of conceiving of education as knowledge for knowledge sake, one approaches education within a concept of knowledge for humans' sake. This means that knowledge as a key social value is conceived as belonging not simply to the student and intellectuals but also to the community and that both the mission of students and the university must relate to and contribute to the historical vocation of human flourishing in the context of a just and good society.

Inherent in this communitarian concept of education is the concept of mission, which has long been a central theoretical pillar in Africana studies' conception of itself. W. E. B. Du Bois' conception of the Talented Tenth stands as a classic example of mission as an inherent aspect of the educational project. Education, he argued, is "a difficult and intricate task" whose "technique is a matter for educational experts, but its object is for the vision of seers" (Paschal 1974: 31ff). The fundamental challenge of education was for him at that time to "develop the Best" to guide the community, and to avoid focus simply on career preparation. The task is not to develop money-makers or even artisans but men and women of intelligence and character, with knowledge of the world that was and is, and commitment to community. Although he later modified stress on the Talented Tenth to deal with its class problem, he still maintained that service to the people was key to any viable and valuable concept of education (Stewart 1984: 306ff).

One can see the concept of mission in Mary McLeod Bethune's (1939: 9) concept of education as a process of searching for truth, critically interpreting it, and then spreading it. In a word, she (1938: 10) says truth is "to discover the dawn and to bring this material within the understanding of the child and the masses of our people." For, she continues, although "we are living in a great age of science and invention . . . we still have the human problem of distribution of natural resources and of seeing that the fruits of science and invention are within the reach of the masses who need it most." The need, she concludes, is an ethically focused education which teaches one obligations not simply to self but to community, society, and humanity and to look forward at the end of one's life to standing tall "on the platform of service" (Bethune 1939: 46).

The stress on the academic and social nature of the educational project was also expressed in the relationship of the university to the community. Early in Black studies history, the relationship of the university to the community was defined as important and even indispensable by Nathan Hare, one of the founders of the discipline. Hare (1969, 1972, 1975), who established the first Black studies program, made essential to his conception of the discipline the joining of the university and the community in a mutually beneficial ongoing relationship. His conception was summarized in the idea, bring the community to the campus and take the campus to the community.

This mutually beneficial exchange between community and campus would involve, at a minimum, several aspects. First, it would require the university to recognize and reaffirm in practice its obligation to serve the communities in which it is located and those from which its students come. This implies not only the teaching of students but also joining with the community in cooperative projects to address critical issues and challenges. Second, such a relationship would necessitate the community's active involvement in the determination of what constitutes quality education. It would also require involvement in ongoing campus-sponsored educational projects and any other projects of mutual benefit. And finally, such an exchange would mean that students again, as Du Bois argued, would use their own experience to understand social and human reality and to enrich the educational process with it.

In such a process of reciprocal engagement on and off campus, students are challenged to frame questions and projects from their own experience and for their own future. They raise and seek to answer questions about the meaning, quality, and direction of their lives, not as abstracted individuals but as persons in community. Therefore, their efforts becomes not simply to understand self, society and the world but to change it. In this education and the corrective social practice it encourages, one discovers a practice of freedom.

Thus a joining of critique and corrective, in both the intellectual and practical sense, poses an important model which contains several components. First, the model focuses on critical thinking, on challenging the given and posing plausible alternatives to the established order of things. Second, this means that the university can no longer be seen and posed as simply a place for the authoritative transmission of sacrosanct knowledge of the Eurocentric world. On the contrary, it becomes a context for contestation and the cooperative discovery and production of knowledge of the real multicultural world. Third, this model encourages the creation of space and process for students to discover and speak the truth and meaning of their own cultural experience. This requires that they locate themselves in social and human history and having oriented themselves, project possibilities of where they wish to go. Fourth, the concept of mission and social obligation removes education from the role of simple transmission of canon and job preparation to one of preparation for a quality life. And it reaffirms the imperative of critical thinking (i.e. below-the-surface searching for new and more ethically and culturally sensitive conceptions of society and human life). Finally, the university defined as a partner with the communities it serves creates the concept of joining the intellectual and practical in a project to create and sustain the just and good society.

The Historical Perspective

Another contribution which the Afrocentric vision of a quality education offers is its emphasis on the indispensability of the historical perspective in understanding social and human reality (Keto 1991). Africana studies is not to be equated with history, but it is considered within this framework as the key social science, given each discipline's dependence on it for grounding (Karenga 1993: 70). As Malcolm X (1965: 8) noted, "of all our studies history is best qualified to reward our research." For history is the central discipline of contextualization and orientation, and the Afrocentric stress on centeredness is both a historical and cultural concept. Thus, the first value and use of such historical stress is its function as a mode and means of centering.

Second, history for Africana studies has been the key means in the central and ongoing project of rescue and recovery. In a multicultural context, this means that African and other cultures are prized as treasure troves of rich and varied experiences, narratives, knowledge, and ways of being in the world. Thus, one rescues and reconstructs one's history as a part of the process of rescuing and reconstructing one's humanity. The study, writing, and discussion of history become ways of giving freedom to suppressed voices. Reconstructing a lost history is, as the ancient Egyptian texts teach, a process of "restoring that which is found in ruins, repairing what is found damaged and replenishing what is found lacking" (Lichtheim 1988: 43).

Central to Africana studies and the Afrocentric concept of education in this respect is the concept of *Sankofa*, an Akan concept of historical recovery. As Niangoran-Bouah (1984 Vol. I: n.p.) notes, *Sankofa* "is made of the words san (to return), ko (to go) and fa (to take). The literal translation is: come back, seek and take or recover." The *Sankofa* ideogram is a bird reaching back with its beak into its feathers and "is a symbol representing the quest for knowledge and the return to the source." Niangoran-Bouah (1984 Vol. I: 210) further states that the ideogram implies that the resulting knowledge "is the outcome of research, of an intelligent and patient investigation." This concept of *Sankofa* with its dual emphasis on the quest for knowledge and return to the source has become a central concept in Africana studies in all its fields (i.e., history, religion, sociology, political science,economics, creative production, psychology, etc.). But the concept of *Sankofa* gets its greatest use in reference to the quest for historical paradigms to place in the service of the present and future.

Such a function of historical knowledge and paradigm is evident in the identification and beginning restoration of ancient Egypt (Kemet) as a paradigmatic classical African civilization. It is Cheikh Anta Diop (1982: 12), the Imhotepian or multidisciplined scholar, who posed ancient Egypt as the essential paradigmatic African civilization, arguing that "a look toward ancient Egypt is the best way of conceiving and building our culture future." In fact, he maintains that "Egypt will play, in a reconceived and renewed African culture, the same role that ancient Greco-Latin civilization plays in western culture." In a word, he concludes, for African peoples "the return to Egypt in all fields is the necessary condition to reconcile African civilizations with history, to build a body of modern human sciences and renew African culture." Afrocentric scholars have accepted the validity and urgency of this task and have begun to do work important to its completion (Asante 1990; Carruthers 1984; Karenga 1984, 1990a, 1990b; Karenga and Carruthers 1986).

The African rescue and recovery of ancient Egypt as a paradigm, which precedes and parallels in intellectual function as well as contributes to the Greek paradigm for Europe, has created an important source of contestation in the academy (*Arethusa* 1989; Bernal 1987; Diop 1982). The importance of this contribution lies in several areas. First, it provides an important creative challenge to Africana scholars who, in presenting and defending the paradigm and the work surrounding it, challenge and are challenged by Eurocentric scholars. Second, the contestation becomes for Africana studies another opportunity to critique domination. For it challenges the cultural hegemony, an exclusive canon, and denial of the historical capacity and achievement of Africans and other peoples of color. In such a struggle, the falsification of African history becomes a metaphor for the falsification of human history. For central to Europe's falsification of human history was its removal of Africa from Egypt, Egypt from Africa, and Africa from human history.

Likewise, the emancipatory, intellectual, and practical struggles to return African to its own history and to human history become a metaphor and model of a similar return of all people to their history as well as to human history. Diop's concept of reconciling African civilization with human history becomes a metaphor and impetus for reconciling all excluded civilizations and cultures with human history. This process of reconciliation returns them to their rightful place, restoring the rich variousness of their voices and learning the complex and often contradictory messages they offer to teach. Such a contestation as both paradigm and process reaffirms the value and function of critical thinking in its demand for intellectual skill and human and ethical sensitivity.

Finally, the Afrocentric conception of history reveals history as a living concreteness. History, as I (1993: 70) argued elsewhere, is not simply a record but rather a struggle and record of specific peoples and humanity as a whole in the process of shaping their worlds and the world in their own image and interest. Here one sees the dynamic and dialectic of the particular and the universal, for as each people shapes its own world, it contributes to the shaping of the whole-world. In this process it is important that no people impose their world view and practice on others or in a rationalized illusion of superiority assert themselves as the single paradigm for human thought and practice. Such has been the history of Europe in its drive for political and cultural hegemony. The history of peoples of color reveals liberational struggles in society and in the academy to challenge, check and end this hegemony.

At this point one sees how history, for Afrocentric scholars (as their critics charge) is not simply a neutral record. On the contrary, it is neither neutral nor simply a record. It is above all a struggle, a lived concreteness. At the heart of this process called history is the struggle to clear and create space for human freedom and human flourishing. Such is the history of Africans, for them history cannot be an abstract intellectual process. It is their lives unfolding or being checked, their perceptions given wings or restrained, and their struggle to be free and productive through emancipatory thought and practice. Such a conception of history offers multicultural education a mode of critical engagement in discourse and practice essential to the concept and process of quality education. For again students are challenged to discover, recover and speak the truth and meaning of their own experience, locate themselves in the larger realm of social and human history, and pose paradigms of human culture and society which contribute not only to our critical understanding of the world but also to our thrust to change it in the interest and image of human good. This, in turn, encourages and cultivates critical thinking, below-the-surface searching, and ethical concerns and conceptions of human life and society.

The Ethical Dimension

A final contribution of the Afrocentric concept of education to the paradigm of a quality and multicultural education is the centrality of the ethical dimension. Again, since its inception, Africana studies has stressed the centrality of ethics to a quality education. This stress has its roots in several basic factors. First, it evolves from the emancipatory nature of the Africana studies project itself, which has at its central thrust a critique and corrective of domination and the posing of paradigms of human freedom and human flourishing. As mentioned earlier, the critique is essentially a moral critique of constraints on human freedom, and the correctives are always undergirded by the moral project of creating a just and good society.

Second, the focus on the ethical evolves from the definition of the dual mission of Black studies (i.e., academic excellence and social responsibility), a social responsibility which conceptually and practically is an ethical obligational task. It is an ethical responsibility to create the kind of community which practices and promotes human freedom and human flourishing. Moreover, one is obligated to create the kind of moral community one wishes to live in. In the earliest stage of Black studies in the United States, Du Bois (1971: 61) argued that education was "primarily scientific, a careful search for truth conducted as thoroughly, broadly and honestly" as possible. However, he noted that in its more expansive form, the educational process was "not only to make the truth clear but [also] to present it in such shape as will encourage and help social reform."

Third, the very practice of generating reflective problematics and correctives from the African experience continuously raises critical ethical questions. For that experience is defined by oppression, resistance, and the creation and maintenance of free space for proactive practices in spite ofsocial oppression. Both oppression and resistance unavoidably generate ethical questions, and thus much of Africana studies discourse revolves around issues of right and wrong and the grounds and meaning of human freedom and human flourishing.

Fourth, the stress on the ethical dimension evolves from an ancient tradition of emphasis on civic moral education. This tradition extends back to ancient Egypt with its concern for moral leadership and a just and good society (Carruthers 1984; Karenga 1989, 1994). Classical African philosophy in ancient Egypt posed the human ideal as a reflection of the universe which was grounded in and ordered by the principle of *Maat*. *Maat* was rightness in the social, nature, and divine sphere and translated as truth, justice, propriety, harmony, balance, reciprocity, and order.

Also key to this is the African world view in general with stress on freedom as responsible personhood in community. It stresses persons in community acting with shared initiative and responsibility to collectively conceive and create a social context for maximum social solidarity and human flourishing (Gyekye 1987; Wright 1984). This communitarian philosophy and emphasis of African culture serves as an essential framework for the conceptualization and pursuit of the just and good society. Such a society is defined by civility, reciprocity, and equality in all areas of human life and practice.

The contribution of this discourse to a quality multicultural education begins with its encouraging students and faculty to frame questions and generate problematics around the quality, purpose, and direction of social and human life. It cultivates an appreciation for framing and discussing issues of life and death in ethical terms rather than vulgarly pragmatic and egoistic ones. Second, such an ethical dimension to the educational process also encourages critical thinking, because only in matters of faith are such issues of life and death exempt from complexity and most often ambiguity. One is compelled to do below-the-surface thinking to confront and be confronted in a mutually benefiting process.

The Afrocentric stress on ethics also becomes a way to begin to integrate the disciplines. For it rightly raises questions about the relevance of knowledge and its pursuit to the human person and the human community. This means that ethical questions about the world or ethical questions of life and death are no longer safely assigned to religion. Rather each discipline raises its own ethical questions as well as participates in discourse on general ethical issues. This would include the hard sciences, which often conceive of themselves as exempt from and beyond valuative discourse and ethical judgment. However, it is the hard sciences—physical and technical—which have produced products and processes of the greatest threat to humankind and the environment. Thus, neither they nor their practitioners can be exempt from discussion of how they conceive, approach, and affect the world.

Finally, the Afrocentric stress on ethics as a fundamental component of a quality education brings to the multicultural process of exchange support for the concept of pursuit of the common good. For pursuit of the common good is at heart an ethical project in the philosophical and practical sense. It translates as democratic multicultural discourse on and pursuit of social policies aimed at creating a context of maximum human flourishing.

African Americans have played a historical and current vanguard role in setting and pursuing the moral and socially progressive agenda in this country. Therefore, it is only logical that they would play a vanguard role in creating space and impetus for a generalized and deepened ethical discourse in the academy. Not only does African culture have the oldest ethical texts in the world, but it is the African American struggle which has been at the heart of fundamental changes in the quality of life in this country. Moreover, this struggle for a just and good society has posed a paradigm which has been both instructive and inspiring to other people of color, women, the disabled, the seniors, and other marginalized groups in this country, as well as peoples in South Africa, South America, the Philippines, China, Eastern Europe, and the Palestinian and Israeli peace movement. In these struggles, the participants borrowed from and built on the moral vision and moral vocabulary of the African American struggle and embraced it as a paradigm for the struggle of human liberation.

Jesse Jackson (1989: 14) contends rightly that the "greater good is the common good," which is clearly "a good beyond personal comfort and position." It is a good created out of the common aspirations of many peoples, groups, and cultures who share this society and want and are willing to cooperate in building a just and good society. This aspiration finds itself needing a public philosophy beyond liberal myths of melting pots and Eurocentric concepts of universality. It seeks and must be grounded in a public philosophy which teaches above all (1) the reality that U.S. society is not a finished white product but rather an ongoing multicultural project, and (2) that each person and people has both the right and responsibility to speak their own special cultural truth and make their own unique contribution to the forward flow of societal and human history. Moreover, such a public philosophy will build on the best ethical traditions of the many cultures that constitute the U.S. social project. These traditions will, of necessity, contain the values of civic virtue, voluntarism, reciprocity, cooperativeness, and social justice. They will stress creative resolution of tensions between the personal and the collective, community and society, the private and the public, and different and common.

Finally, these traditions must merge in the public sphere in redefining politics in the classical African sense as an ethical and collective vocation to create a just and good society. Such an ethical vocation will be one of shared responsibility in a shared public life of mutual benefit and cooperation. Such a vocation will also seek to create a democratic political and economic sphere. All this, of course, requires public debate and discourse, and the academy becomes an indispensable context for conception and discourse based on civility, reciprocity, and equality. The challenge is to initiate and sustain such a discourse and the companion practical project which gives such discourse its relevance and ultimate reality.

REFERENCES

Arethusa. 1989. Special issue (Fall).

Asante, Molefi. 1980. *Afrocentricity: The Theory of Social Change*. Buffalo: Amulefi.

Asante, Molefi. 1987. *The Afrocentric Idea*. Philadelphia: Temple University Press.

Asante, Molefi. 1990. *Kemet, Afrocentricity and Knowledge. Trenton*, NJ: Africa World Press.

Bernal, Martin. 1987. *Black Athena: The Afro-Asiantic Roots of Classical Civilization*. Vol. I. London: Free Association Books.

Bethune, Mary McLeod. 1939. "The Adaptation of the History of the Negro to the Capacity of the Child." *Journal of Negro History* 24: 9-13.

Blassingame, John. 1973. *New Perspectives on Black Studies*. Chicago: University of Illinois Press.

Breasted, James. 1934. *The Dawn of Conscience*. New York: Charles Scribner's.

Brisbane, Robert. 1974. *Black Activism*. Valley Forge, PA: Judson Press.

Carruthers, Jacob H. 1984. *Essays in Ancient Egyptian Studies*. Los Angeles: University of Sankore Press.

Cooper, Anna Julia. 1988. *A Voice from the South*. New York: Oxford University Press.

Cope, Trevor. 1968. *Izibongo: Zulu Praise Poems*. New York: Oxford University Press.

Diop, Cheikh Anta. 1982. *Civilization ou Barbarie*. Paris: Presence Africaine. English translation, *Civilization or Barbarism*. Brooklyn, NY: Lawrence Hill, 1990.

Du Bois, W. E. B. 1971. *The Dusk of Dawn*. New York: Schocken Books.

Du Bois, W. E. B. 1975. *The Education of Black People: Ten Critiques, 1906-1960*. New York: Monthly Review Press.

Ferguson, Russell, Martha Gever, Trinh T. Minha, and Cornel West. eds. 1990. *Out There: Marginalization and Contemporary Cultures*. Cambridge, MA: MIT Press.

Finnestad, Ragnhild B. 1989. "Egyptian Thought about Life as a Problem of Translation." In *The Religion of the Ancient Egyptians: Cognitive Structures and Popular Expressions*, Gertie Englund, ed. Uppsala: Acta Universitatis Upsaliensis.

Giroux, Henry. 1992. *Border Crossings: Cultural Workers and the Politics of Education*. New York: Routledge.

Gyekye, Kwame. 1987. *An Essay on African Philosophical Thought: The Akan Conceptual Scheme*. New York: Cambridge University Press.

Hare, Nathan. 1969. "What Should be the Role of Afro-American Education in the Undergraduate Curriculum?" *Liberal Education* 55(March): 42-50.

Hare, Nathan. 1972. "The Battle of Black Studies." *Black Scholar* 3(May): 32-37.

Hare, Nathan. 1975. "A Black Paper: The Relevance of Black Studies." *Black Collegian* 6(September/October): 46-50.

Hassan, Ihab. 1987. *The Post Modern Turn: Essays in Postmodern Theory and Culture*. Columbus, OH: State University Press.

Hicks, Florience J., ed. *Mary McLeod Bethune: Her Own Words of Inspiration*. Washington, DC: Nuclassics and Science Publishing Company.

Hooks, Bell. 1990. *Yearnings: Race, Gender and Culture Politics*. Boston: South End Press.

Hornung, Erik. 1985. *Conceptions of God in Ancient Egypt*. Ithaca, NY: Cornell University Press.

Jackson, Jesse. 1989. "A Call to Common Ground." *Black Scholar* 20(1): 12-18.

Karenga, Maulana. 1984. *Selections from the Husia: Sacred Wisdom of Ancient Egypt*. Los Angeles: University of Sankore Press.

Karenga, Maulana. 1988. "Black Studies and the Problematic of Paradigm: The Philosophical Dimension." *Journal of Black Studies* 18, 4(June): 395-414.

Karenga, Maulana. 1989b. "Towards a Sociology of Maatian Ethics: Literature and Context." *Journal of African Civilizations* 10, 1(Fall): 352-395.

Karenga, Maulana. 1990a. *The Book of Coming Forth By Day: The Ethics of the Declarations of Innocence*. Los Angeles: University of Sankore Press.

Karenga, Maulana, ed. 1990b. *Reconstructing Kemetic Culture*. Los Angeles: University of Sankore Press.

Karenga, Maulana. 1993. *Introduction to Black Studies*. 2nd ed. Los Angeles: University of Sankore Press.

Karenga, Maulana. 1994. *Maat, The Moral Idea in Ancient Egypt: A Study in Classical African Ethics*. 2 Vols., Ph.D. Dissertation. University of Southern California.

Karenga, Maulana, and Jacob H. Carruthers, eds. 1986. *Kemet and the African World View*. Los Angeles: University of Sankore Press.

Keto, C. Tsehloane. 1991. *The Africa Centered Perspective of History: An Introduction*. Laurel Springs, NJ: K. A. Publishers.

Lichtheim, Miriam. 1975. *Ancient Egyptian Literature*, Vol. I. Berkeley: University of California Press.

Lichtheim, Miriam. 1988. *Ancient Egyptian Autobiographies Chiefly from the Middle Kingdom*. Feiburg, Switzerland: Universitatsverlag.

Locke, Alain. 1968. *The New Negro*. New York: Atheneum.

Malcolm X. 1965. *Malcolm X Speaks*. New York: Merit Publishers.

Malcolm X. 1968. *The Speeches of Malcolm X at Harvard*, Archie Epps, ed. New York: William Morrow and Co.

Mbiti, John. 1970. *African Religion and Philosophy*. Garden City, NY: Anchor Books.

Menkiti, Ifeanyi. 1984. "Person and Community in African Traditional Thought." In *African Philosophy: An Introduction*, 3rd ed. Richard Wright, ed. Lanham, MD: University Press of America.

Ming, Tu Wei. 1985. *Confucian Thought: Selfhood as Creative Transformation*. Albany: State University of New York Press.

Morenz, Siegfried. 1973. *Egyptian Religion*. Ithaca, NY: Cornell University Press.

Niangoran-Bouah, G. 1984. *The Akan World of Gold Weights: Abstract Design Weights*, Vol. I. Abidjan, Ivory Coast: Les Nouvelles Editions Africaines.

Paschal, Andrew, ed. 1974. *A W. E. B. Du Bois Reader*. New York: Macmillan.

Ravitch, Dianne. 1990. "Multiculturalism." *American Scholar* (Summer): 337-354.

Report. 1991. *The Challenge of Diversity and Multicultural Education: Report of the President's Task Force on Multicultural Education and Campus Diversity*. Long Beach: California State University.

Robinson, Armstead, C. Foster, and D. Ogilvie. 1969. *Black Studies in the University*. New York: Bantam Books.

Schapera, I., ed. 1965. *Praise Poems of Tswana Chiefs*. New York: Oxford University Press.

Schlesinger, Arthur. 1991. *The Disuniting of America: Reflections on a Multicultural Society*. Knoxville, TN: Whittle Direct Books.

Simpson, William K., ed. 1973. *The Literature of Ancient Egypt*. New Haven, CT: Yale University Press.

Stewart, James. 1984. "The Legacy of W. E. B. Du Bois for Contemporary Black Studies." *The Journal of Negro Education* 53: 296-311.

Turner, James. ed. 1984. *The Next Decade: Theoretical and Research Issues in Africana Studies*. Ithaca, NY: Africana Research and Studies Center, Cornell University.

Woodson, Carter G. 1969. *Mis-Education of the Negro*. Washington, DC: Associated Publishers.

Wright, Richard. 1984. *African Philosophy*. 3rd ed. New York: University Press of America.

Part Two

AMERICA'S OTHER CULTURES

However we look at this nation's and the world's demographics, the multicultural character of all social worlds is a reality that we simply cannot ignore. Yet we now face the next century with a higher educational institution deeply rooted in the nineteenth-century presumptions of European superiority and dominance over all other cultures and peoples. It is no coincidence that African Americans, who were brought to this country as slaves and whose presence predates all European immigrants except the original English settlers, have the oldest and most developed critique of the Eurocentric world view. But to pose an alternative and equally closed centric world view based on the African diasporic experience would be an ironic flattery of nineteenth-century European racism. This is why Maulana Karenga's chapter is so important. The ultimate acceptance and reconstruction of African diasporic cultures, histories, and communities will have to be part of a multicultural corrective.

To critique the exclusive European cultural basis of the university paradigm does not show how America's other cultures can be a genuine part of a new and more inclusive university model. In Chapter 4, Bonnie Mitchell and Joe Feagin provide a historic and cultural overview of how America's other historic cultures have not only survived European Americans' efforts to ignore and destroy them but have been transformed and made unique contributions to American life. What Native Americans, African Americans, Mexican and Puerto Rican Americans, and Asian Americans have are not soon to be lost inferior cultures. They are American co-cultures with much to offer. Two illustrations are provided by Milga Morales-Nadal, who writes in Chapter 5 about Puerto Rican culture, and by Donald Fixico, who shares with us (in Chapter 6) an Native American world view. What is unique about these chapters is that they suggest to us what their historic communities have to offer a culturally inclusive university model. Again, these are only illustrations of an untapped potential that has always been a part of American history and life. A series of anthologies could be written on this topic. In Part Three we will use these insights to propose a new and multicultural model of the American university.

Chapter 4

America's Racial-Ethnic Cultures: Opposition within a Mythical Melting Pot

Bonnie L. Mitchell
Joe R. Feagin

THE MYTH OF THE INCLUSIVE MELTING POT

Prior to the establishment of national governments, North America was populated by a diverse admixture of Europeans and Africans together with hundreds of Native American tribes. The nature of the relations between these peoples differed widely, sometimes taking the form of slavery or genocide, at other times taking the form of the geographically and culturally distinct hybrids of Spanish-speaking and native societies of the Southwest, and at yet other times taking the form of respectful coexistence. In the two centuries since a national U.S. government was established a powerful nation has emerged and great racial and ethnic diversity has persisted.

In this chapter, we view culture as including both the "patterns . . . of behavior" (Kroeber and Kluckhohn in Schneider 1973: 121) and the "underlying attitude toward themselves and their world" (Geertz 1973: 127) that operate within a particular group. The cultural bandwidth may be as broad as U.S. society or as narrow as a specific urban immigrant enclave. Whether preexistent or immigrant, European or non-European, all groups other than the English faced heavy pressure to acculturate to the English language and culture. Later white groups, such as Jewish and Italian immigrants, took advantage of economic opportunities and gained substantial political power as they adapted to the dominant North European culture. Yet people of color have been forced to remain in a subordinate position politically and economically and have assimilated much less to Euro-American culture. This chapter is an examination of the character and dominance of Euro-American culture and of the ways in which certain oppressed racial-ethnic groups are carriers of cultural traditions oppositional to dominant values. We will examine how the dominant culture has drawn on these oppositional cultures for enhancing the social health of the United States and has simultaneously ignored those elements that call into question its hegemony.

ASSIMILATION PRESSURES: SCHOLARLY PERSPECTIVES

In spite of the cultural richness and diversity of the United States, much social science theorizing has accented more or less inevitable assimilation of in-
coming groups to the so-called core culture. In response to the posited
inevitability of assimilation, some scholars have focused on racial-ethnic inequality as an alternative foundation of this society. Among U.S. scholars,
Hirschman has noted, the assimilation perspective "continues to be the primary
theoretical framework for sociological research on racial and ethnic inequality"
(Hirschman 1983: 397-423). According to Gordon (1964, 1981), substantial acculturation to the dominant culture has usually been completed by the second or
third generation. Gordon's view has been viewed as correct because most white
immigrant groups have been able to succeed in integrating themselves into U.S.
economy and politics. Gordon also suggested that the impact of existing non-
European cultures and of those of later immigrants on the core culture has been
minor.

While agreeing with Gordon on the dominance of Euro-American culture,
more radical power-conflict theorists have accented the persisting inequality
and conflict features of the pressured adaptation process, particularly for those
groups that have not been allowed equal participation in the U.S. economy and
polity. Internal colonialism analysts have rejected the assimilationist view that
non-Europeans are more or less like white European groups in their potential for
cultural assimilation and structural inclusion. Also rejected is the assimilation-
ists' bias toward focusing on deficits within non-European cultures as barriers to
integration into U.S. society. Blauner (1972) argues that there are major differences between Americans of color and the white immigrant groups at the center
of traditional assimilationist analysis. Africans were not allowed to assimilate
like the white immigrants; they were forcibly brought across the Atlantic Ocean
to become part of an internally subordinated colony; slave owners incorporated
them against their will. From the internal colonialism perspective, the current
condition of African Americans is far more oppressive than that of any white
immigrant group because of its roots in the enslavement of Africans. Once a
system of extreme subordination is established historically, those in the superior
position in the hierarchy continue to inherit and to monopolize disproportionate
socioeconomic resources over generations. There is no progressive assimilation
at the structural level of the economy and polity. From this perspective, Gordon's model of assimilation cannot be applied easily to people so subordinated.

THE DOMINANCE OF EURO-AMERICAN CULTURE

These received perspectives agree that the dominant culture has been northern European at its core. They see this impact in dominant linguistic, political,
economic, and religious institutions. During the first century of colonial development, an English heritage integrated the imperial colonies but not, of course,

the outlying areas of the continent, where not only Native American cultures prevailed but French and Spanish cultures as well. However, by the 1600s colonial linguistic, religious, economic, political, and legal institutions were mostly based on English models.

The pressure to learn the English language in the colonies and, after the 1780s, in the new nation was great and accelerated acculturation for many European immigrant groups. George Washington believed in a homogeneous citizenry, and Thomas Jefferson and Benjamin Rush expected those immigrants who were educated to fit into a culturally homogeneous mass of citizens. But such unity could be accomplished only by the substantial subordination of other ethnic identities to that of the dominant culture and by considering peoples of color as racially and culturally inferior (Feagin and Feagin, 1993).

The lasting dominance of the English language in the United States makes conspicuous the impact of the English immigrants. Warner and Srole conclude that "our customary way of life is most like the English, and our language is but one of the several English dialects" (1945: 287). While this reflects the Eurocentric view of many Euro-American scholars, it is true that the central language of the United States is not an equal blend of the many immigrant languages of Europe and Africa. The pressures on non-English-speaking immigrants have often taken the form of language barriers. From the beginning to the present, the dominance of the English language over other languages has been a major concern of Euro-American nativists. There was also great pressure on the schools to Anglicize later immigrant groups. This pressure signals the uneasy dominance of the English-speaking majority. From the beginning, subordinate racial and ethnic groups struggled against this dominance.

The English religious influence on the United States has also been of great importance. For the first 200 years English churches, or derivatives thereof, dominated the colonial and U.S. scenes. The disproportionate number of Anglican and Congregational churches was obvious at the time of the Revolution, although other northern-European-origin churches were by then more numerous. Yet again this religious dominance has been uneasy and vigorously challenged. In the centuries since 1776, northern European dominance of American religious institutions has, to a substantial degree, been forced to yield in the face of the numerous Catholic and Jewish immigrants (Gaustad 1962: 1-20) and most recently in the face of successful legal battles to preserve Native American religious freedom (U.S. Congress P.L. 95-341, 1978).

The superiority of European economic—especially property—perspectives in North America is so profound that it is usually not even considered. Yet Native American concepts of stewardship over rather than ownership of the land have from the beginning come into conflict with European notions of private property. Among most people of color within the United States today, there persists a markedly greater emphasis on gift giving and reciprocal obligations within extended kinship structures as opposed to reliance on the contractual agreements of Euro-Americans. In addition, North American political and legal institutions have been shaped in critical ways by the British heritage through the laws inherited from the English and through the influence English immigrants and their descendants have had on important political organizations and government institutions (Morison, 1965: 48-68). Yet, as we will see later, the Euro-American legal and political tradition has also come under major challenge from oppressed groups, who have pressed for the expansion of civil liberties beyond those envisioned by the Whites who crafted the basic institutions.

In spite of the dominance of English linguistic, economic, political, and religious patterns, there have been major influences and challenges from the dozens of major racial and ethnic groups that have contributed to American society and culture. Recognition of the importance andviability of cultures not at the core of Euro-American society is important for understanding the cultural past, present, and future of U.S. society.

A THEORY OF CULTURES OF RESISTANCE

Essential to the conceptualization of cultures of resistance is the recognition that the history and cultures of subordinated groups cannot be reduced to mere contributions to the mythical melting pot. To take this "me-too" approach to America's racial and ethnic groups is to dilute and co-opt the past and present realities of both the oppression and the resistance efforts of these peoples (Aptheker 1978: 144).

Historical control of the means of production of both material and intellectual values, whether through ownership or positions of authority within institutional hierarchies, has given members of one U.S. group—those of northern European descent—decided material and power advantages over members of other groups. While the material disadvantages associated with membership in a U.S. subordinate group beg for serious constructive attention from public policy makers and members of the dominant group as a whole, there is a serious problem inherent in focusing exclusively on the shared history of oppression of peoples of color. As Gutman (1987: 357-358) has noted, this mode of analysis is "incomplete, misleading, reductionist, and overdetermined." When we examine only the structural inequalities between groups, it is easy to make helpless victims out of the oppressed.

At the micro level, individuals who are denied access to forms of formal power, such as decision-making positions in economic, political, and military spheres, will usually become adept at forms of informal power by using interpersonal strategies such as humor, persuasion, manipulation, and other means of influencing those with the real power (Janeway 1980; Wolf 1974). At the macro level, groups denied access to formal power have responded by developing an informal arena in which they are powerful. These abilities can be termed an *oppositional culture* or a culture of resistance. A culture of resistance embodies a coherent set of values, beliefs, and practices which mitigates the effects of oppression and reaffirms that which is distinct from the majority culture.

Concurrently with the development of cultures of resistance, actual challenges to the physical power of the oppressor are mounted. The numerous slave revolts documented by Aptheker (1939) are one example. For centuries, numerous Native American tribes resisted encroachment on their lands with amazing ferocity in the face of massive opposition. African Americans, Native Americans, Latino Americans, and other non-European groups have formed associations and clubs for mutual betterment and cultural maintenance. Subordinated groups have not passively accepted the inferior lot assigned to them by Euro-Americans. They have actively resisted both extermination and assimilation, using the means available.

In this chapter our focus will be on how peoples of color have consistently used their cultures as tools of resistance, sometimes influencing and reshaping the dominant culture in the process. Our thesis is that under conditions of oppression, subordinate groups tend to emphasize existing cultural concepts, norms, and practices which are in opposition to the majority group's culture. In time new elements of oppositional culture develop and become interwoven with the traditional beliefs and practices of oppressed peoples. Subordinated racial and ethnic groups come to emphasize world views and behaviors that contradict or redirect those of the prevailing Euro-American culture. These elements of oppositional culture within each non-European group operate to preserve dignity and autonomy, to provide an alternative construction of identity (one not based entirely on deprivation), and to give members of the dominant group an insightful critique of the their own culture. From this perspective, members of oppressed subordinate groups are not powerless pawns that merely react to circumstances beyond their control, but rather are reflective, creative agents that construct a separate reality in which to survive.

We contend that a more productive theoretical perspective on racial and ethnic relations must take into account the simultaneous pressures to assimilate to the dominant Euro-American ideal and to preserve distinct and protective cultural identities. This process results in both accommodation and opposition, in varying degrees under varying conditions. The primary predisposing condition for the maintenance of separate group identity within the U.S. context seems to be the lack of economic and political power for people of color: The greater the barriers to structural assimilation in the economy and polity, the more likely that elements of a culture of opposition and resistance will develop and persist.

A theoretical perspective on the maintenance and development of cultures of resistance may be constructed from the writings of Hechter (1975), Eco (1986), de Certeau (1984), and Fiske (1989). These theorists outline a dynamic process in which subordinate groups selectively appropriate and transform elements of the dominant culture, to which they are of necessity related. Working on the English colonization of Ireland, Hechter (1975: 9-12) developed a theory of internal colonialism dealing with how a subordinated group uses its culture to resist subordination. Cultural as well as racial markers have been used to set off subordinate groups such as African Americans in the United States and the Irish in the United Kingdom. As a result, resistance to the dominant group takes the form of cultural solidarity in opposition to the dominant culture.

Racial and ethnic groups may engage in "semiotic guerilla warfare" (Eco 1986) in which they maintain their opposition to Euro-American culture by assigning unique cultural meanings to imposed products, including elements of the language of the dominant group. Specific evidence of this process can be seen in both the nonstandard English syntax of various subordinate groups and in the alternate usages of English words, which have unique meanings in subordinate group contexts. Likewise, de Certeau (1984: 18, 31) argues that the culture of everyday life may be seen in the ways one uses imposed systems. Selective consumption may be viewed as a tactical raid on the system, especially when one uses a cultural product for other than the uses intended by the producers. Subordinated racial and ethnic groups are experts in the use of this strategy to maintain their separate cultures. Each group selects its own array of material items and social forms supplied by the dominant group and then endows these commodities with meanings which are contrary to the intent of Euro-American producers. According to Fiske (1989: 15), this strategy may be viewed as "an excorporation of the commodity" into a culture and an "assertion of one's right to make one's own culture out of the resources provided."

That the production of cultures of resistance takes place within the dialectical relationship between dominant and subordinate racial and ethnic groups is significant. Today's European American, African American, Native American, and Mexican American cultures are not merely repositories of distinct cultural elements that have survived after centuries of intermingling. Rather, they embody the results of dynamic processes of interaction in tension-filled relationships between groups characterized by differential access to critical resources. Just as the material conditions of production condition ideology in a Marxist sense, or physical characteristics of the environment condition certain ecological forms, so in complex modern societies the presence of peoples of various cultural backgrounds influences the belief systems and practices of those around them.

The term *culture of resistance* signifies a culture that has evolved and continues to evolve under conditions of oppression. This in no way negates or diminishes the authenticity or primacy of the cultures of subordinated groups. In the words of one of Gwaltney's (1980: 18) black male informants, "We are our own nation . . . . We are not no one tenth of some white something! The [white] man has got his country and we are our country." We recognize the twofold nature of cultural persistence and that no culture in today's world exists in complete isolation. While maintaining strong links with the past, all cultures are in a constant process of reformation in response to pressures of the context in which they operate. These cultures of resistance retain some precontact elements, most noticeably in their systems of meaning and in subtle aspects of appropriate interpersonal interaction. At the same time, they alter the usage of elements of the larger culture to conform to their specific attitudes toward themselves and their world. The interplay of these forces and the ensuing conflicts and diverse formulations of racial and ethnic cultures provide the wealth of lived experience from which social change continues to emerge. The most prominent theme that emerges from the writings of U.S. peoples of color is pride in their principled survival. By this we mean physical survival accompanied by the persistence of values and beliefs that are substantively distinct from those of the majority.

Subordinated racial and ethnic groups are necessarily bicultural. This contrasts greatly with the dominant group, which mostly knows only its own culture (and that not very well, due to lack of comparative perspective). Biculturalism is thus a key aspect of the greater knowledge that people of color have about U.S. society. The dominating need only know their own culture; the dominated need to know both their own and that of their oppressors in order to survive. From this biculturalism flows an ability to see issues from multiple perspectives and to have insights that only those in marginal positions can provide. Intimate acquaintance with, and often rejection of, aspects of Euro-American culture is reflected in many of the elements of oppositional cultures of subordinate groups. The process is interactive to a limited degree, with the dominant group sometimes making modifications along the way.

In this chapter we emphasize the wealth of cultural resources present among subordinated racial and ethnic groups. We focus on three major groups representing different areas of the globe: African Americans, Native Americans, and Mexican Americans. We summarize the forms of physical protest that people of color in the United States have launched against their oppressors. We describe salient elements of their cultures of resistance, accenting selected major continuing critiques of Euro-American culture and noting the responses of the dominant group. We summarize the commonalities among critiques by these diverse cultures of resistance, and we end with an illustration of the costs of not heeding the call for cultural inclusiveness. Since the scope of this project is broad enough for several volumes, the focus in this chapter is on a few recurrent themes common to cultures resisting Euro-American dominance. The groups and examples we have chosen are meant to be illustrative, not comprehensive.

AFRICAN AMERICANS: OPPOSITION UNDER THE WORST FORMS OF OPPRESSION

Unlike all white immigrant groups, black Americans have not been allowed to assimilate substantially into the basic economic and political institutions. Even though most wish full economic and political integration, black Americans have not desired to give up African American culture. The African heritage of African Americans is complex and diverse, since those enslaved came from many different tribes in West Africa and often spent some time in the Caribbean before they (or their descendants) were imported to North America. This African tradition has many important features that have only recently received much scholarly attention and are still unknown to most white Americans. Historically, Whites systematically attacked the African culture of the slaves. Without parallel in North American history, this cultural attack was seen as necessary by the oppressors to root out the oppositional possibilities of an alternative culture.

Williams (1987: 415) has underscored the dramatic difference between the oppression faced by the enslaved immigrants and that faced by white immigrants: "The black slave experience was that of lost languages, cultures, tribal ties, kinship bonds, and even of the power to procreate in the image of oneself and not that of an alien master."

In spite of great oppression, the many peoples of Africa among the slaves—the Yorubas, Akans, Ibos, Angolans, and many other groups—became a single African American people with a distinctive African American oppositional culture. First, slave families maintained kinship practices that were distinct from those of their oppressors. As Gutman (1987: 360-67) noted the typical slave household was double-headed and lasted until the death of a spouse, slave marriages were exogamous with respect to blood cousins (contrasting with planter endogamy), women who bore children outside of marriage were not rejected by their families of origin, and a distinctive and enlarged kinship system—in which great importance was attached to relations between families and among different generations—developed. Parents and other adults taught slave children to address all older slaves as aunt and uncle. Thus, when children were separated from blood kin by death or sale, fictive kin were prepared to assume parenting responsibilities. This practice not only socialized children to recognize the importance of the larger slave community, as opposed to the nuclear family, but it also inculcated a respect for the older ones. Respect for persons with more life experience was shown by giving these individuals symbolic or fictive kin titles. The effectiveness of this cultural strategy for physical survival is evidenced by the fact that during the Civil War northern soldiers and missionaries found very few orphaned black children—most were being cared for by their black neighbors.

One of the most important if misinterpreted contributions of black Americans to America has been the reality and the image of the strong black female. Black freedwomen after the Civil War doubtless wanted to stay home with their children and wanted to pursue the so-called ideal of womanhood, but their labor was needed in the fields, so they were viewed as lazy if they sought to implement those ideals (Jones 1985). They became strong in order to survive. And in this sense the strong black female is part of the oppositional culture. Wages for farm (and later, urban) labor were kept low enough that entire black families were required to work in order to survive—under conditions that did not differ in many respects from those under slavery. So black women have managed the dual roles of wage earner and nurturer since the Civil War. Black families survived under oppressive conditions; strong extended biological and fictive kinship ties provided and continue to provide mutual emotional support and pooling of economic resources as a strategy for coping with conditions impossible for individuals to manage alone (Stack: 1974). It remains to be seen whether the adaptive strategies developed by African American women will be incorporated into the Euro-American mainstream.

African Americans have shaped their own version of English, their own syncretic form of Christian and African religions, their own art and music, and their own philosophical and political thinking about oppression and liberation. A centuries-long struggle for the maintenance of a separate culture, part African and part African American, has provided the foundation for black resistance to oppression since 1619. For example, in his analysis of slave revolts, Stuckey (1987: 42-46) has shown that African culture and religion were a major source of the black revolutionaries' (i.e., the great Nat Turner's) philosophy and inclination to rebellion. From colonial days to the present, pressures on African Americans to conform to white culture have encouraged the maintenance of a black culture of resistance and forced most to be bicultural, to know both the dominant Euro-American culture and their own culture as well.

One of the most important and fascinating elements of African American oppositional culture is its critical assessment of the dominant culture. According to Gwaltney's (1980) informants, white people are too concerned with getting paid for everything, to the exclusion of appropriate humanitarian concern for the well-being of others. Moreover, according to Gwaltney's informants, white folks often pretend that they know what they're doing when they obviously don't, and they do a lot of things that just don't make any sense: The foolishness of whites involved in Watergate—who kept a written record of illegal acts committed—was repeatedly mentioned. No black person, the black respondents asserted, would do something so silly. Such a critical perspective on U.S. politics may be one reason why black Americans have often been correct in their early and critical assessments of national white politicians, such as Richard Nixon and Ronald Reagan, whose corruption and weaknesses were not recognized by most Whites until long after the damage was done.

A fundamental part of Afro-American culture is a deep respect for civil rights and for personal and communal liberty. The Euro-American political institutions put in place by the early waves of North European immigrants were remarkable in their assertion of political and civil liberties. Yet it has been the organized activities of black and other subordinated Americans that has kept that tradition alive and expanding. Historically, black protest strategies have ranged from legal strategies, to the ballot, to nonviolent civil disobedience, to violent attacks on the system. Criticizing the accommodationist position of such leaders as Booker T. Washington, W. E. B. Du Bois and other black and white liberals formed the Niagara movement in 1905 to work on legal and voting rights as well as economic issues. Not long thereafter, some of these leaders played a role in creating the National Association for the Advancement of Colored People (NAACP), the organization which became the major civil rights organization in the United States for decades. Its name has been associated with many of the most important federal court decisions expanding civil rights in the twentieth century.

Black Americans, under the leadership of Dr. Martin Luther King, Jr. and his associates in the 1960s, launched a series of demonstrations against discrimination in Birmingham, Alabama. Later came the massive 1963 March on Washington, in which King dramatized rising black aspirations in his famous "I have a dream" speech. There were boycotts in Harlem, sit-ins in Chicago, school sit-ins in New Jersey, and mass demonstrations in Cairo, Illinois. The Congress of Racial Equality (CORE) accelerated protest campaigns against discrimination in housing and employment. School boycotts, picketing at construction sites, and rent strikes became commonplace. The Student Nonviolent Coordinating Committee (SNCC) germinated the Black Power movement. Pride and consciousness grew in all segments of the black community in the North, particularly among the young (Feagin and Hahn 1973: 81-85; Miller, 1966: 250-56).

In 1983 Jesse Jackson announced his candidacy for president of the United States. Jackson and many of his supporters had learned political skills in various civil rights efforts in the past. Jackson put together a remarkable campaign grounded in an organization of various U.S. racial and ethnic groups called the Rainbow Coalition. Here was a view of what meaningful cultural pluralism could actually look like, for the Coalition included not only African Americans but also Latinos, Asians, Native Americans, Jewish Americans, and an array of sympathetic Whites from both north and south European heritages. By the end of his campaign in 1984, Jackson had registered 2 million new voters, many of them formerly excluded people of color, and had won nearly 4 million votes in the primaries, a fifth of all the votes cast. With Rainbow Coalition support, Jackson was the first black person in U.S. history to make it to that level in the political arena. Jackson succeeded in creating multiracial organizations in states from Vermont to Washington, and he won political power at the party and local levels in some southern states. In 1988 Jesse Jackson again campaigned for the Democratic presidential nomination, with the Rainbow Coalition as his base, and took many delegates to the Democratic national convention. The voters he registered helped elect numerous moderate Whites to the U.S. Congress from 1984 to 1992 (Collins 1986).

The roots of this civil rights activity lie in the centuries-old history of revolts against slavery (Aptheker 1939) and in part in the history of religion of black Americans. Many slave owners encouraged white missionaries to convert slaves in order that they might be better controlled. Yet Stuckey (1987: 27) has demonstrated that the religion of the slaves mixed African and European elements and that the African values prevailed over the European. The view of God that many slaves held—for example, the emphasis on God's having led the Israelites out of slavery—was different from what slave holders had hoped for. Religious meetings sometimes hatched conspiracies to revolt. Like liberation movements before it, the nonviolent civil disobedience movement from the mid-1950s to the 1970s had religious underpinnings.

The effectiveness of black churches in providing leadership and in mobilizing masses of disenfranchised voters is due in large part to recognition of the power of emotions and warm relationships to generate collective action. Both ministers and congregations in black churches are more likely to openly express deeply felt emotions than their white Euro-American counterparts. The call/response format allows the congregation to participate in and give feedback on the sermon. Thus when Dr. Martin Luther King, Jr. called out his dream, he had the support of a people with a heritage of putting religious fervor into their dreams for a better world. When Jesse Jackson gives speeches, complete with "altar calls" (to come down to the front and register to vote), there is a religious tradition which gives both form and substance to the message. In this manner, such political leaders have harnessed the religious sentiments of an oppressed people to mobilize support for political action. Protest has been part of black religion from the beginning.

The emotional component of life, so valued by black churches, makes sharing dreams with the larger community a valued activity. By the same token, those who can most effectively articulate dreams, whether their own or someone else's, are appreciated for their talents and contribution to the whole. Black churches value the role of charisma, which Weber (1946) identified as a leadership characteristic that taps into the emotional commitments of listeners and has the potential for changing oppressive bureaucratic structures. The Euro-American focus on rationality may increase the dominant group's vulnerability to demagoguery, precisely because emotions are not supposed to enter into rational discussions, and therefore structures for appropriate inclusion of the healthy emotional aspects of social life are often missing.

NATIVE AMERICANS: RESISTANCE BY THE MOST MISUNDERSTOOD

After millennia of cultural separation between western and eastern hemispheres, the European colonization process encountered the original inhabitants of the Americas, whom the (lost) Europeans erroneously called Indians. Euro-Americans then proceeded to promote extremely biased renderings of historical realities. Reflect for a moment on Europeans "discovering" an ancient continent already peopled by several million inhabitants. Note also the Euro-American concept of "undeveloped" land, which promoted the destruction of ecologically critical natural habitats in order to fulfill their manifest destiny. Native Americans sometimes speak with pride at having survived genocidal attacks, enforced incarceration on the worst agricultural land in the nation, corrupt Indian agents, insensitive Bureau of Indian Affairs officials, and systematic efforts to destroy native cultures (Witt 1981). Given the sad statistics on income, education, and health, even in recent decades, mere physical survival has been a remarkable feat.

As with African Americans, reliance on expanded kin networks for physical survival has been key. This is illustrated in Navajo and Hopi societies. Among the Navajo, whenever resources come to a traditional member of an extended kin group, the whole network of family members sees some immediate benefit. Feasts are often provided and the most pressing physical needs of individuals within the group are met. Among the Hopi, there is a common saying that "if you're Hopi, you've always got family." This is because each Hopi is born into both a physical and a ritual set of relationships with attached responsibilities and benefits. If one leaves one's biological kin, there are ritual parents and siblings with whom one has relationships. In any location a Hopi has duties regarding others, and others have reciprocal obligations toward him or her. Both Hopis and Navajos are fundamentally oriented to ensuring the collectivity.

Native Americans have managed to retain very strong cultures of resistance. They are strong because most tribes have stayed together geographically, because their precontact world views were so diverse and distinct from European perspectives, and because, lacking opportunities for economic assimilation, their cultures are still a primary vehicle for preserving a positive sense of identity. Many Native Americans have been very critical of Euro-American culture: Europeans are newcomers to the continent. They killed off many animal species. They betrayed the Native Americans who had aided them in establishing a place on the continent and even in subduing other hostile tribes. They destroyed the ecosystem.

Native American reservations in the United States encompass about one third of all low-sulphur coal reserve, one fifth of oil and gas reserves, and half of all known uranium reserves. Historically, when mineral resources have been found on Native American land, the land has been taken over and exploited by white entrepreneurs and corporations (Churchill and La Duke 1986: 51-57). In the 1970s, a member of the Hopi tribe wrote to President Richard Nixon protesting strip mining and other forms of destruction of the western lands: "The white man, through his insensitivity to the way of Nature, has desecrated the face of Mother Earth. The white man's advanced technological capacity has occurred as a result of his lack of regard for the spiritual path and for the way of all living things" (quoted in Olson and Wilson 1984: 219). Many Native Americans now argue that the solution to problems of environmental damage and social isolation lies in recognizing the superiority of Native American values, including a respect for the environment and a strong sense of community.

According to Shirley Hill Witt, one Mormon child-placement program was reportedly aggressive in seeking the placement of Indian children. The president of the Mormon church reportedly commented in this way: "When you go down on the reservations and see these hundreds of thousands of Indians living in the dirt and without culture or refinement of any kind, you can hardly believe it. Then you see these boys and girls [placed in Mormon homes] playing the flute, the piano. All these things bring about a normal culture" (Witt 1980: 31). Here again we see the white culture held up as the normal culture against which Native Americans are judged. This is ironic, for the poverty and dirt in the lives of Native Americans are fundamentally the result of the destruction of Native American resources, the taking away of land, and the rank discrimination in urban areas over hundreds of years of rapacious white, capitalistic oppression.

The Reagan administration in the 1980s made an attempt to foster the "entrepreneurial spirit" on the reservations (Cook 1987: 68-71). In 1987 *Forbes* magazine ran an article on the difficulties of development projects such as industrial parks in the Native American communities called reservations. Reservation resources are usually administered by tribes rather than individuals and any benefits are shared equally among the families. This comment in the premier magazine of U.S. capitalism recognizes that the values of most Native American tribes accent the group rather than the individual. Capitalism is alien to most traditional tribal value systems because it requires basically greedy individuals. Tribal values often include a marked tendency toward "anti-acquisitiveness" (Steele 1973). Whites seem to always want more things. Most traditional Native Americans value work only insofar as it helps maintain a stable environment or improves quality of life. In fact, acquiring too many possessions is often viewed as a burden, as adding unnecessary complications to one's life, and as creating responsibilities which limit freedom.

Among most tribes it is expected that understanding of sacred teachings increases with age, that certain experiences are required for increased comprehension. In the Euro-American world one can, at least theoretically, study any topic and come to complete understanding, limited only by one's intelligence. Yet most Native American traditions, like those of Africa, place greater value on life experience. This provides a good metaphor for the critique Indians often give: Whites often proceed quickly with projects that make rational, linear sense (much planning and calculating has gone into them) without taking time to consider the long-term effects these projects might have on future generations. For this reason Native Americans think it wise to consult with the elders before proceeding with such projects.

In addition, like many African Americans, most Native Americans have preserved a tradition of balancing the nonrational with the rational aspects of life and view Euro-Americans as weak in this regard. Within most Native American frameworks, the logico-deductive mode of thinking does not have dominance over intuitive or metaphorical thinking. Acknowledging and valuing emotions and intuition is part of the concept of walking in balance, staying in harmony, being on the right path. This positive valuing of the nonrational can be seen in oral traditions and in the modern Indian literature (Allen 1986; Cameron 1981; Silko 1977).

The object of most healing rituals is to restore the individual to a state of psychic harmony with all that surrounds him or her. Whereas a Euro-American doctor of medicine treats primarily physical symptoms of illness, a Native American medicine person would be more likely to treat both the body and the psyche. Recognizing that emotional problems are causes of physical distress, native medicine people seek to discern the emotional difficulty of a client and what needs to be done to restore psychic balance in the client's relationships with persons, places, and things. Native Americans have tenaciously clung to rituals preserving balance between the rational and nonrational. The larger society has much to learn from Native Americans in this area.

An example of the persistence of the culture of resistance, combined with the influence of the majority culture, can be seen in the recent growth of Native American powwows. The dominant culture has defined that what it means to be Indian is "to put on feathers and dance" (Seeger 1990). At present, members of tribes that do not have a tradition of such dancing may be observed attending powwows across the country. While one might conclude that even the rituals and identity of subordinate groups are structured by dominant group beliefs, this would be a misreading. On close examination one notices an appropriation of the outward forms dictated by the dominant group, but accompanied by the continual transformation in cultural meaning by the subordinate group. To be a tribal princess carries meaning far removed from European notions of royalty and luxury. To dance to the sound of an eagle whistle may be experienced quite differently from the contest performance to win prizes. To receive gifts from a family sponsoring a give-away has nothing to do with maximizing one's individual profits and everything to do with reciprocity and concern for the collective. Powwows are replete with jokes about the white people and their foolishness and with much advice to the young about traditional ways. The particular proscriptions and prescriptions vary at powwows, but the oppositional culture is apparent.

Many Native American tribes have preserved their languages, and these have sometimes served the vital interests of the U.S. government. This was the case with the Navajo "code talkers" during World War II who succeeded in transmitting strategic information—using the Navajo language—that the Japanese were unable to decode. Today there are hundreds of Native American tribes; their various cultures could provide extremely vital resources to U.S. society. But their cultural vitality has been largely ignored by U.S. society and has yet to be appreciated or incorporated into the Euro-American mainstream.

MEXICAN AMERICANS: RESISTING CULTURAL IMPERIALISM

"Mejicanos" were in the Southwest long before the northern Europeans invaded the area. In 1848 the Mexican government was forced by U.S. military pressure to give the northwest area of Mexico to the imperialistic United States. The existing Mexican residents mostly stayed in their homes, assured in print of protection and citizenship rights by the Treaty of Guadalupe Hidalgo. However, soon thousands of Euro-American in-migrants flooded the area and used legal and illegal means to take most of the land owned by the Mexican occupants. By force Mexicans became part of the complex mosaic that is the United States.

Legal scholar Perea (1992) has noted that this nation has long been a country of many different languages and cultures. In the beginning, several languages were recognized. The Articles of Confederation were officially published in English, German, and French. In 1849 the state of California's first constitution required that all laws be published in English and Spanish. The laws of the territory of New Mexico were published in Spanish and English, and most schools used Spanish. But Euro-Americans eventually succeeded in labeling once-dominant Spanish as a foreign language, in direct contradiction of historical and geographic reality. In addition, treatments of Mexicans and Mexican Americans in schoolbooks have often distorted the history of the Southwest in the myths that glorify heroic Texans confronting a backward Mexican people. Much lawlessness by Euro-Americans against Mexicans had an official status, as when Texas Rangers terrorized Mexican Americans (Paredes 1958: 3).

Mexican American culture has long included elements of opposition and resistance. There is a long history of actively protesting against injustices. The League of United Latin American Citizens, organized in Texas in the 1920s, has pressed vigorously for better conditions. After World War II, The American G.I. Forum was established to organize Mexican American veterans and to work for expanded civil rights. Several groups were formed in the 1960s, including the Mexican American Political Association and the Political Association of Spanish-Speaking Organizations, with explicit political goals. Also in the 1960s, Corky Gonzales and others in Denver worked for school reform and against police brutality; new Chicano organizations were formed throughout the Southwest, including the Mexican American Youth Organization and the Brown Berets, a militant organization with a program of better education, employment, and housing. These groups articulated an oppositional ideology of Chicanismo that accented the ancient presence of Mexican culture and people on southwestern soil and espoused decolonization (Feagin and Feagin 1993). Among the aggressive decolonization protests were those led by Reies Lopez Tijerina, who founded the Alianza Federal de Mercedes in 1963. He and his followers engaged in civil disobedience in New Mexico to dramatize the need for the return of the land to its original Mexican owners.

For many decades a steady immigration of Mexicans looking for work in the United States has buttressed existing Mexican culture and encouraged the maintenance of Spanish as a primary language. This emphasis on retention of ties with Mexico must be viewed from within the social and economic context. While white ethnic immigrants learned English and successfully worked their way into Euro-American economic and politicalstructures, Mexican Americans for the most part have mostly been permitted to assimilate into the lower levels of the U.S. economy and polity. The preservation of fluency in Spanish thus became a key component of Mexican American oppositional culture. Surveys in Los Angeles and San Antonio have found that most Mexican Americans wish children to retain ties to Mexican culture, particularly to language, customs, and religion. Mexican American parents want their children to know and maintain their important cultural heritage (Grebler, Moore, and Guzman 1970: 384, 430).

Euro-American society has been relentless in its attempts to force linguistic assimilation; schools with high percentages of Mexican American students have often been rigid in prohibiting manifestations of Mexican American culture. Bilingual programs specified by laws have mostly been weak (Ramirez and Castaneda 1974). The Mexican American emphasis on linguistic traditions has precipitated a thinly disguised racist attack, as in the promotion of laws making English the only official language. Nativist organizations such as the California English Campaign and the national group called U.S. English have argued that they are not trying to discriminate against Latino Americans, but Latino civil rights groups have vigorously pointed out that pro-English advocates advocate stopping the spread of Spanish as a major language and cutting off governmental expenditures for bilingual programs mandated by the U.S. Supreme Court. These nativists also fear the large numbers of Mexican immigrants who come in each year and thereby reinforce the Latino culture throughout the Southwest.

As with Native Americans, the oppositional culture of Mexican Americans provides the potential for even greater contributions to mainstream culture than has so far been permitted. Whether fluency in Spanish will be recognized by white Euro-Americans as a cultural resource vital for U.S. effectiveness in an increasingly globalized economy and polity is yet to be seen. Without the maintenance of a strong language diversity, the United States will not be able to relate to the linguistic diversity of the world scene. Without an understanding of other cultures, the U.S. government (and corporations) will be increasingly unable to understand overseas firms, governments, and peoples—especially peoples of color.

In addition to preserving Spanish as the primary language in their homes, Mexican Americans have resisted many other sociocultural aspects of U.S. society. Perhaps one of the most important distinguishing characteristics of Mexican Americans, according to Keefe and Padilla (1987: 94), is the substantial size of local kin networks and the frequency of kin visits. Mexican Americans tend to have many relatives who live nearby, and they tend to visit these relatives more often than Euro-Americans. Among Mexican Americans, as among Native Americans, fictive kin relationships form an important part of the extended family. The practice of obtaining godparents for each child, in rituals marking the lifecycle, brings close friends into relationships characterized by affection and kinship obligations. Beneficial as a strategy for survival, such practices become fundamental to Mexican American communities and thus underscore the importance of reciprocal family-type obligations, in contrast to Euro-Americans' typically greater reliance on contractual agreements. Again Euro-Americans may be viewed as spending too much time earning and spending money and not investing sufficient time developing lifelong friendships.

The Mexican American critique of the too-materialistic Euro-Americans is shared with most Latin Americans: most Euro-Americans are so concerned with material things that they forget about the nonrational aspects of life. This critique was stated succinctly by one informant cited by Keefe and Padilla (1987), who said that Anglos are very "materialistic" because "you are what you have." Others stated that Anglo-Americans did not show their feelings as readily as Mexican Americans. Anglos were characterized as less affectionate and more concerned about showing off their purchases, while Mexican Americans emphasized respect and loyalty to elders. Mexican Americans see themselves as more likely to express feelings physically than Euro-Americans. There is greater physical contact between individuals, and hugging and kissing are more frequent and ritualized than among the dominant group. This can be seen in the work of Nobel-prize-winning author Gabriel Garcia Marquez. One of the recurring themes in his work is that physical matter is infused with emotional, nonrational qualities which generate sequences of actions not logically explicable. From the Latino perspective, insufficient attention to the intuitive aspects of life leaves members of the Euro-American group with unbalanced, unhealthy perspectives.

Whether Euro-Americans are capable of seriously considering the cultural critiques offered by Mexican Americans is hard to determine. At this point, it can only be said that the oppositional culture of Mexican Americans has persevered and prospered and can provide valuable cultural resources for the ultimate cultural and physical survival of the United States.

COMMON CHARACTERISTICS AND CRITIQUE FROM CULTURES OF RESISTANCE

A common theme that repeatedly emerges in the histories of subordinated peoples, especially as told by their own chroniclers, is that they, as separate peoples, have managed to survive physically and to maintain their distinct cultures in the face of overwhelming white Euro-American oppression. They have survived the inhumanity of slavery, extermination orders, wars, and forced removals; they have survived denial of voting rights, educational opportunities, and housing. For each of the groups we have addressed, we have shown that subordinated peoples not only have survived these great injustices but have actively fought against them by launching protests, forming political organizations, and refusing to assimilate to inferior identities. They have withstood harsh punishment for holding to their cultures in the face of intense physical and acculturation pressures.

In the face of denial of economic and political opportunity, people of color have resisted the oppression of the majority by maintaining their oppositional cultures. One oppositional element common to the groups discussed is the tendency to value extended kin networks, whether biological or fictive. This tendency has been both culturally encouraged and economically beneficial for subordinate groups in the United States. For example, concluding her study of a black community, Stack (1974: 128) writes, "When economic resources are greatly limited, people need help from as many others as possible. This requires expanding their kin networks—increasing the number of people they hope to be able to count on." Angel and Tienda (1982) document a similar process among Mexican Americans and conclude that nonnuclear family members contribute critically to household income. In addition, Native American groups have been known for their communalism, to the extent that individuals who become wealthy have been scorned by their relatives—who assume that if they were taking proper care of all their relatives, they would not be wealthy. The particular mode of extending kinship ties varies among groups—enlisting the help of boyfriends and significant others among African Americans, respecting reciprocal obligations between clan members among many Native Americans, and incorporating godparents among Mexican Americans—but the tendency is remarkably common in subordinate groups. Such practices recognize the importance of the collectivity in insuring the survival of the individual.

Emphasis on real and fictive kin relationships suggests possible strategies for coping with current U.S. social problems. Subordinated racial and ethnic groups have preserved a way of life that is an antidote for the problem Bellah and his associates (1985) have described as the excessive emphasis on individualism and the lack of a strong sense of community among white Californians. Partly as a result of shared histories of oppression and partly as a result of prior commitment to a set of values that differs from Euro-Americans, people of color have developed strong and complex real and fictive kin networks that bind communities together, especially during times of economic and social distress. From their perspective, the Euro-Americans would do well to learn from these practices, to recognize the value of collective economic interdependence as opposed to individualistic economic independence.

Another common strategy for fighting the unequal distribution of power is for the subordinated group to assert cultural and moral superiority. One manifestation is the moral claim that white Americans too often act like foolish children. Euro-Americans are seen to behave in ways that American persons of color would never consider. Usually this involves brutality, insensitivity, impatience, too much attention to minor details while avoiding weightier matters, pretending to know in the absence of real knowledge, or just doing things that don't make sense: the foolishness of white Americans involved in Watergate, the failure of whites to consider the long-term consequences of attempts to dominate the natural environment, the impulsiveness of Euro-Americans. Another example of moral inferiority, seen through the eyes of subordinate peoples, is Whites' excessive concern with money. African Americans, Mexican Americans, and Native Americans all poke fun at the importance Euro-Americans place on accumulation of money and material objects. The perspective from below is that most Euro-Americans are more worried about getting their money's worth than they are about anything else, including human suffering or even death. For example, those whites who dominate the U.S. health care system often worry more about getting paid for their service than they do about saving a life. White Americans are typically said to value the accumulation of material possessions more than the acquisition of good character, refined sensitivities, or spiritual growth.

A final and related common critique of Euro-American culture is that it privileges logico-deductive modes of thinking. People of color often point out the absurdity of white Euro-American attempts to make all of their behaviors appear rational, when barely obscured emotions (such as fear and guilt) appear much of the time. Peoples of color speak of the need to walk in balance, to acknowledge both intuitive and empirical realities.

CONCLUSION: THE PROCRUSTEAN BED OF WHITE EURO-AMERICAN CULTURE

In the United States, the pressures of white Euro-American nativists for conformity to the Euro-American linguistic, political, and religious norms persist. This can be seen in the economy, in government, and in educational institutions. There is still much white Euro-American resentment of the views and values of American with different racial and ethnic backgrounds. There is clearly a major failure to recognize the significance of the contributions of African Americans to the protection of the civil liberties of all Americans, of Mexican Americans to healthy linguistic diversity, and of Native Americans to respect for land and environment. More fundamentally, there is a failure to recognize the importance of cultures of resistance within the framework of U.S. society. These cultures provide models for coping with and reversing the oppressive excesses of the dominant culture. They provide alternative modes of structuring reality and conceptualizing problems such that novel strategies for bringing about social change can emerge.

For many Euro-Americans, the potential contribution's of these oppositional elements are neither recognized nor respected. The Procrustean bed of Euro-American culture remains a powerful framework pressing on those Americans not rooted therein. A clear example of the great tragedy of this forced acculturation to Euro-American ways of doing things can be seen in the dilemma faced by all middle-class black Americans as they become the pioneers of initial integration into White-controlled economic organizations. For many decades, Whites would not allow black Americans to move beyond a certain level of economic and political assimilation. As the most rigid barriers to economic and political integration have given way before the assault of black political and civil rights organization, Whites have had to allow some movement of Blacks into institutional arenas where they were formerly prohibited. Yet, most whites today either resist black integration or put great pressure on black Americans to assimilate completely to Euro-American culture. There is little thought that dominant white persons should make major adaptations to other Americans' ways of seeing and doing.

Commenting on the white world around her, an African American college student interviewed in a recent study by one of the authors expressed this problem eloquently: Everything, everywhere I look, everywhere I turn, right, left, is white. It's lily white, it's painted with white. And it's funny, because I was reading this article about how America is synonymous with white people. I mean, I'm sure when Europeans or Asians, or Africans for that matter think of America, they think of white people, because white people are mainstream, white people are general. "White is right," as my daddy tells me. White is right, at least they think it is. So, if you're a black person trying to assert yourself, and express your culture, there's something wrong with you, because to do that is to be diametrically opposed to everything this country stands for. And everything this country stands for is what is white.

This quote sums up the basic problem of Euro-American culture. In a large public college with a student body overwhelmingly white, this student expressed the feeling of being hemmed in. When she and other students talk about everything around them being "lily white," they are reporting being overwhelmed by an alien and often hostile cultural environment of white ways of being and of thinking. In institutions of higher education, there are few mirrors that reflect the achievements and identities of subordinated racial groups. Overwhelmingly white images are reflected, regardless of the backgrounds of the individuals admitted. It is miraculous indeed for an individual from a black, Native American, Latino, or Asian background to have command of sufficient skill and guile to outwit the majority's system. Yet individuals in these diverse racial and ethnic groups daily continue to perform such miracles.

This is the ultimate problem of U.S. educational institutions and U.S. society. The integration of non-Europeans into the core institutions cannot be on European terms. If Americans of color are to thrive and prosper, the dominant white, mostly north European American culture itself must be radically changed to recognize the major contributions already made by, and the validity of the critiques still offered by, America's diverse peoples of color. Yet it is not just the latter who will benefit from a central recognition of the viability of the cultures of resistance and the limitations of the white Euro-American culture, for in a world increasingly dominated by peoples of color and of non-European cultural backgrounds, the survival of white Euro-American culture itself is contingent on the recognition that European culture is only one culture among many that contain knowledge pertinent to survival and prosperity. Indeed, a recognition and positive valuation of the values and practices of others will help white Euro-Americans to better understand their own habits of mind and behavior, which remain at present unconscious to them.

REFERENCES

Allen, Paula Gunn. 1986. *The Sacred Hoop*. Boston: Beacon.

Angel, Ronald, and M. Tienda. 1982. "Determinants of Extended Household Structure: Cultural Pattern or Economic Need?" *American Journal of Sociology* 87(6): 1360-1383.

Aptheker, Herbert. 1939. *Negro Slave Revolts in the United States*. New York: International.

Aptheker, Herbert. 1978. *The Unfolding Drama*. New York: International.

Bellah, Robert N., et al. 1985. *Habits of the Heart*. New York: Harper and Row.

Blauner, Bob. 1972. *Racial Oppression in America*. New York: Harper and Row.

Blauner, Bob. 1989. *Black Lives, White Lives*. Berkeley: University of California Press.

Cameron, Anne. 1981. *Daughters of Copper Woman*. Vancouver: Press Gang.

Carter, Thomas P. 1968. "The Negative Self-Concept of Mexican-American Students." *School and Society* 96(March 30): 217-20.

Churchill, Ward, and W. La Duke. 1986. "Native America: The Political Economy of 'Radioactive Colonialism.'" *Insurgent Sociologist* 13(Spring): 51-57.

Collins, Sheila D. 1986. *The Rainbow Challenge*. New York: Monthly Review Press.

Cook, James. 1987. "Help Wanted—Work, Not Handouts." *Forbes* 139(May 4): 68-71.

de Certeau, Michel. 1984. *The Practice of Everyday Life*. Berkeley: University of California Press.

Drinan, Robert F. 1986. "The Supreme Court, Religious Freedom and the Yarmulke." *America* 155(June 12): 9-11.

Eco, Umberto. 1986. *Travels in Hyperreality*. London: Picador.

Feagin, Joe R., and C. B. Feagin. 1993. *Racial and Ethnic Relations*. 4th ed. Englewood Cliffs, NJ: Prentice Hall.

Feagin, Joe R., and H. Hahn. 1973. *Ghetto Revolts*. New York: Macmillan.

Fiske, John. 1989. *Understanding Popular Culture*. Boston: Unwin Hyman.

Gans, Herbert J. 1979 "Symbolic Ethnicity." *Ethnic and Racial Studies* 2: 1-20.

Gaustad, Edwin S. 1962. *Historical Atlas of Religion in America*. New York: Harper and Row.

Geertz, Clifford. 1973. *The Interpretation of Culture*. New York: Basic Books.

Gordon, Milton. 1964. *Assimilation in American Life*. New York: Oxford University Press.

Gordon, Milton. 1981. "Models of Pluralism." *Annals of the American Academy of Political and Social Science* 454: 178-188.

Grebler, Leo, et al. 1970. *The Mexican-American People*. New York: Free Press.

Gutman, Herbert G. 1987. *Power and Culture*. New York: Pantheon.

Gwaltney, John Langston. 1980. *Drylongso*. New York: Random House.

Hechter, Michael. 1975. *Internal Colonialism*. Berkeley: University of California Press.

Herberg, Will. 1960. *Protestant-Catholic-Jew*, rev. ed. Garden City, NY: Doubleday/Anchor.

Hirschman, Charles. 1983. "America's Melting Pot Reconsidered." *Annual Review of Sociology*. 9: 397-423.

Janeway, Elizabeth. 1980. *Powers of the Weak*. New York: Knopf.

Jones, Jacqueline. 1985. *Labor of Love, Labor of Sorrow: Black Women Work and the Family from Slavery to the Present*. New York: Vintage.

Keefe, Susan E., and A. M. Padilla. 1987. *Chicano Ethnicity*. Albuquerque: University of New Mexico.

Leacock, Eleanor. 1978. "Women's Status in Egalitarian Society: Implications for Social Evolution." *Current Anthropology* 19(2): 247-275.

Lenski, Gerhard. 1970. *Human Societies*. New York: McGraw Hill.

McBee, Susanna. 1986. "A War over Words." *U.S. News and World Report*, October 6: 64.

Miller, Loren. 1966. *The Petitioners*. New York: Random House.

Momaday, N. Scott. 1968. *House Made of Dawn*. New York: Harper and Row.

Morison, Samuel Eliot. 1965. *The Oxford History of the American People*. New York: Oxford University Press.

Murguia, Edward. 1991. "On Latino/Hispanic Ethnic Identity." *Latino Studies Journal* 2(3): 8-18.

Olson, James S., and R. Wilson. 1984. *Native Americans in the Twentieth Century*. Provo, UT: Brigham Young University Press.

Paredes, Americo. 1958. *With His Pistol in His Hand*. Austin: University of Texas Press.

Perea, Juan F. 1992. "Demography and Distrust: An Essay on American Languages, Cultural Pluralism, and Official English." *Minnesota Law Review* 77(2): 269-373.

Ramirez, Manuel, and Alfredo Castaneda. 1974. *Cultural Democracy, Bicognitive Development, and Education*. New York: Academic Press.

Schneider, Louis. 1973. "The Idea of Culture in the Social Sciences: Critical and Supplementary Observations." In *The Idea of Culture in the Social Sciences*, Louis Schneider and C. M. Bonjean, eds. Cambridge: Cambridge University Press.

Scott, James. 1990. *Domination and the Arts of Resistance*. New Haven, CT: Yale University Press.

Seeger, Anthony. 1990. Curator of the Folkways Collection for the Smithsonian Institution, Washington, DC. Comments made during roundtable discussion sponsored by the Institute of Latin American Studies at the University of Texas at Austin.

Silko, Leslie Marmon. 1977. *Ceremony*. New York: Penguin.

Silko, Leslie Marmon. 1981. *Storyteller*. New York: Seaver.

Stack, Carol B. 1974. "Sex Roles and Survival Strategies." In *An Urban Black Community, Woman, Culture and Society*, Michelle Rosaldo and L. Lamphere, eds. Stanford, CA: Stanford University.

Steele, C. Hoy. 1973. "The Acculturation/Assimilation Model in Urban Indian Studies: A Critique." In *Proceedings of the 1973 Annual Spring Meeting of the American Ethnological Society*. St. Paul, MN: West.

Stuckey, Sterling. 1987. *Slave Culture*. New York: Oxford University Press.

U.S. Congress P.L. 95-341. 1978. American Indian Religious Freedom Act. 95th Congress. Vol. 92, Pt. 1.

Warner, W. Lloyd, and L. Srole. 1945. *The Social Systems of American Ethnic Groups*. New Haven, CT: Yale University Press.

Waters, Frank. 1963. *Book of the Hopi*. New York: Ballantine.

Weber, Max. 1946. *From Max Weber: Essays in Sociology*. New York: Oxford University Press.

Williams, Patricia. 1987. "Alchemical Notes: Reconstructing Ideals from Deconstructed Rights." *Harvard Civil Rights and Civil Liberties Review*. 22: 401-434.

Witt, Shirley Hill. 1980. "Pressure Points in Growing Up Indian." *Perspectives* 12(Spring): 31-32.

Witt, Shirley Hill. 1981. "Past Positives, and Present Problems." In *Words of Today's Indian Women*, Sedelta Verble, ed. Wichita Falls, TX: Ohoyo Resource Center.

Wolf, Margery. 1974. "Chinese Women: Old Skills in a New Context." In *Woman, Culture, and Society*, Michelle Rosaldo and L. Lamphere, eds. Stanford, CA: Stanford University.

Woocher, Jonathan S. 1986. *Sacred Survival*. Bloomington: Indiana University Press.

Chapter 5

Puerto Rican and Latino(a) Vistas on Culture and Education

Milga Morales-Nadal

Puerto Ricans living in the United States have often responded to their social, economic, and political situation with intense polemical debate, grass-roots organizing, and coalition building. This method of responding to a situation of exploitation is congruent to the traditional cultural mores of Puerto Rican society. It includes our tradition of intense discussion on controversial issues, a belief in the personal versus the impersonal, and working collaboratively at home and in our communities. While this type of response has served Puerto Ricans well, particularly in periods of crises, it has left us with less time to devote to recovering much more of our history and reflecting on the richness and the diversity of our culture. Generally, efforts to promote scholarly study in the history and culture of diverse peoples have, in this country, met resistance and even ridicule. Yet every day, at one college campus or another, the stories of Puerto Ricans and other groups are being told and generations of younger people are listening. This is happening thanks to ethnically based programs and departments constituted through student struggles since the civil rights era of the 1960s and 1970s.

But there is something missing in our histories. They are not complete since much has been left out. Little is said of the Africanness of our people, and we know even less of our Native American ways, customs, and folklore. In fact, much of what has been disseminated in many schools and classrooms is biased and reflects the notion, for example, that Puerto Rico is a small island, too small to be significant, and conditions under U.S. rule have been idealized. This lack of information and diversity of viewpoints on the sociohistorical development of a people leaves a vacuum which must begin to be filled by institutions committed to multiculturalism.

Puerto Rico was occupied militarily by the United States in 1898, and subsequently Puerto Ricans were made U.S. citizens by decree. Despite citizenship, we do not fail to hear cries of "go back where you came from" when something unpopular or unsettling happens which involves us and mainstream America.

The message is "you are not able to survive independently" but, on the other hand, "we don't really want you here." This is what our younger students often hear. Of course, if they affirm their ethnicity and native language, they are accused of being un-American. At the same time, we have been discouraged from participating with our Caribbean family and their counterparts in Latin America. Paradoxically, there are still many in this country who do not know anything about Puerto Rico and its people, and unfortunately some of those are our own Puerto Rican children, born and raised in the United States. For these and other reasons, who we are and how we become are issues we struggle with daily in the Puerto Rican community. These issues speak to our search for an authentic explanation of our identity. Searching for that explanation or explanation(s) will, it is expected, allow us to understand the caution, the cynicism, and the passion often expressed in a diversity of ways by our people and often misinterpreted by mainstream American society.

This chapter will address the broad cultural, linguistic, and political issues which impact the Puerto Rican community on the mainland United States. Puerto Ricans are the largest Latino group in the Northeast. This chapter is a personal and scholarly attempt to come to some understanding of the reality of Puerto Rican and Latino communities from the perspective of a Puerto Rican woman, born in Puerto Rico but whose identity was formed in the cauldron of the U.S. ethnic and racial reality. An expected outcome of this discussion would be to provide additional vistas that may be considered in the forging of a truly multicultural university.

THE BROADER LATINO(A) PERSPECTIVE

The numbers of Latinos(as) in this country are growing by leaps and bounds. Latinos are considered the fastest-growing minority group in the United States. Currently, over 22 million reside within U.S. borders (Garcia and Montgomery 1991). This, of course, does not include Puerto Rico, a U.S. territory with a population of over 3.5 million. Generally, all Latinos(as) are lumped together without regard to differences in class, race, language, ethnicity, and gender. In fact, the term Hispanic has been used often to obfuscate our diversity and implies a false homogeneity based on the language and culture of Hispania (the Roman name for Spain). This term also emphasizes the dominant European (Caucasian) heritage while more often than not excluding the African and Arabic peoples central to Spanish development and society. The lack of a serious commitment to the study of and education about Spanish-speaking peoples in the United States has resulted in stereotypical images portraying Latinos(as) and Puerto Ricans, as violent, knife-wielding gang members (the movie *West Side Story* contributed to this development), hot-blooded, and promiscuous (the Latin lover image), crazy and procrastinating ("Frito Bandido," stereotyping Mexicans and other Latinos as "loco" and leaving everything for "manana"; see Perez 1990). For the urbanized Latino child who may watch television for several hours a day, there are few positive role models to look to. Moreover, when these children seek out role models in the elementary school, the high school, or the university, they are fewer and far between. While we work to dispel myths such as these, it appears to us as more consequential to the overall development of our children that we attempt to recover, understand, and advance our distinct and identifiable characteristics as a people.

LATINOS(AS) IN THE U.S. CONTEXT

In the United States, the Latino/a population is composed of Mexican Americans, Puerto Ricans, Cubans, Dominicans, and Central and South Americans. Mexicans are by far the most numerous, with Puerto Ricans, Dominicans, and Cubans in lesser numbers. A networking, research, and advocacy group which has attempted to direct itself to researching the demographic and socioeconomic trends of Puerto Ricans and other Latinos in the United States has been the Institute for Puerto Rican Policy, Inc. (IPRP). This organization, along with ASPIRA of New York, Inc. (an educational agency concerned with developing Latino youth leadership), has interjected Puerto Rican issues and concerns into the political agenda of the United States. IPRP has designed surveys and compiled data on the various Latino groups and has shown the divergence between them.

Mexican Americans, for example, are by and large indigenous to the North American continent. Over 16 percent in the 25+ age group have less than five years of schooling, and 31 percent of the males, and 21 percent of females are operators, laborers, and fabricators. This contrasts sharply with the Cuban population in the United States of which only 4.3 percent of the 25+ group have less than five years of schooling and only 23 percent of the males and 14 percent of the females are in lesser skilled jobs. Moreover, over 25 percent of Cuban males are in managerial and professional specialties, but less than 9 percent of Mexican males and less than 13 percent of Mexican females occupy this position (IPRP 1990). These discrepancies are of particular concern when politicians hasten to demonstrate the progress or achievements of the entire Latino/a community. This attention to diversity certainly adds complexity to the issue. However, it also generates a more vivid description of the context in which Puerto Ricans live within the United States.

In 1988, over one third of all Puerto Ricans were living in poverty. Most of these impoverished households were headed by females with children. Less than half of this figure reflected the Cuban reality. Mexicans were slightly better off. Approximately 28 percent were living in poverty (Torres 1989). These variations in socioeconomic condition cannot be attributed to lack of skills, motivation, or "ganas" (the term used by the character of Jaime Escalante in the movie *Stand and Deliver*, meaning "desire to do"). Puerto Ricans have demonstrated their ability to work successfully in all sectorsof the economy from agricultural labor to computer programming. The migratory movements of the 1940s dem-

onstrated their willingness to overcome poverty. Puerto Ricans have since set-
tled in all fifty states. They had left their tropical climate for the snow and cold
flats of New York City, encountering their share of bias and discrimination from
those who had themselves weathered storms to reach Ellis Island in New York
harbor. In spite of this, Puerto Ricans have survived and most have raised their
families in the United States. Yet Puerto Ricans have not achieved the same high
socioeconomic status as Cubans. If skills or motivation are not missing ingredi-
ents, what characteristics of this population make it difficult for Puerto Ricans
to achieve as even more recently arrived Latino immigrants have? Historical,
linguistic, and racial differences may provide some insight and direction.

EMERGENCE OF THE *BORICUA*: A SYNCRETISM OF CULTURES

Many of us acknowledge that long before Cristobal Colon arrived in
Guanica Bay on November 19, 1493, indigenous populations lived in *Boriken*
(the Taino or Native American name for what today is referred to as Puerto
Rico). But only a handful of local and mainland scholars recognize Native
Americans as significant to our development as a people. This is not surprising,
however, since most textbooks brush aside or quickly dismiss accounts of their
presence, their legacy, and their part in our formation as Puerto Ricans. Re-
claiming this heritage has been the lifelong work of Ricardo Alegria and other
founders of the Instituto de Cultura Puertorriquena in Puerto Rico. Most recently, Antonio Stevens-Arroyo of Brooklyn College has written about the importance of Arawak myth construction and its relevance to a Puerto Rican world
view utilizing Jung's theory of archetypes and the collective unconscious
(Stevens-Arroyo 1990).

A visit to Tibes, one of the most recently uncovered indigenous ceremonial
grounds located in the southern part of Puerto Rico, invites us to shed our preconceived notions and partake in an appreciation of who we are as a people. A
walk through the grounds of Tibes allows us a look back, for example, at the
figures made on stone petroglyph, symbolizing our regard for the human spirit,
and harmony with the earth. Open areas, which the indigenous people referred
to as a*batey*, were a common ground for recreation, a place to meet or celebrate.
If you listen closely, the language of the Arawak whispers through the Ceiba
trees, and the names of the *Caciques* (chieftains) of the Tainos are heard:
Caguax, Guarionex, and Ana Caona. We are reminded that the names of many
of the towns of Puerto Rico reflect our Indianess—Caguas, Mayaguez, Arecibo,
and my hometown Guayanilla. We remember the names for the fruits and vege-
tables found on this land, such as yuca, batata, and mamey, and we feel close to
those who planted, conserved the earth, and made it richer for us. These original
inhabitants were known as Arcaicos. Subsequently, the Igneris, different in that
there were more agriculturalists among them, joined the community. The Mayas
may have also come to this land, and samples of Mayan-type art have been

found. These Native Americans also inhabited other countries of the Caribbean as well, such as the Dominican Republic, Cuba, and Haiti (Coll y Toste 1968).

Whether we have dark-colored hair and dark colored skin or light-colored hair and light colored skin, Puerto Ricans are known as *Boricuas*, from the indigenous name for our country. As opposed to underestimating the significance of this population to our formation, we have come full circle, and now younger *Boricuas* are forming Taino cultural groups to recover and study the art and culture of our indigenous ancestors.

A continuous focus on indigenous victimization by the Spaniards from the middle of the sixteenth century requires us to now retrace and recover our history. We are recapturing indigenous customs and traditions that often go unrecognized or, equally negative, are considered exotic and mythical. There is another complementary cultural force. The indigenous need to be in balance with and respect nature's forces is also central to the African world view. In this case, our indigenous ancestors could not be in disharmony with our African family forcibly taken from the African lands of the Yorubas and of the Congo and sent to Brazil, Cuba, Santo Domingo, and Puerto Rico. Their beliefs in the Yoruba deities are part of our heritage and our religious traditions and rituals. They are evidenced today in the maintenance of the color codes (white and red) used in Santerismo in Puerto Rico when the spirit of Chango is to be invoked.

In addition, Marta Moreno Vega writes that the Ceiba tree was of religious significance to the Native American in Puerto Rico as well as the African Yoruba (Moreno-Vega 1989). Rene Marques, an acclaimed Puerto Rican playwright of this century produced a modern three-act play, *La Carreta* (The Oxcart), which ends with a reference to the strength of the Puerto Rican and compares that strength to the endurance of the *ausubo*, the Arawak name for a tree native to Puerto Rico whose bark is so strong as to be virtually impenetrable with an ordinary ax. This contemporary work reflects our continued belief in and respect for the land (Marques 1955). A distinctive Puerto Rican (*Boricua*) nationality has emerged from this historical interweaving of peoples to create mestizos (the blend of Arawak and European) and mulattos (the blend of African and European) and a combination of all of these. Because there are those who consider themselves pure Indian, pure European (Caucasios), or pure African, the question is always asked, "Y tu abuela, donde esta?" (Who was your grandmother?).

Familiar to Puerto Ricans of all social classes in Puerto Rico are three concepts, which may have evolved from the Spanish *Pundonor* (Point of Honor, an unwritten code that governs behavior at the interpersonal level). The first is *Respeto*. Uppermost in each person's mind is achieving respect and conserving it. *Dignidad* is the dignity inherited by virtue of keeping respect and giving it. The expectation is that we will hold our heads high and no one will *doblegarse* or bend over to anyone. The attribution of *machismo* to the Latin American may have had its basis in these ideas. *Relajo*, on the other hand, is related to humor and is a way of being that shows one is not frustrated or overly concerned but relaxed and in control. These concepts appear central to our Puerto Rican culture, but it would be difficult to attribute their origin to any one particular segment of our heritage (Lauria 1963).

The interweaving of the African, Spanish, and indigenous cultures is reflected in the folklore and traditions of Puerto Rico as well. For example, African and indigenous expressions may be found in the folklore, the music, the art, and the dance of the Puerto Rican people. The *plena*, an Afro-Puerto Rican folk and dance form, is a case in point. Traditional call and response of West African singing and drumming is interwoven with lyrics recited in Spanish using Andalusian versions of the copla and decima. An indigenous Arawak taino instrument, the guiro, is often used in plena to provide rhythmic accent along with the pandero, a small, hand held drum similar to the tamborine. This form of artistic syncretism is replicated in various sociocultural contexts (Nadal 1976).

Religion is a prime example in the blending of traditional Spanish Catholicism with the polytheistic Yoruba and Ashanti folk religious practices of West Africa. In Cuba and Puerto Rico, this form of religious syncretism has taken the names of Santerismo and Espiritismo, respectively. Similarly, the Spanish language incorporated the diversity of expressions, intonations, and pronunciations that reflect the three cultures. Words such as *nagua* (half slip), *hamaca* (hammock), *huracan* (hurricane), commonly in use in Puerto Rico, may be traced to the Arawak language. In like manner, *bembe* (festive occasion), *fufu* (hex), and *bomba* (large drum) may be traced to Yoruba (African) culture (Alvarez-Nazario 1972).

These experiences do not in and of themselves make us unique. It is the intersection of these sociohistorical events with the politics and people of North America that make this Latino/a population different. As a result of the Spanish-Cuban-American War, the United States occupied Puerto Rico in 1898. With the exception of a few months prior to the U.S. invasion when the Spanish colonizers had granted Puerto Rico a form of limited political autonomy, the island territory has never achieved complete sovereignty from U.S. rule. This particular historical occurrence has impacted immensely on the development of the Puerto Rican people. While some have acquiesced to U.S. rule, others continue to resist culturally and politically.

A particular tool of both oppression and resistance has been education. There has been an attempt to use schooling to assimilate and acculturate Puerto Ricans both at home and on the mainland. The language policy in 1898 changed the language of instruction in Puerto Rico to English almost overnight. But Puerto Ricans have resisted over the generations by continuing to speak and value Spanish. Some have educated each other using the writings of revolutionaries from throughout the world (Osuna 1949). The university, both in Puerto Rico and in the United States as well, has, as in many other countries, served for many as a vehicle for liberation and consciousness raising.

CULTURAL VIEWS AFFECTING THE PERCEPTION OF EDUCATION

Prior to the Second World War, higher education in Puerto Rico was primarily for the upper classes, although there were some exceptions. Similarly, it was not always the sons and daughters of the lighter skinned that reached professional status. One notable example was the teacher Rafael Cordero, an African Puerto Rican who against all odds fought to teach the poorest children in the country (Babin 1958; Tuck and Vergara 1969). My father attended a rural grade school for only two years and my mother for four years. Poverty prevented many of them attending school beyond the sixth grade. This does not mean that Puerto Ricans do not have a history of education. Many are self-taught. My hometown of Guayanilla boasts of several talented personalities who were not famous outside of their community and had little or no schooling. They were poets, orators, musicians, writers, historians, and teachers.

In both the Southern Spanish (Moorish) and West African parts of our cultural heritage, there is a vibrant oral tradition. It combines improvised verse forms of varying rhythmic and metric schemes with musical backgrounds incorporating vocal-percussive ensembles accompanied by native stringed instruments. So strong is this tradition that the community accords respect and recognition to the person who can spontaneously recite verse or improvise song on a given theme at any time. Such is the case with Puerto Rican verse and musical forms like the *aguinaldo*, *copla*, *plena*, and *controversia*. An individual's literate ability, though highly regarded, cannot substitute for the *don de la palabra* or gift for language.

Nowhere is this more evident than in the bowl-faced expression of Puerto Rican children when they listen to elders' accounts of the legendary Puerto Rican character Juan Bobo (Cadilla de Martinez 1979). The word *bobo* in Puerto Rican Spanish means "feeble minded or extremely naive." Actually, this character's name belies an ingenuity and craftiness that allows him to be perceived as a fool or simpleton while astutely manipulating a situation to his advantage. Concha Melendez, an expert on the Puerto Rican short story and its roots in the oral tradition, states that Juan Bobo could more appropriately be named *Juan que se hace Bobo*, or a Juan who feigns ignorance and naivete (Pitre 1993). This character is said to have derived from the Puerto Rican highland culture of the *jibaro*, a mountain-dwelling peasant with little formal education but who possesses a trove of worldly knowledge that is passed down via storytelling, poetry, song, pithy, and epigrammatic sayings known as *refranes*. The *jibaro's* world view is conditioned by a strong Christian ethic of *caridad* (charity) and *amistad*, friendship based on mutual respect and reciprocity. However, one must not mistake this charity and goodwill with submissiveness and passivity. In the face of dishonesty and chicanery, the *jibaro* exercises *jaiberia*, the quality to be circumspect and remain silent while evaluating one's intentions.

The definition and view of education from the Puerto Rican perspective has been investigated by Sonia Nieto (1992). She suggests that the definition Puerto

Ricans and other Latinos give to education has different connotations. When, for example, one says in Spanish that a person is *educado* (educated), one is really referring to a person who is gentle, kind, generous, and polite. A person with very little schooling may be *educado*. Puerto Rican parents often have difficulty understanding how their children pick up negative attitudes in schools toward them and toward their communities. If they are in school they should learn *modales* (loosely translated as "manners" but meaning a whole comportment or behavior). Oratory or *saber hablar* is also considered important. A man should be able to get up in front of a group at a wedding and toast the bride and groom with a very flowery speech. Or a man should be able to toast his new compadres when he has baptized a godchild. Poetry and song are valued as a means of communication with your family and community. Puerto Rican men who can sing or recite are prized as invaluable members of their family and community. A man who knows how to speak to women with respect is regarded highly as well. Early on men learn to deliver *piropos*. These are flowery comments about women, how they look, and their fantasies about them. One *piropo* often heard is *Dios bendiga el jardin que engendro esa flor* (God bless the garden in which that flower bloomed). Men as well as women are usually impassion about their loves, their lives, and their beliefs. Passion is not a negative but seems to be at the core of the culture. To stand and deliver a speech without involving your body and your soul (*alma*) is to be *seco*, (dry, without feeling).

Associated with being *educado* is to be knowledgeable about politics, sports (boxing and baseball), and music. Men should be able to speak about these topics with some assuredness. Women, on the other hand, are not necessarily required to know very much about the world, be able to give fiery or flowery speeches, or be the poets and leaders of the country and community. In spite of these lower levels of expectations, however, women have in our history risen to greatness. Mariana Bracetti and Lola Rodriguez de Tio were Puerto Rican revolutionaries who fought against Spanish colonialism; Luisa Capetillo organized women workers at the turn of the century; Lolita Lebron battled U.S. intervention in Puerto Rico; and Pura Belpre wrote stories about Puerto Rican life and culture, including life in the United States (Acosta-Belen and Christensen 1979; Ortiz 1989-1990).

Hospitality and relatedness are also associated with a person that is *educado*. You are not *educado* if someone comes to your house and you do not invite him or her in and offer that person at least a glass of water. Your home should always be open to the stranger, as long as you are familiar with his or her background. Knowing what family one comes from is very important. The expression *De tal palo, tal astilla* signifies the interest in knowing what tree that branch is from or what family you are from.

In addition to being hospitable, it is important to be informed about your own family. Where are they living now? What work is each person doing? Who passed away? Who is coming to the United States? Who is getting married? My husband often tells an anecdote about the time that a childhood friend of his was alone in his house and a family acquaintance came by to inquire about the whereabouts of his father. When he asked "where is your father?" my husband's friend, at that time a senior in high school, answered that he did not know. The father's friend said, "Hah! Four years in high school and you don't know where your father is at 7 o'clock in the evening."

While these values are still found at the core of Puerto Rican culture, they are played out differently as Puerto Ricans encounter the experience of the migration. Clashes between what is expected of the Puerto Rican male, for example, and the values with which he has been raised give way to clashes between the concept of education and schooling and being *educado*. What was valued in the community previously may no longer be valued. In this regard, the male's perceived role as the provider and protector is important. He is expected to protect the women in his life: mothers, sisters, and daughters. This may mean physically fighting for them, or leaving school in order to work and provide for the family. These expectations color the extent to which formal schooling may be identified as important in a young person's life.

Women are not measured with the same standard. They are not expected to speak up or speak out except as it relates to their families, particularly regarding their children. In a society like the United States, where the dominant culture expects people to have voices, to say what they mean, Puerto Rican women do not always find the support they need to do so. Whereas women may have talent for poetry, singing, and dancing, assertive skills may not be favored because they may impinge the woman's role as wife and mother. Many of the second generation of Puerto Ricans in the United States and some of the first generation have rebelled against some of these traditional values. But when intergenerational familial gatherings occur, somehow the women are still found in a different part of the room or in another room in the house, separated from the males.

The effect of some of these traditional ideas on the behavior of Puerto Rican students in the college classroom becomes apparent to those familiar with the roots of the culture. More often than not, the Puerto Rican or Latino/a student does not actively participate in the classroom setting unless he or she is asked or directed to do so. The issue of voice is particularly relevant here because not speaking up may be interpreted as not knowing. In fact, the relationship is often established linking a lack of language to intellectual deficiency. There is also a disregard or lack of understanding of the linguistic pluralism that exists in the Puerto Rican and Latino community.

LANGUAGE PLURALISM IN THE PUERTO RICAN AND LATINO COMMUNITY

Given the relationship of Puerto Rico to the United States, Puerto Ricans could be characterized as bilingual. In fact, the research carried out in the Puerto Rican and Latino community suggests that various levels of bilingualism are present. In addition, some researchers argue for the presence of a dialect that has emerged due to the interaction of different languages and peoples with different cultures. The work of Attinasi et al. (1982) indicates that Puerto Rican Latinos are not speaking Spanish all the time in particular contexts or domains (Fishman et al. 1971). Rather this group has begun to construct a new form of expression that incorporates both Spanish and English, sometimes intrasentencially and at other times intersentencially. This use of language is shaped by the race, class, and gender of the speaker.

To characterize this new form of expression as code switching does not do justice to the complexity of language use in this community. In some instances, both the professional and layperson have assumed that this emerging code of expression arises due to a linguistic deficiency or disorder in the child or student. As a teacher-educator, I have heard one too many stories of children being amateurishly diagnosed as language handicapped by a teacher or other professional who is attempting to assess the language development of a child without cognizance of the sociolinguistic features characteristic of the child's community.

Some research has emerged which demonstrates, for example, that an urban Puerto Rican child given a set of pictures may label some in Spanish and some in English. This choice may be a product of a child's individual decision to use the label in the language he or she first acquired, or to provide the term in the second language. In either case, it is a decision based on context. A child may respond to the picture of a broom with the word *broom* or *escoba* or even *e'coba* (Puerto Ricans and Cubans often engage in segment deletion). This same child may start a story about a party in his grandmother's house in English and interject whole sequences of the story in Spanish. He or she may even do this within sentences. In another example, as he or she recounts a story to an English-dominant teacher with little knowledge of Spanish, he or she may say, "I went to *abuela's* [grandma's] house *y comi pavo y pernil* [and I ate turkey and roast pork]." If asked, the child could probably translate *pavo* to turkey, but in translating *pernil* to roast pork, the festivity and celebration that is associated with certain kinds of foods is not as apparent.

This constructing of language is not just structural or lexical. The class and racial position of Puerto Ricans and Latinos contributes to making such language choices in multiple social linguistic environments. African American adolescents, particularly many of those raised in mixed cultural neighborhoods, have acquired Spanish expressions and are conversant in the language itself. Young Puerto Ricans and Latinos raised in these same neighborhoods are often heard speaking black dialectical English with Spanish phonology (Zentella 1982).

This growing linguistic plurality may be especially disconcerting to university professionals witnessing a transformation in the language paradigms to which they have been accustomed. As a Puerto Rican teacher-educator, I have been approached by faculty members attempting to enlist support in condemning the influx of nontraditional students into the university. More often than not, these nontraditional students are native speakers of languages other than English and are people of color. In directing myself to these comments, I have reminded colleagues that linguistic pluralism comes along with the territory of diversity. If we are to embrace the notion of cultural pluralism and not the old program of assimilation, then bilingualism, dialectalism, and diversity of language codes must be taken into account.

All of these various linguistic codes ought to be the object of serious study by secondary school and university instructors, who are often too quick to label Puerto Rican Latino students as lacking a coherent linear style of writing in the standard English language code. This is particularly disturbing when Puerto Rican students are given back papers that point to stylistic flaws such as circumlocution and awkward phrasing. Within the sociocultural context of their language code, Latino students see nothing wrong with statement, restatement, and redundancy, often creating new metaphors that stem from their dual language background that are deemed unacceptable by the Anglo teacher. I like to call this the "bottom linism" inherent in what English teachers characterize as good, economical writing devoid of flowery and excessive language. As James Banks has emphasized, and many are now beginning to realize, the dominant WASP culture and language has been influenced and transformed by those who are often seen as marginal to it as well as those who appear to be part of it. As language is a maker and bearer of culture, it becomes transformed and transforms in its very use. Therefore, those that embrace cultural diversity ought to be aware that the dominant language, English, is itself changing as languages always do. However, resistance to this notion is understandable particularly when one examines the dialectical relationship between language, culture, and politics (Banks 1991).

NO SOMOS NI CHICHA NI LIMONADA: IDENTITY AND POLITICS IN THE PUERTO RICAN AND LATINO COMMUNITY

The words of a prominent African-Puerto Rican leader of the twentieth century, Pedro Albizu Campos, "Esta sobre el tapete la suprema definici'on: o yanquis o boricuas" (Yankee or Puerto Rican: the time to decide is upon us), have served to remind us of the relationship of language, culture, and politics even as we approach the twenty-first century (Campos 1971: 126). A plebiscite on the issue of the political status of Puerto Rico appears to be forthcoming. Puerto Ricans living on the island may be asked by the U.S. Congress to decide whether to continue the Commonwealth relationship, to become the fifty-first state, or to opt for political independence. The plebiscite has not quelled the passionate debate surrounding the issue of identity. In fact, in determining whether or not Puerto Rican Latinos residing in the United States could participate in the plebiscite, a controversy has emerged as to who are real Puerto Ricans.

Puerto Ricans in the United States have never hyphenated their national origin (Puerto Rican-American) for themselves. Those who live in Puerto Rico, be they statehooders, advocates of independence, or supporters of the status quo, visualize the Puerto Rican Latino(a) in the United States as *Newyorican*, on one side of the scale, or *asimilado*, on the other side. Both assertions communicate an attitude of nonacceptance. In spite of this, young Puerto Rican Latinos continue to immerse themselves in the music, folklore, customs, and traditions of their culture. The emergence of salsa music in Puerto Rican and Latino communities throughout the United States may be considered a tool of resistance to assimilation as well as a vehicle for indirectly promoting and maintaining indigenous language and traditions. Moreover, recent examples of popular bilingual and bicultural rap music demonstrate the dynamic and protean quality of this creative expression. "Mentirosa" and "La abuela," popular rap songs in both Puerto Rico and New York City, reflect the meshing of culture and language as it occurs in the urban barrios, both in Puerto Rico and the United States (Flores 1991).

An unfortunate circumstance in the Puerto Rican and Latino communities is that the hometown clubs of the past, which served to provide sanctuary for the uniting of politics, language, and culture, now exist in few communities (Sanchez-Korrol 1986). However, educational organizations, such as ASPIRA, continue to provide a forum for discussion and a platform for debate on issues of concern to young Puerto Ricans. While the focus of such an organization is not directly interrelated with concerns of political status, it serves to ensure that Puerto Ricans that come into contact with it emerge as knowledgeable participants in the political process, whether on the island or in Puerto Rican communities in the U.S. This is of extreme importance in the context of the colonial relationship of Puerto Rico to the United States because the families of these young Puerto Rican Latinos have in many cases been marginalized from the political process in their own country as well as in the United States. Some with pro-independence views, in particular, have been discouraged from exercising their right to struggle for self-determination. It is incumbent, then, that young Puerto Rican Latinos become actively engaged with the political process in this country and with the many strategies and tactics necessary to become subjects and not objects of their existence (Freire 1970). This is particularly germane to the Puerto Rican and Latina woman, particularly in light of her perceived role within the community. In what follows, we will look at how Puerto Rican and Latina women appear to fit within a society that has attempted to lock them out.

YO MISMA FUI MI RUTA: THE PUERTO RICAN LATINA SEARCHING FOR A VOICE

A loose translation of the subtitle of this section might be read as, "I did it my way." However, Julia de Burgos, the poet who wrote these words, was expressing much more than staunch individualism (Jimenez de Baez 1966). She used the medium of poetry to express her rejection of oppression—be it male chauvinism or colonial domination. Her voice has been echoed by a new generation of young Puerto Rican Latinas seeking ways of expressing their anger, frustration, and seeming double powerlessness. They are to be found in the performing arts, education, politics, and community struggles. Victims of dwindling resources, they often juggle jobs, schooling, and family. Almost half of all Puerto Rican households are headed by females and are among the poorest of all people of color in the United States (Garcia and Montgomery 1991). In spite of all the hardships, these women are attempting to get the education required for a career and decent job. It is not uncommon for some women to take their children with them to college classes when they do not have the resources for child care. Given these circumstances, it is also not surprising that many Puerto Rican and Latina women do not relate to a feminist movement in the United States that they consider to be dominated by white, middle-class females. The agendas for each are not only different in content, but they differ as well in strategy and tactics. As Celina Romany notes, "Our experience with gender intersects with the social marginality that is a product of racial, ethnic, and class oppression and, in the case of the Puerto Rican woman, colonial oppression" (1989).

Nonetheless, it is encouraging to note that as more Puerto Rican Latina and other women of color enter the ranks of the traditional feminist movement, the face of the movement is changing and a diversity of voices will soon be heard. Women's centers throughout the country are beginning to listen to the call for a movement that incorporates the lived reality of the Puerto Rican Latina and other women of color. They are including the history and struggles of these women in women's studies, joining efforts to secure day care for women attending school, and, in some cases, allowing space for the unique cultural expression of individual women. There is still room and a need to provide young Puerto Rican Latinas with role models and support networks that attend to the economic, cultural, and social aspects of their daily lives. Yet inclusion should not be patronizing. The feminist movement must understand that it will be transformed by the very participation, activism, and leadership of Puerto Rican Latinas and other women of color. Some of the voices will be a true expression of the hurt and the heat of the struggle felt by poor women of color every day. What will be needed is a rapport and an enabling commitment that will ensure the empowerment of the young Puerto Rican Latina. The university will have an opportunity to reach into communities and provide the necessary educational and financial resources that will allow for a multiplicity of women's voices and make their message its own.

CONCLUSION

Finally, it should be encouraging to all that this quest for inclusion is off to a good start. A new paradigm has been generated, and it is homegrown. It requires, however, that the university become truly universal, that it encourage the uncovering and the recovery of our history. It must consider the codes of the communities that it seeks to integrate and create space for the diversity of voices that have been quieted for all these years. Moreover, if universities are ready to move into the twenty-first century, they will be transformed into dynamic, colorful, and cultural repositories of lived realities that will make sense to all of us, and we will all be enriched by the change, although it will not come easily to many or without pain.

Recommendations for a Multicultural University

Awareness of cultural difference is not sufficient to create a hospitable or encouraging climate for Puerto Rican and Latino students in the university. Respect for the students must be at the foundation of the new university. This can be achieved through the recognition and valuing of a person's identity, culture, and language. An underestimation of a student's worth because of his or her diversity in culture or language suppresses the valuable exchange of experiences and the expansion of ideas and shortchanges all of those who seek an enriched educational experience.

Faculty members and staff who understand the diversity and the dynamics of culture and can immerse themselves in the socio-cultural reality of the Puerto Rican and Latino world are essential to this new university. For this to happen (viewing the world through the eyes of a Puerto Rican Latino), both white faculty and faculty of color may be instructed and sensitized to expressions of circumspection, passion, and search for belongingness that characterize our young people. Recreational and study areas may be staffed by students and faculty that reflect the university's diversity and use can be made of the expertise of ethnic and women's studies departments and programs to establish the *ambiente* or social climate conducive to the needs of students and in deference to the variety of languages and cultures.

Puerto Rican and Latino students generally demonstrate a commitment to and concern for community that should be fostered in the university. A university without walls may be an empowering institution since the student is not cut off from his or her primary source of identity, strength, knowledge, and inspiration. All areas of concentration or majors could include community-based internships and activities which cultivate this link and strengthen the reciprocity of the relationship of school and community.

An invitation to students to contribute from their wealth of literature, folklore, and customs to the university's curriculum, in the broadest sense, must come not just from ethnic studies or minority faculty members but from the institution's highest levels without qualification. Presidents and other officers of the university may provide leadership in this area while serving as examples for their own ethnic constituencies. Acknowledgment of the favorable outcomes of bilingualism could be realized in a variety of ways. However, simply encouraging faculty, staff, and students to utilize a second language, even for the purpose of greetings at official functions, is a small but progressive step in the right direction.

Literacy and language issues, as discussed in this chapter, may be addressed through university seminars. But more practically, the inclusion of students in conversations privy only to faculty, and more specifically to white faculty, would encourage students of color to become active participants in the transformation of the university. Such a recommendation, however, involves the opening of segregated enclaves within the institution, such as faculty lounges and cafeterias, and the provision for structures that encourage dialogue independent of rank and social status. A variety of language codes may then be appreciated as contributing to the development of a diversity of repertoires (i.e., different ways of viewing the world).

The sounds of different cultures should emanate from multicultural universities. Artistic expression, like the university's athletic endeavors or sports, may provide common ground for the development and conscious reappraisal of the traditional meaning of aesthetics. Wind, percussion, and strings, as well as dance and song, are instrumental in telling all of our stories. Visual images of our past and present, via paintings, murals, and sculpture, validate our uniqueness of creative expression and serve to correct our indigenous African and European heritage in the lives of young Puerto Rican Latinos in search of their cultural roots.

Our traditional plaza or *batey* may be at the center of such a university, providing the space for the interchange of cultural lore and the acquisition and sharing of a multiplicity of perspectives.

Finally, I envision collaborating and cooperating study circles forming in our communities around the themes, issues, and problems discussed or alluded to in this chapter. To that end, the university must provide and assure that students have the tools to uncover knowledge and recover their history, with the proviso that it is not theirs to keep but to pass on in the tradition of our ancestors.

REFERENCES

Acosta-Belen, Edna, and E. Christensen. 1979. *The Puerto Rican Woman*. New York: Praeger.

Alvarez-Nazario, Manuel. 1972. "La Naturaleza del Espanol Que Se Habla en Puerto Rico." *Revista Ceiba* 1(1). Mayaquez, Puerto Rico.

Attinasi, John, et al. 1982. *Intergenerational Perspectives on Bilingualism: From Community to Classroom*. Centro de Estudios Puertorriquenos Language Policy Task Force. New York: Hunter College, Research Foundation of CUNY.

Babin, Maria T. 1958. *Panorama de la Cultura Puertorriquena*. New York: Las Americas Publishing.

Banks, James. 1991. *Teaching Strategies for Ethnic Studies*. Boston: Allyn and Bacon.

Cadilla de Martinez, Maria. 1979. *Los Cuentos de Juan Bobo*. Mayaquez, Puerto Rico: Ediciones Libero.

Coll y Toste, Cayetano. 1968. *Prehistoria de Puerto Rico*. S. A. Bilbao (Spain): Editorial Vasco Americana.

Campos, Pedro A. 1971. "Interview." In *Republica de Puerto Rico: Libros de Bolsillo*, Carlos Rama, eds. Montevideo: Uruguay.

Fishman Joshua, et al. 1972. *Bilingualism in the Barrio*. Bloomington: Indiana University Press.

Flores, Juan. 1991. "Latin Empire: Puerto Rap." *Centro de Estudios Puertorriquenos Bulletin* (Hunter College, New York) 3(2): 75-85.

Freire, Paulo. 1970. *Pedagogy of the Oppressed*. New York: Continuum.

Garcia, Jesus, and P. Montgomery. 1991. "The Hispanic Population in the U.S." *Current Population Reports*, Series P-20, No. 455.

Institute for Puerto Rican Policy. 1990. *Datanote on the Puerto Rican Community*. No. 3-4, March.

Institute for Puerto Rican Policy. 1992. *Datanote on the Puerto Rican Community*. No. 9-10, March.

Jimenez de Baez, Yvette. 1966. *Julia de Burgos: Vida y Poesia*. San Juan, Puerto Rico: Editorial Conqui.

Lauria, Antonio. 1963. *Respeto, Relajo and Inter-personal Relations in Puerto Rico*. Paper presented at the Central State Anthropological Society Conference, Detroit, MI.

Marques, Rene. 1955. *La Carreta*. San Juan: Edil.

Moreno-Vega, Marta. 1989. *Cultural Identity: The Contributions of Africans and African Descendants in the Latino Caribbean*. New York: Caribbean Cultural Center.

Nadal, Antonio. 1976. "Brief History of Puerto Rican Music." *Sing Out Magazine* 25(3): 4-8.

Nieto, Sonia. 1992. *Affirming Diversity: The Socio-Political Context of Multicultural Education*. New York: Longman.

Ortiz, Altagracia. 1989-90. "The Lives of Pioneras: Bibliographic and Research Sources on Puerto Rican Women in the U.S." *Centros do Estudios Puertorriquenos* (Hunter College, New York) 2(7): 40-47.

Osuna, Rafael. 1949. *A History of Education in Puerto Rico*. Rio Piedras: Editorial de la Universidad de Puerto Rico.

Perez, Richard. 1990. "From Assimilation to Annihilation: Puerto Rican Images in U.S. Films." *Centro de Estudios Puertorriquenos Bulletin* (Hunter College, New York) 2(8): 8-27.

Pitre, Felix. 1993. *Juan Bobo and the Pig*. New York: Lodestar Books.

Romany, Celina. 1989. "Ellos, Ellas y Nosotras: Breve Paseo per las Autopistas y Callejones Sociales." *Centro de Estudios Puertorriquenos Bulletin* 2(7): 101-106.

Sanchez-Korrol, Virginia. 1986. *Politics: Issues of Participation in Puerto Rican Colonias before the Second World War*. Paper Presented at the Organization of American Historians Conference.

Stevens-Arroyo, Antonio. 1990. *The Cave of the Jaqua*. Westport, CT: Greenwood Press.

Torres, Andres. 1989. "New York in the Year 2000: A Sober Assessment." *Centro de Estudios Puertorriquenos Bulletin* 2(6): 48-54.

Tuck, Jay Nelson, and N. Vergara. 1969. *Heroes of Puerto Rico*. New York: Fleet Press.

Zentella, Ana. 1982. "Code Switching and Interactions among Puerto Rican Children." In *Spanish in the United States: Socio-Linguistic Aspects*, Amastae and Lucia Olivares, eds. London: Cambridge University Press.

Chapter 6

American Indians (The Minority of Minorities) and Higher Education

Donald L. Fixico

Of all the people in the United States, American Indians are considered one of the least educated minorities, and their students have alarmingly high dropout rates. Few understand why, and the situation becomes worse with every year. Simultaneously, a growing number of people in America, including teachers, fail to realize that American Indians are still present and a part of this country, and they know little about them. In the eyes of many Americans, Indians once existed in the Wild West and have just disappeared (Berkhofer 1978). Surprisingly, this complete disappearance does not alarm people. Nor does it seem to affect many institutions of higher learning, in spite of their professed mission to educate people about the histories of various cultures, including American Indians. Ultimately institutions of higher education have the responsibility to educate and to stress the importance of teaching about American Indians so that the general public might benefit as well as future generations of American Indians.

This chapter has three purposes: (1) to address this critical problem of Indian heritage being omitted from the curriculum, (2) to state the concerns of Indians, and (3) to outline the role of higher education from the point of view of American Indians. This agenda requires discussing a general Indian viewpoint, relating it to the American mainstream of education, and analyzing the dynamics of the interactions of the Indian educational and mainstream systems. Finally, this agenda suggests recommendations for preserving American Indian knowledge in a multicultural university. Putting forward such a generic point of view is based on personal observations of Indian people from numerous tribes and teaching Indian students and non-Indians in the classroom from the viewpoint as an instructor and visiting professor at nearly half a dozen universities. More specifically, my own experiences as an American Indian offer insights into such a perspective, particularly drawing from the tribes of the Seminoles and Muscogee Creeks in Oklahoma, from which much of my ancestry is derived.[1] This subject is difficult to research for insightful knowledge since very few publications offer such delicate information; hence the following discussion contains my views, with objective analysis interceding as a guiding conscious. [2]

POLARIZATION OF WORLD VIEWS

There is no single American Indian point of view. Theoretically, such a viewpoint infers that all Indian people perceive all issues in the same manner—an impossibility. In reality, American Indians represent over five hundred Native American groups who possess distinctive cultures. In this century, an astonishing almost two thirds of the total Indian population of nearly 2 million persons lives in cities. Furthermore, a developing urban Indian culture differed from rural Indian life on the 287 reservations in the United States and approximately fifty native villages in Alaska. Urban Indian cultures are becoming more Indian oriented and less tribal (Snipp 1989).

Moving toward a generic Indian identity even with an impressive variety of tribal backgrounds, American Indians categorically share some common experiences as Indians living in coexistence with the Anglo-American mainstream society. It is from this position of a common Indian education experience that the incongruence becomes apparent between American Indians and the Anglo-American mainstream. These incongruent differences reach such a degree of contrariety that they advance two opposite sides that have been erroneously understood to be two points of view (e.g., the American Indian viewpoint and the mainstream viewpoint). Like the American Indian multiple views, all Anglo-Americans do not profess the same viewpoint. However, the case of American Indians juxtaposed to the American mainstream, and the latter's benign neglect of the Indian presence, is the point of concern here.

After the obvious realization of the differences between the American Indian minority and the American mainstream, it is important to concentrate on the coexistence of American Indians with the mainstream and how Indian people are distinctive in their functionary. This approach presumes common knowledge about the American mainstream (i.e., values, motivation, ideals, etc.); thus the objective is to investigate the distinctiveness of American Indians and to examine the dynamics of exchange with the mainstream. Traditional American Indian views and mainstream views of the world function at polar ideological opposites. In fact, some specific points about the term *world* are in order. Each world view consists of the gamut of each society's heritage and includes the learning experience of education composed of pertinent knowledge. In particular, understanding a general world view of traditional Indian life requires comprehending the approach of Indians toward education, but it bears repeating that each tribal nation professed its own view of the world, and in most cases they include the universe (Hassrick 1946; Ortiz 1969; Wallace 1970; Waters 1963). The following commentary and analysis covers general observations about American Indian to point out significant similarities for comprehending the polar differences between how traditional American Indians and Anglo-Americans perceived and intellectualize.

American Indian life has evolved and changed considerably from historical times of traditionalism to a modern traditionalism in the twentieth century which stresses increasing identification with the label *Indian* and less with *tribe*. This evolutionary change of every American Indian tribe adapting to external influences is complex, and using one case helps to illustrate the juxtaposition of Indian minority and mainstream.

THE MUSCOGEE CREEKS

Among the Muscogee Creeks, origin myths proclaim that the people emerged from the earth only to become lost in a mist or fog. Unable to see and stricken with fear, the people and even the animals cried out until the wind blew away the fog so that they could see. Perceiving animals and people to be equal, the Creeks named groups of people after animals and became members of clans, and the savior wind became the highest recognized clan (Debo 1941). In all four cardinal directions, the forces of fire confronted the people, and they had to make a decision. From the south, a blue fire faced the people, a black fire burned in the west, a white fire was aflame in the east, but the people elected to choose the red and yellow fire from the north (Swanton 1922, 1928). The fire of the north warmed the people and provided light over the world and enabled the plants to grow, so that the Muscogee Creeks learned to respect all of the elements for life and celebrated the harvest of the green corn (busk) in ceremonials. Should the people fail in their respect for nature and forget the busk ceremonies, the people would disappear from the land and it would fall beneath the waters of the ocean. The Muscogee Creeks stressed the importance of community, and generations of ceremonialism reinforced it. As the ceremonies became ritualized, the Muscogees developed ceremonial laws to maximize the community's confirmations of successful ceremonies, and thus the way of life of the Creeks was the correct way (Debo 1941; Green 1982; Howard and Lena 1990; Perdue 1980).

The true direction of life, however, came from above. Ceremonies served as an emotional and official vehicle for the community to respond in unison for the paying of homage to the supreme creator *Hemsektevsee* (translated as "Master of Breath"). The ceremonies also represented a learning process and manifested group celebration as well for the blessing of life from high, stressing positive over negative and good over evil. It was critical that all of the Muscogees thought in these terms and that this was their mindset (to show this, they took medicine to purify themselves from the influence of negativism and evil). To think otherwise than group homage to the Creator singled out individuals and led to self-centeredness. Continued energy and action toward individuals led to egotistical criticism of the Creek membership and eventually opposition to the community and Creek world view.

In this light, Muscogee Creek life in the community also limited free thinking, as any society's members would think with a similar attitude to perpetuate the community's basic ideology. Such a reinforcement of community might inhibit intellectualism, as group conformity is preferred in all aspects of thought on religion, economy, sociology, and so forth. But does this limit intellectualization of the community members? Presumably yes, since numerous examples of national ethnocentrism can be referred to such as Amerocentrism. Consider theoretically the possibility of tribal centrism exhibited by all of the 500 American Indian tribes.

In such a community culture as the Muscogee Creeks, knowledge is accepted rather than intellectually pursued outside the sphere of Muscogee Creek life. From a traditional point of view, to live outside a Creek community (or *etalwa*, meaning "town") invited negative influences. Because the individual is sociologically weaker than the group, then the ostracized person becomes more susceptible to the external influences. For example, in the late 1800s government boarding schools realized the importance of keeping Indian children away from their communities, particularly their families, so that they could be educated like Anglo-American children while missionary teachers tried to convert the Indian youths from their heritage of ceremonial life to Christianity (Qoyawayma 1964).

This conversion or transformation represents a stage that has entrapped many Indian students in public and private mainstream schools. Theoretically, the Indian children are caught between two worlds, but in reality the traditional tribal world is rapidly disappearing as the Indian youth forgets his or her culture and is psychologically forced to identify with the dominant non-Indian culture. The world view of traditional Indians projects its own reality of life that the mainstream finds difficult to comprehend due to its alien nature.

CONCRETE AND ABSTRACT DIMENSIONS OF TRADITIONAL LIFE

In traditional Indian life, two dimensions of the world exist, the concrete and abstract, despite the belief of some observers that this was not possible (Diamond 1964). Traditional Indian groups maintain a constant interaction between the two, creating a unique reality as a combined manifestation of both dimensions. Reinforced in the tribal community, members of the same world view experience the same reality, which includes the rest of the universe. This perspective is perpetuated by the continuous cultural practice within the native community as long as it may exist.

Although culture is the overall determining agent of world view, at a deeper level a certain set of basic values determines the view. The priority of these values produce culture and is germane to influencing the world view of the concrete and abstract. In the concrete sense, the basic values are determined by the continual (normally daily) needs of the people. The people are in control of defining their needs, but the natural environment and the tribal relation to it are the ultimate factors in the final determination. It is important to realize that traditional Indians are practical due to their daily life's needs such as finding a sufficient food supply to sustain the community and obtaining suitable materials for constructing shelter. This mundane practicality considers the basics for life, and afterward the community sets the determining factors for cultural expressions of ideology, philosophy, art, religion, and other aspects of culture. As a result, basic elements affecting life, such as water, fire, air, space, and mass, are at the core as a culture reflects the importance of these elements.

Among the Muscogee Creeks and Seminoles, the abstract dimension is philosophical and symbolic in the cultural context. A thematic thread of socialization bonding all of life and the supernatural led to a common belief in the metaphysical world of spirits. Living in communities bonded through kinships of generations, Indian people interlink themselves with other communities throughout regions representing all parts of the universe. At the philosophical level, the tribal communities define themselves as distinct worlds within a grand system as ordered by a supernatural force, generically referred to as the Creator. Most important, each tribal world has its own philosophy, explanation of the universe, and set of values, guiding the lives of the people between right and wrong, and good and evil. Several generations ago, human survival depended group cooperation, wherefore laws, ceremonies, and a philosophical world view avoided chaos and established a balanced order for life (Kerney 1984).

Overall, traditional native communities have developed their own world views and produced distinct identities with certain advancements in technology, art, music, and philosophy, depicting products of cultural development. Due to the distinct identity, the desire of American Indians to assimilate into American society is not as compelling as it is among other minorities who share the same values as those of the mainstream. Assimilation has had to be forced (Prucha 1912; Szass 1974; Trennert 1988). While other minorities pursue the American Dream of comfortable wealth, American Indians of traditional backgrounds operate from different criteria and establish different objectives and goals in their lives. It is imperative to realize that they may be content in a special way apart from the American mainstream. Accumulation of materialism and monetary wealth is not essentially germane to their objectives in life, and to judge them to be unsuccessful if they do not live according to mainstream materialism and capitalism indicates a prejudiced society.

THE AMERICAN INDIAN MINORITY AND PERSONAL IDENTITY

Since American Indians are not totally assimilated into the mainstream capitalistic society, they are a minority. But are they different from other minorities? While the United States is a nation of many immigrant and racial groups who strive to assimilate into the mainstream, American Indians have a choice of assimilating or remaining in their communities. The decision is difficult, and even afterward one wonders if the right choice was made. This personal dilemma confronts American Indian youths, and many have not matured sufficiently to realize the full consequences much less anticipate the struggle of a minority living and competing in the mainstream. Considering this situation, there are three main types—the traditional Indians, assimilated Indians, and persons caught in between cultures. Furthermore, urban Indians and interracial marriages have produced mixed bloods representing all of these groups. Thus, a wide variety is represented by traditional mixed bloods, assimilated mixed bloods, marginal mixed bloods, and urban mixed bloods. Actually, it is insensitive to describe Indian people in this manner, but perhaps the rest of this chapter will help American Indians and non-Indians to understand what has happened and will illustrate the complexity of the American Indian minority.

This chapter addresses mainstream education and the assimilating person, urban Indian, and marginal individual since these people more commonly pursue an education at colleges and universities. But the cultural ideal outlined throughout most of this chapter will focus on one form of American Indian traditionalism. What nontraditional Indians are confronted with as well as what one Indian culture might offer a multicultural university will become apparent. Educators do not understand the struggle within the Indian person who attempts to resolve the question "Who am I?" in college. As individuals, the Indian youths descend from tribal backgrounds that are rapidly becoming less traditional, yet many young Indians search for their past heritage in hope of stabilizing their identity. It is this search to fill the void that affects many urban Indian students, while reservation Indians have a stronger sense of identity. For this reason, academic institutions have begun to discriminate against reservation Indians, who they see as likely to have more academic problems. Thus the nonreservation or urban Indian is preferred student. But regardless of cultural orientation, the struggle of personal identity must be waged first or the educational experience in college will be plagued with personal and academic problems. Perhaps all young people ask themselves this fundamental question, but the focus in this chapter is on the complexity of the situation involving a young Indian minority encountering a quasi-receptive mainstream university while dealing with generational and cultural gaps. The difficulty is even more complicated for young Indian women confronting the gender issue as well.

Wrestling with oneself, the Indian college student finds himself or herself separated from family and community. Living as an individual becomes a harrowing experience for many Indian students, whose identities were secured in the tribal communities and defined for them. As a former community member, now they are a person alone. Unfamiliar with college life, their family and community likely do not know how to support them morally. This is a familiar cultural and psychological barrier until another family member attends college and the family and community are educated in sending their loved ones off to college. To a lesser degree, this loneliness and alienation would occur if the Indian student commuted to college. For those Indian students who attended government boarding schools as children, the mainstream has traumatized them forever, leaving them with unforgettable bad memories.

If they become confident with their personal identity away from home, Indian students then face the struggle of learning in a mainstream college or university. New barriers appear, consisting of stereotypes, peer pressure, mainstream pressure, pressure from home to succeed, discrimination, perhaps gender prejudice, and racism. From a traditional standpoint, maintaining balance and keeping things in a healthy perspective is essential.

BALANCE IN LIFE FOR PERSPECTIVE

A traditionalist must also find balance within the self. Keeping things in perspective becomes most significant to achieving this balance, resulting in a steady mental calmness after experiencing happiness and sadness, good and bad—the opposites of emotions and anxieties. This achievement of balance may require many years, but it is expected that adults and children will learn the trials of life while maturing.

The tribal community provides emotional balance and a mature personal outlook within the cultural context. Moral support from family and community helps individuals to realize their roles and to understand life's expectations. When removed from the community, Indian people jeopardize the balance of their state of mind, and confusion results.

A person strives to maintain a social balance between self and the community, and it is the philosophy of equilibrium that is important for learning about life. To learn about balance, one must first learn about oneself, such as one's role in the family, responsibility, purpose, and place in the community. This is an education in itself, de-emphasizing the ego and self-interest for the sake of the family and community. Due to group emphasis, a person's self-confidence is more fragile than a mainstream Anglo-American since ego consciousness is not as important (Kelsen 1943: 6-8). This condition subjects a lonely Indian student in a mainstream classroom to tremendous peer pressure and negative racial stereotypes. Most people do not understand American Indians and know very little about them, except for harmful stereotypes.

In regard to this struggle, American Indians of traditional backgrounds are content in their tribal communities. Within the tribal communities, one is a member of the family structure (which is often an extended family). One's relations with other kins promote socialization and encourage moral support, humor, and sharing, especially when one requires food and shelter. Beyond the family unit are clans and societies—interlinked themselves within the community and other communities of the same tribal nation. This order creates a tribal world with its own values, cultural norms, economy, belief system, tribal perspective, and world view. Having a role of responsibilities in a community enables a personal balance of membership within a group and order of life.

STEREOTYPES AND RACISM

Stereotypes about American Indians are primarily negative or patronizing—the "dirty savage," "drunken Indian," or "noble Red Man" and "brave warrior" (Berkhofer 1978). These common stereotypes are potentially dangerous and can penetrate the psyche of American Indians. The origin of stereotypes about Indians derives from the earliest frontier relations between Indians and white settlers, who both experienced mostly hostile relations that periodically resulted in war. Such ill relations fostered poor attitudes against each other throughout the eighteenth and nineteenth centuries. Since the turn of the twentieth century, the media and film industry perpetuated American Indians as the "bad guys" in westerns on television and in cinemas, early popular western literature added to the prejudice against Indians.

Stereotypes about Indians have led to mistreatment of Indian people, especially when teachers or advisers try to advise Indian students. Beliefs that "Indians work best with their hands," "Indians are natural artists," "Indians are incapable of intellectualization," and "Indians are natural athletes, drunkards, or have low self-esteem," influence the non-Indian treatment of Indian youths. Indian youths are prone to listen to the non-Indian, who is an elder and in a respected position of authority and therefore must have more knowledge.

The negative stereotypes have also led some Indian young people to believe them, especially when they fail in mainstream life (such as dropping out of school). Failure shatters their confidence and leads to self-doubt. At this critical juncture, the Indian youth may begin a course of psychological feelings of bitterness against the mainstream and self-hatred. In the end, self-destructive behavior such as alcoholism and drug abuse could result, or the result may be the ultimate self-destruction of suicide.

The path leading to suicide is more shocking than the mainstream realizes, since most tribes are proud people and their traditionalism has instilled in their membership a personal internal strength. Among certain tribes, the native is extraordinarily proud to the point of an ethnocentrism of prejudice against other Indian groups and other ethnic and racial groups. Demeaned and degraded from such a proud position to self-doubt, confusion, frustration, failure, and escape to alcoholism or drugs, then suicide represents a lengthy emotional and psychologically exhausting struggle that has been lost—the death of the spirit and life of an Indian person.

NATIVE INTELLECTUALISM

Among many tribes, like the Seminoles and Creeks, the quest for knowledge correlates with the practical needs for life. One's skills and pursuits involve survival and thinking naturally inclined toward understanding life. People's energy and efforts focus on life as the positive force and explore their relationship with it. This process and experience assists in intellectualizing knowledge at the physical and philosophical levels in both concrete and abstract. In attempting to relate their experiences to life in general, Muscogee and Seminole people viewed the world and beyond in a social context of human terms, thus reinforcing the kinship networks and political alliances. Hence, the past controls the present.

The emphasis in life and direction of knowledge is on cooperation within one's family and within the community. Except on specific occasions (such as a vision quest among many plains tribes), a traditionalist sought and developed a strategy for forming positive relations with community members. Socialization bonded the community so that the native intellectualizing occurred within the confines of cultural and social norms. Furthermore, the supernatural existed as a part of the real world, and native intellectualism derived from both the physical and metaphysical realities. In this sense, it might be concluded that other tribes who functioned accordingly would possess a similar native intellect.

Attempting to understand spiritualism in human social terms stressed a kinship with congruent elements in the natural inhabitant. Western scholars have called this approach "animism," where everything possessed a spirit. The Seminoles and Creeks would agree with this term. For example, animals have spirits as people do, but they also have special biological qualities and inherent powers that the Seminoles and Creeks respected. In many instances, these two native groups imitated certain animals by creating clans named after specific animals and ranked them, with people belonging to the clans according to bloodlines (e.g., a child would become a member of the mother's clan, a matrilineal lineage). Inanimate objects could possess a spirit as well, if deemed by the Master of Breath, who would give life to it. Respectful of the spirituality of life, people treated animals and certain inanimate objects with respect, as they would another person with certain powers. All beings had roles according to the Creator, and each role was equally respected. Disrespect would cause mishap, bad luck, and confusion throughout one's life.

If all people and things have spirits, the American Indian traditionalist does not necessarily inquire why something happened, but who did it. This orientation would dispute cause-and-effect logic since the traditionalist is social oriented in relating everything to kinship and communal social relations. Hence native logic assumes that the spirit of the causer in the causality of action is responsible. This native type of deductive reasoning is based on the cultural training of the traditionalist, who has accepted the generations of knowledge based on social relations with all things in the universe.

LEARNING METHODS AND OBTAINING KNOWLEDGE

In the educational process of American Indian students attending mainstream schools, students are compelled to understand or perceive everything from the mainstream point of view. But the instructor should be cognizant that traditional Indian youths also possess a native perspective that is likely incongruent with mainstream thinking. For these Indian students, they are learning in an alien culture. This unacknowledged and unaccounted-for conflict between perspectives has resulted in many Indian students doing poorly in school and dropping out.

There are three general methods for traditional American Indians to obtain knowledge: (1) personal desire, (2) cultural mechanism, and (3) direct revelation. In the first method, people can teach themselves and learn to the limit that they wish, if they assert sufficient effort. In the second, the educational system of traditional Indian societies has been deliberately designed to be simple in order to be efficient. This method consists of observation in the manner of a master crafts person and the apprentice. In comparison, the learning methods of traditional American Indian societies are less complicated than those of the American mainstream. Within Indian education, it is always advantageous to keep things simplified to avoid misunderstanding and prevent confusion.

Historically, American Indians commonly learned by the observation and imitation method. For instance, after a length of time of watching an elder weave a basket, listening to an uncle tell a story, or observing a curer prepare medicine, a young person then imitated the elder as an apprentice. Learning the procedure was important to reproduce the final product, which was understood also to be important, but questioning the procedure was not considered. Among the Muscogee Creeks, the people wash and drink medicinal herbs with the realization that it is important (without questioning the procedure), and they realize that the important results will bring purification and protection (Hudson 1979). Formatters that are not bound by tradition and passed-down practice, trial and error and deductive reason are not important means of learning. Again, mainstream teachers of Indian students need to be aware of this situation and recognize the apprehension of the Indian student and encourage the student's progress.

For Indian traditionalists, the third method of education, direct revelation, is the ultimate method of knowledge. Among many traditional Indians, obtaining knowledge through dreams, visions, and metaphysical manifestations happened frequently. This information came from the metaphysical world of the Creator—the world beyond normal life on earth. This information has been interpreted as gifts of knowledge to help people. Sometimes these gifts of knowledge are piecemeal and bestowed upon certain individuals, compelling selected ones to become medicinal persons, but such lessons can be halted at any point, especially if the person of such knowledge fails to respect the gifts.

Normally, the accumulation of knowledge is limited by the person (unless a greater force intercedes, such as the Master of Breath among the Seminoles and Creeks). This limitation is self-imposed by each individual in accordance with personal interest, and it is restricted by their tribal cultural norms. The basis of the limit of knowledge is practicality—what is revealed is based on need according to daily life until a new level of awareness is established. Theoretically, revealed knowledge is limitless and is therefore confined by the perimeters— person, culture, and direct revelation.

In receiving knowledge, it is also imperative to understand the difference between knowledge and information. Information (such as news on television) is meaningless, without substance, and has no intellectual value. In contrast, knowledge is determined by a society's culture as it will benefit the community. Among Indians in a traditional society, the culture may render importance to news or information, allowing it to become knowledge. As knowledge helps the community, it is influential and becomes powerful. In a helpful situation, the knowledge is positive, but in a destructive situation, the power of knowledge becomes negative or evil and can be reversed against the evil practitioner abusing knowledge. For instance, among the Muscogee Creeks and Seminoles, the medicine maker is a good example of a practitioner of positive and negative power, depending on his or her reputation. This is an example of the potential of knowledge, but traditional knowledge does not help American Indians in the practical life of the mainstream. In the process of assimilation, American Indian students have to realize the important potential of the mainstream education.

Concepts of the Oral Tradition and Written Word

Long ago, Indian communities maintained an oral history tradition of myths, legends, stories, and tales to pass knowledge to new generations (such as the Muscogee Creek belief in The Master of Breath). Oral history depended on the verbal skills of storytellers, who relied on their memories. In fact, certain persons became well known for their oratory, and they systematically told the stories, legends, and myths so that the people would not forget this knowledge. Each presentation invited a degree of variation, and this possibility did not distract from the basic truth or moral to be learned from the oral episode. The oratory skills of the storyteller and the listening ability of the community stressed the importance of communication via language in a nonliterate society.

Oral history accounts could be compared to further illustrate the truth (Vansina 1980, 1985). The oral tradition disseminated knowledge to the listeners, who were usually youths, and they learned history, morals, and truths. Creating an entertaining mood, the oral tradition became exciting when the storyteller commanded a talent of different voices, humor, facial expressions, and effective gestures to capture his or her listeners. Verbal and bodily gestures enhanced the story, specifically as the elder twisted his or her face, changed voices to mimic characters of other persons or animals, and simultaneously sometimes contorted the body to re-create the characters. At its utmost, the oral tradition cast multiple dimensions to the spoken word, expressing emotion, light or serious meaning, philosophy, history, morality, and entertainment.

In contrast, in a written language the written word is singular in dimension. Moreover, the information is subject to interpretation as any reader is the lone participant in the knowledge that is transmitted, whereas in the oral tradition the knowledge is passed deliberately from the storyteller to the listener. In oral transmission, two participants increase the degree for accuracy of what is to be learned within the cultural sphere, so that the external influence of culture plays a greater role than the internal influence of self (as in reading or writing).

Furthermore, the singular dimension of the written tradition presents cold, inhuman factual information and depends on how the information was written (such as for entertainment purposes, solely historical facts, philosophical lessons, and so forth). Again, the risk for misinterpretation is increased until the information obtained from the reading can be corroborated by an authority like a teacher, instructor, professor, elder, or another knowledgeable person. Until such corroboration, time elapses and literate individuals may be misled by their own logic.

Overall, the advantages of the oral history tradition are direct revelation of knowledge, less confusion, and no misinterpretation (thus the importance of accuracy). At the social or community level, the oral tradition functioned as a group process and bonded the community. The tradition also established group identity and transmitted heritage and history. Hence, the language had to be simply and direct with such importance placed on the "spoken word."

In both the Indian and mainstream worlds, language is imperative to learning and expression of knowledge. Learning in an alien culture stressing a written language should not be underestimated for students from a nonwritten culture (i.e., traditional Indians). Learning English becomes a difficult barrier for Indian students since it represents a foreign language of expressing ideas and thoughts. Language is involved in reading and speech development, yet learning to read and speak a different language adds another level of difficulty. More than mere words are expressed as ideas, patterns of thought, values, and philosophies. Indian students frequently experience problems in expressing themselves while struggling with cultural retention, grammatical problems, and thinking in the mainstream mode. Furthermore, the traditional emphasis on listening rather than articulating puts an Indian person at a disadvantage in today's society, which praises impressive eloquence even more so than significant ideas and creative thinking from a different culture.

American Indians are the least-heard-from minority because they are fewer in number than other minorities, and those of them from traditional backgrounds were taught not to be outwardly demonstrative in complaining and expressing their unhappiness. From a traditional perspective, continually venting one's frustration causes a negative reaction, and people would disassociate themselves from the chronic complainer. Afterward, the community would ostracize or isolate the complainer as an outcast. Being an accepted and respected part of the community is imperative, since life's struggle on one's own is exceedingly difficult when the universe contains numerous physical and metaphysical destructive forces. In such cases, an imbalance occurs, thus it is important for all (people, animals, and environment) to know how to keep things in their proper place and perspective and thus to restore the balance of order and peace. The intelligence of the traditional American Indian included an open perspective accounting for all things.

Circular Thought and the Mainstream

Circular thinking among Indian traditionalists involves using more than one example to illustrate a point of knowledge. This type of thought is a slower process in comparison with the mainstream's linear thinking. However, it reinforces the point to build confidence in the students and negates misinterpretation. Circular thinking is more inclusive of how an item such as the letter A is a part of the entire universe as a system. Linear thinking extracts A and places the importance on A as an individual item, so that the two emphases are on A as a part of the whole system and A as an individual. Symbolically, the equation A+B=C can represent anything, such as man and woman produces a child, an action and reaction produces a law of physics, and so forth. It is important to realize how both linear and circular schools of thought serve Indian traditionalists and the mainstream and that they are incongruent, but they can both be utilized as teaching methods if used appropriately in a class.

In circular thought, if a circle is envisioned and items are placed within it, we realize that each item or element has a relationship with each other in a fixed order within the system. If the elements are of equal substance, then they are equally treated and respected since they belong to the system or universe, but if the qualities and powers of some of the elements are superior or unknown, then they are respected and might hold a higher ranking. As a result, native people of America have found it best to treat the unknown with respect since it has a spirit and unknown powers bestowed by the Creator that could be greater than those of the people. The concept of the circle and all things treated democratically equal is a longstanding philosophy that is applicable to most of life. Yet this perspective remains at an introductory stage to Amerocentric mainstream educators and non-Indian scholars.

Unwisely, mainstream thinking yields to the same ideas and perpetuates one linear way of thinking. In the educational system of the mainstream, instructors teach a singular pattern of learning instituted by the dominant culture, and this monointellectualism negates other patterns of learning and nonmainstream intellectualism. As a result, American education, even at the university level, may slip into a general pattern of intellectualism which will hinder opportunities to find solutions to difficult problems, especially when answers are needed in times of crises.

FROM GOVERNMENT BOARDING SCHOOLS TO URBAN INDIAN EDUCATION

Unfortunately, ethnocentric presumptions led to underrating the intelligence of American Indians and other races of darker color. For instance, Victorian evolutionists such as Sir Edward B. Taylor and Herbert Spencer professed that the Anglo race was superior to races of darker skin and referred to them as primitive societies. By using anthropometric studies of cranial sizes and measuring amounts of brain capacity, these bias evolutionists promoted the scientific theory that the Mongoloid and Negroid races were of lower intelligence than the Anglo race (Diamond 1964; Radin 1927).

This view supported the prevailing frontier attitude in the American West during the late 1800s that American Indians lived as savages and were inferior, without respect to their advanced philosophies and world views. Negative stereotypes about Indians combined with the concurrent scientific belief and perpetuated Anlgo racism against Indians. As Indian children attended government boarding schools in the late nineteenth century and in the twentieth century, they learned racist societal and scientific views about their people (Hoxie 1984). This education led to many Indians' belief that they were intellectually and culturally inferior. Obviously, such an Amerocentric education does not improve Indians; instead it is destructive of their sense of self, their culture, and their heritage.

Traditionalism in its purest form among the Indian population does not exist today, especially due to evolution and desired or forced changes. A significant number of members from tribal communities left their reservations and rural homes to live in cities. After World War II, the federal government developed the Relocation Program (in 1952) to assist in relocating American Indians to cities and find them jobs and housing (Bernstein 1991; Fixico 1986). Becoming urbanized, these individuals joined the American mainstream and adopted values, norms, dress, and other characteristics of the dominant culture.

Indian urbanization has meant the decline of traditionalism, simultaneously giving rise to the urban Indian population, which has grown steadily. Relocated Indians who survived the street life of the cities during the 1950s and 1960s have produced a second generation of urban Indians and in 1990, a third generation began. Presently two thirds of the Indian population live in cities, a remarkable demographic change (most Americans still believe that most Indians live on reservations in the West).

Urban survival and a promising future mandate an education in the mainstream. Since 1945, American Indian youth have had more opportunity to attend schools, although their achieved level of education has remained much lower than the national average. Since 1960, a significant number of Indian youth has been attending postsecondary schools. Between 1960 and 1970, the number multiplied fivefold. An estimated 8,000 Indian students attended universities or postsecondary colleges in 1970. During the late 1970s, the average level for Indian students ranged from 8.9 to 11.2 years of formal education—a low level, but an increasing number of Native Americans realized the importance of a mainstream education. Approximately 35 percent of the mean age group, (eighteen to twenty-one) completed secondary schools, and 20 percent of this age group entered universities. The crucial drawback was the lack of funding to attend school, with families' incomes averaging below the national average. To offset this disadvantage, the Bureau of Indian Affairs (BIA) in 1969 awarded scholarship grants to 3,432 young people, with an average of $868 per student. By 1975 the amount of scholarships had increased to 15,000 dollars with an average of 1,750 dollars per student. During 1975, 1,497 Indian students who graduated from four-year colleges had received BIA scholarships (Havighurst 1978). From this group came the small pool of BIA students for entering graduate school in the last of the 1970s—a very small number to produce Indian scholars in the 1980s. Obviously, some Indian students attended college without BIA assistance, but the potential for the 1980s continued to remain small.

In addition to BIA grants, in the early 1970s the Ford Foundation began offering academic fellowships to minority students for graduate studies. The foundation offered scholarships to Blacks, Hispanics, Puerto Ricans, and American Indians with the goal of producing minority academics for the future. A research survey conducted by educator Dean Chavers in the 1970s for American Indians in professional positions indicated that there were two podiatrists, three veterinarians, six dentists, thirty pharmacists, 115 physicians and an estimated 191 Ph.D.s of Indian descent. [3]

Another problem depressing the number of Indians who attended college in the 1970s was Indian adjustment to school life in the cities. Indian youths applied traditional learning methods in the classroom, and this proved impractical (Guilmet 1976). Indian youths were poorly advised, families had never sent anyone to college, Indian youths were ill prepared and had not set educational goals, and attending public schools in the mainstream was a lonely experience. Many Indian students simply gave up when they continually faced negative stereotypes about their people.

Results of Substandard Performances

Substandard performances have produced negative views about educating American Indians: They are incapable of being educated, difficult to teach, have short attention spans, lack motivation, and are intellectually inferior. Measuring youths from another culture against mainstream standards is unfair, and focusing on the progress of American Indian education and how to improve it should be the emphasis. The truth is that most of the current Indian population lives in cities—not on reservations. American Indians are not disappearing in numbers, but rather are the fastest-growing minority population in the United States in proportion to their low numbers when compared to other minority groups. An important visual fact is that the stereotype of the full-blooded Indian person with long black hair and a copper complexion is no longer the dominant characteristic among Indian people. Many American Indians are now biracial as a result of lengthy contact primarily with Anglo-Americans.

With each decade and each generation, Americans learn less and less about American Indians, making our society increasingly ignorant about American Indians. Much of this ignorance can be blamed on our educational system at all levels. American history textbooks present history from a biased point of view and have at the most one or two chapters on Indians (sometimes just a few paragraphs about American Indians). State history courses teach students that Indians were vanquished in the 1700s and 1800s and fail to mention deliberate military policies and wars to exterminate Indians (and never mention their present-day existence and contributions to America). Political science texts and civics courses teach that there are three governments within the United States—the federal, state, and local levels. None to date, explain that over 400 tribal governments govern their people and have a legal status higher than that of the state governments. The scant material that is presented is often misleading and stereotypical, and no one seems interested.

CONCLUSIONS

The needs for education among American Indians pertain to two types of circumstances: (1) for the individual living in the mainstream, and (2) for the tribal person on the reservation. Involving the latter, twenty-seven tribally controlled colleges operate today, and one urban Indian college (Native American Educational Services, Inc.) was established to educate the urban Indian community in Chicago. Many Indians want an education and want to return to their communities in order to help their people by participating in their tribal governments, courts, industries, or teaching in the reservation schools. This desire is made possible by obtaining an education in the tribal community college or obtaining an education in the mainstream college and university and then returning to the tribal community. Evidence from Scholastic Aptitude Test scores in 1990 reveals that American Indians earned a nine point increase in math skills to 437 from 428 (remaining twenty-nine points below the national average). The average verbal scores among Indian youths were at 384 previously and improved to 388, four points better than the national average (Cellis 1990).

To improve the situation for American Indians, it will require the involvement of many people for Indian young people to obtain an education in the mainstream university. But the real need for college education for American Indians is different from what mainstream educators think the need is (Fuchs and Havighurst 1972). For American Indians wanting to return to tribal communities, doing graduate work or completing a Ph.D. may not be what they want. Tribal communities are not impressed with doctorates but stress how one fits into the community and how one helps others. Currently, tribal communities seem to need two professional groups, teachers and lawyers. Another area of need that has emerged in recent years is business administration. With teachers, tribal communities can educate their youth. Business administrators can advise the tribal government on investments, and lawyers can protect the civil and treaty rights of the communities.

Recommendations for a Multicultural University

The diversity of minority groups in America is one of the potential strengths of this country. It is puzzling how America has held itself together as a nation of individuals and various ethnic and racial groups. Yet in times of crises, especially war, this nation identifies a common cause and unites with patriotism and national commitment.

A large body of new knowledge can be learned from diversity. But first, our educators must realize that there are other ways from different ethnic and racial groups for arriving at answers to problems. It is important to recognize that different intellectualism from other cultures can contribute new ideas and propose new theories and provide solutions to current problems.

In theory, if two groups are culturally alike, it is probable that they think and solve problems similarly. Furthermore, it has been professed that individuals of different racial backgrounds, but who spend a long period of time in the same culture, will develop ways to communicate. But when one group holds its culture over others, a mutually harmful conformity occurs. This is what happens when minority groups assimilate into the American mainstream, particularly when the mainstream professors at universities and mainstream educators at all levels try to restrict minorities to only think in a western linear fashion—the method of Western thought. However, individuals from the Mongoloid race experience difficulty in analytically thinking in a linear fashion even after a lengthy experience of living in the mainstream. This is because of the insistence that Western intellectualism is the only correct way to scholarship. The potential for fresh ideas and creativity from different cultures is suppressed and regarded as nonintellectual by discriminatory mainstream intellectuals. This type of academic discrimination must be put behind us.

Theoretically, the more different two cultures are, the broader the range of thinking and the greater the resources for solutions for problems. Different cultures have different approaches and their own way of thinking—intellectualism—which should be recognized and respected. Imagination and creativity result from cultural differences. The greater the differences, the greater potential for contribution to knowledge. In many instances, mainstream professionals and researchers are learning from American Indians and their various cultures. One example of learning from American Indians is psychiatrist Carl Hammerschlag, who is using the approach of American Indian healing practices of connecting the human mind and the immune system. This new science is called psychoneuroimmunology (Hammerschlag 1989). This is just one example of similar cases of mainstream professionals learning from American Indians and their culture in medical science areas and other areas, like environmentalism and philosophy.

Lack of Indian and other minority scholars is a serious problem. No element of the university should be excluded from this problem. Faculty, administrators at all levels, and minorities at all levels need to meet, discuss, cooperate, form solutions, and act. In some cases, such action may have to be drastic to produce improvement for the overall situation. During the late 1980s, alarmed university officials developed innovative programs to encourage the numbers of minorities in universities. Rigorous efforts brought a summer program at Ohio State, the Big Ten Conference set aside a certain number of fellowships for minorities,

Stony Brook spearheaded a national program to hear from minority professors to encourage mainstream faculty involvement, and Stanford University intensely recruited minority students for several years. Texas Christian University's History Department established special fellowships for American Indian History, and the Wisconsin Plan encouraged minorities in universities.

By practice and design, universities produce graduates who are out of touch with the reality of daily life of other cultural communities. They are often out of touch with life in their own communities. Furthermore, since non-Indian students and instructors have little first hand knowledge of traditional American Indians and urban Indians, it might be proposed that interested students and instructors spend a part of their college education interacting within an Indian community. For example, graduate students who want to teach could teach for one year on reservations or at one of the twenty-seven tribally controlled colleges. The benefits are numerous and include obtaining teaching experience, learning about American Indians and a different culture, broadening the perspective of a graduate student preparing for academic life, and influencing the mainstream attitude about American Indians as a minority in mainstream America.

Such a teaching experience must to be administrated at a college or university with faculty that is multicultural in both perspective and experience. The recommendation is for the institute of higher learning to have a mixture of American Indian and non-Indian faculty so that they could strengthen each other's skills and press their ideas beyond the singular cultural dimension of their background. Furthermore, the program would best operate in a cross-disciplinary approach, since all avenues of knowledge about an Indian community should not be obstructed and disseminating knowledge from multidisciplines would be advantageous to the Indian community. The time is now for the faculty and administrators of higher institutions to act, and they are urged to formulate a plan. Each Indian youth is one more day farther away from his or her traditional heritage of the past, and the traditional knowledge of Indian people is rapidly disappearing—a past that is very much a part of American history and this nation's legacy.

Universities and American mainstream society need to be informed about the history and current conditions of American Indians. This is important to their education, because they will likely work at some point with American Indians on a reservation or in an urban Indian organization. American Indians and their history of struggle in this country should not be forgotten, yet we continue to forget. As students fill classrooms in increasing numbers, fewer Indian students will be present, and the lives of American Indians before Christopher Columbus and their history of relations with non-Indians and the United States will be dismissed as not important and will be inexcusably forgotten. Knowledge of American Indians and their native intellectualism offers much in the fields of ecology and environmental concerns (teaching us to conserve natural resources), medicine (providing remedies from the use of herbs and native knowledge), sociology (teaching the significance of community spirit in place of alienation and individuality), and psychology (showing how to deal with one-self more effectively for an optimistic outlook for the future). If American Indian students are to succeed in a non-Indian academic setting, then an atmosphere free of racism and harmful stereotypes is essential for overcoming a racist history against them and their heritage.

NOTES

1. Originally the Seminoles of northern Florida were an offshoot of the Muscogee Creek confederacy in the Southeast, and they migrated to northern and central Florida, where they occasionally met the Mikasukee Seminoles. The Muscogee-speaking Seminoles share the same cultural history of the Muscogee Creeks, and they were both removed to Indian Territory during President Andrew Jackson's Indian removal policy years of the 1830s and 1840s.

2. For valuable insight to American Indian student life during the late 1800s, see Charles Eastman (1916).

3. These statistics are from a survey conducted by Dr. Dean Chavers with the assistance of several agencies during the mid-1970s.

REFERENCES

Berkhofer, Robert Jr. 1978. *The White Man's Indian, Images of the American Indian from Columbus to the Present.* New York: Alfred Knopf.

Bernstein, Alison. 1991. *American Indians and World War II: Toward an Era in Indian Affairs.* Norman: University of Oklahoma Press.

Cellis, William. 1990. "Scholastic Test Scores Show Drop in Verbal Skills." *New York Times,* August 28, p. A14.

Debo, Angie. 1941. *The Road Disappearance.* Norman: University of Oklahoma Press.

Diamond, Stanley. ed. 1964. *Primitive Views of the World: Essays from Culture in History.* New York: Columbia University Press.

Eastman, Charles. 1916. *From the Deep Woods to Civilization: Chapters in the Autobiography of an Indian.* Boston: Little, Brown and Company.

Fixico, Donald. 1986. *Termination and Relocation: Federal Indian Policy, 1945-1960.* Albuquerque: University of New Mexico Press.

Fuchs, Estelle, and R. Havighurst. 1972. *To Live On This Earth: American Indian Education.* Garden City, NY: Doubleday.

Green, Michael. 1982. *The Politics of Indian Removal: Creek Government and Society.* Lincoln: University of Nebraska Press.

Guilmet, George. 1976. *The Non-Verbal American Indian Child in the Urban Classroom.* Unpublished disseration, University of California, Los Angeles.

Hammerschlag, Carl. 1989. *The Dancing Healers: The Doctor's Journey of Healing with Native Americans.* New York: Harper and Row.

Hassrick, Royal. 1946. *The Sioux: The Life and Customs of the Warrior Society.* Norman: University of Oklahoma Press.

Havighurst, Robert. 1978. "Indian Education Since 1960." *The Annals of the American Academy of Political and Social Science* 436 (March).

Howard, John, and W. Lena. 1990. *Oklahoma Seminoles, Medicine, Magic and Religion*. Norman: University of Oklahoma Press.

Hoxie, Frederick. 1984. *A Final Promise: The Campaign to Assimilate the Indians, 1880-1920*. Lincoln: University of Nebraska Press.

Hudson, Charles, ed. 1979. *Black Drink, a Native American Tea*. Athens: University of Georgia Press.

Kelsen, Hans. 1943. *Society and Nature: A Sociological Inquiry*. Chicago: University of Chicago Press.

Kerney, Michael. 1984. *Wordview*. Novato, CA: Chandler and Sharp Publishers, Inc.

Ortiz, Alfonso. 1969. *The Tewa World: Space, Time, Being, and Becoming a Pueblo Society*. Chicago: University of Chicago Press.

Perdue, Theba. 1980. *Nations Remembered: An Oral History of the Five Civilized Tribes, 1865-1907*. Westport, CT: Greenwood Press.

Prucha, Paul. 1912. *The Churches and the Indian Schools, 1888-1912*. Lincoln: University of Nebraska Press.

Qoyawayma, Polingaysi. 1964. *No Turning Back: A Hopi Indian Woman's Struggle to Live in Two Worlds*. Albuquerque: University of New Mexico Press.

Rabin, Paul. 1927. *Primitive Man as Philosopher*. New York: B. Appleton and Company.

Snipp, Matthew. 1989. *American Indians: The First of This Land*. New York: Russell Sage Foundation.

Swanton, John. 1922. *Early History of the Creek Indians and Their Neighbors*. Bureau of American Ethnology Bulletin 73. Washington, DC: U.S. Government Printing Office.

Swanton, John. 1928. *The Social History and Usages of the Creek Confederacy*. Forty-Second Annual Report of the Bureau of American Ethnology. Washington, DC: U.S. Government Printing Office.

Szass, Margaret. 1974. *Education and the American Indian: The Road to Self-Determination Since 1928*. Albuquerque: University of New Mexico Press.

Trennert, Robert. 1988. *The Phoenix Indian School: Forced Assimilation in Arizona, 1891-1935*. Norman: University of Oklahoma Press.

Vansina, Jan. 1980. *Oral History*. Madison: University of Wisconsin Press.

Vansina, Jan. 1985. *Oral Tradition as History*. Madison: University of Wisconsin Press.

Wallace, Anthony. 1970. *The Death and Rebirth of the Seneca*. New York: Alfred Knopf.

Waters, Frank. 1963. *Book of the Hopi*. New York: Viking Press.

Wright, J. Leitch, Jr. 1986. *Creeks and Seminoles: The Destruction and Regeneration of the Muscogulgee People*. Lincoln: University of Nebraska Press.

Part Three

PROPOSALS AND IMPLEMENTATION

In Parts One and Two, we presented the case that the American university is indeed Eurocentric and will have to undergo major revisions of its curriculum, mission, and organization. These changes will not be based on some notion of political correctness or affirmative action. Change will be made because of popular pressure to do so, pragmatism, and the best interest of the nation. There will be a virtual sea of change in the nation's demographics that will bring America's non-European cultural groups into greater prominence. Demands will be made on the university community to educate meaningfully, respond to the intellectual needs of those cultural groups and respect and include the cultures of those groups in the education formula. Part Two provided samples of some of these potential perspectives, concerns, and demands. The nature of genuinely inclusive demands will call for a domestic multiculturalism. Changes in this nation's place in the international community will make new demands on the university community. We will have to educate American students toward a greater international multiculturalism as well.

Two questions remain: First, if multiculturalism will have to become part of the mission and role of the American university community, how do we get from here to there? Second, how do we do it without bitter insurgence, shaking public confidence in higher education, chaos, or eroding rather than improving quality? Part Three responds to these questions. In the six remaining chapters, authors with extensive administrative experience have taken the perspectives, suggestions, and recommendations of Parts One and Two and generated proposals for how the university might be made multicultural in the course of generally improving the quality and character of higher education in the United States.

In Chapter 7, Benjamin Bowser and Octave Baker translate the content of the prior chapters into a series of faculty and administrative actions that can, in stages, move a university or college from here to there. In Chapter 8, Etta Hollins offers suggestions for a more appropriate and developmental way to assess students from a variety of domestic and overseas cultures. In Chapter 9, Arthur Paris discusses how the new revolution in computer and communications technologies can complement and encourage multiculturalism in the university. In Chapter 10, Benjamin Bowser outlines a revised university organization based on advisement from the prior chapters. In Chapter 11, Terry Jones and Gale Auletta-Young synthesize the prior chapters and their own research and experience into proposals on how teaching and the curriculum can be changed. In Chapter 12, Benjamin Bowser, Terry Jones, and Gale Auletta-Young suggest that the implications of these proposals are based on a universalism within education that is broad enough to be inclusive of all of America's European, African, Indigenous, and Asian cultures.

Chapter 7

Toward a Multicultural University: Using Strategic Planning for Change

Benjamin P. Bowser
Octave Baker

How do we rationally, purposefully, and fairly transform a Eurocentric university curriculum, faculty, and organization into a culturally more inclusive and effective institution? This is the most important issue facing higher education in the United States today. Its strategic importance is far more critical than our immediate budgetary crisis and constraints. It is hoped that the answer to this important question will take shape in three ways within each college and university. It will come out of open and honest debate, trial and error, and administration action, and each sector of the university (faculty, students, administration, community) will come to see the value of planned change and action toward a more inclusive university.

The university community is not the first to undertake this process. The challenges of a multicultural nation and world are facing the American business community as well. But in the business community, tradition is secondary. The bottom line is remaining profitable and in business. It is clear that if American corporations are to remain profitable and in business, they will have to operate successfully in culturally diverse domestic and international markets. So people of color will not be the only ones demanding more effective multicultural education. Eventually employers will as well. Because the necessity of multiculturalism is more apparent in business, the business community is ahead of the university in responding. This chapter draws on the experiences and lessons of implementing multiculturalism from the business community. What university faculty and administrators can learn from business is to use strategic planning and implementation as a way to achieve a long-term goal. This chapter outlines a series of strategic processes and actions that can be taken by faculty and administrations to move toward a culturally more inclusive university based on the counsel of the prior chapters in this book.

OBJECTIVES

The overall question is, How do we transform a Eurocentric university to a multicultural one? But the operative question is, How do we transform a Eurocentric faculty and curriculum into culturally more inclusive ones? As a statement of principle to reiterate Maulana Karenga's earlier point, the end result of this transformation must be ethical, must be liberating to all involved, and must result in high-quality and socially responsive institutions. The way to achieve such an inclusive university is to do the following:

1. Develop long-term plans with gradual short-term goals spelling out the specific actions to be taken to achieve each goal. These plans and goals should come out of open debate and discussion among students, faculty, administration, and community (trustees, alumni, and community advisory groups).
2. Execution of the plan will require faculty leadership and must be the day-to-day responsibility of administrators with budgetary authority. It cannot be the responsibility of either junior faculty or middle-level administrators.
3. The planning and execution process must be iterative. All aspects of the process must be open to revision based on experience, the unique strengths and weaknesses of each institution, and appropriate incentives and disincentives.
4. Finally, the process of transition toward a multicultural university cannot take place without a related opening of the educational pipeline—kindergarten through twelfth grade (K-12). This opening is not simply a training of more minority students for undergraduate and graduate education. It is to also provide a culturally more inclusive education to all students throughout their education (Harold Hodgkinson pointed out practical ways to do this in Chapter 1).

The strategic planning and the actions taken to transform each university must take place from within and over time in order to be genuine and effective. The alternative is to have the transformation imposed from without after years of stagnation. The proactive choice can take place in stages. The following are proposals for each sector based on ideas and perspectives from the prior chapters in this book.

LEVEL ONE

Students and administrations come and go, but faculties remain. The strongest academic institutions have strong faculty governance. Ultimately, what is taught and what research and scholarship are produced come from the faculty. Thus, the initial steps toward multiculturalism should come from the faculty after extensive discussion, debate, and consensus building among students, faculty, administration, and communities. Once there is a consensus and there are faculty prepared to take leadership, it is the role of the administration to see that the consensus is supported and carried out. Optimally, the move toward multiculturalism might begin with faculty development.

The Faculty

Faculty may be trained in specific disciplines, and, if there are graduate programs, they may train graduate students in those disciplines. But undergraduate education should not be a lesser mirror image of such a fragmented world. One of the points that the cultural perspective authors (Morales-Nadal, Fixico, Mitchell and Feagin) made is the need to study and arrive at understandings of historic and cultural events and developments. There is a need to understand the past that has defined one's historic and cultural identity, place in history, and circumstance in the present. There is also a great need to have the same understanding of domestic and foreign racial and ethnic groups other than one's own. This is not simply taking one or two courses in ethnic or women's studies. Nor is the development of such an educated perspective of self and the world achieved by a few courses on the history of Europe, Africa, or Asia. Students will have to learn across the disciplines, time periods, and locations. So instead of a first course in European or African history, which is appropriate later in upper-division courses, students should take courses such as Contact and Exchange in the Middle Ages or The Development of the Modern World Order. A year-long course might be developed on contemporary exchange and contact that studies in an interdisciplinary fashion the cultural, political, and economic relations between the first, second, and third worlds.

There are several things that would distinguish these new courses. The first objective is to place oneself in several different cultures and histories at the same time. The second objective is to study the exchange and relations between these cultures and nations. How did they view each other? How do they view each other now? What kind of exchange did they have? What kind of exchange do they have now? How did isolation from one another affect later contact? The third objective is that every effort should be made to view each culture as it saw and now sees itself and other cultures. How did the Chinese, Africans, Europeans and American Indians see themselves and how did they view contact with one another? Have these historic perceptions changed when compared to their present views? Such courses may require introducing students to examples of the literature, oral traditions, histories, language, and arts of each major cultural group under study. The final objective would be to relate both historic and contemporary developments of each group in the international community to the present status and circumstances of their descendants in the United States.

Similar cross-discipline and cross-cultural courses could be developed to better understand contemporary race and ethnic relations in the United States. What have been the historic circumstances of each group from their own points of view? The relations between groups could be studied in detail at specific points in history, including evidence and documentation of how they viewed one another and what kind of contact they have had. A second course could study the contemporary circumstance of each group, allowing students to make rich comparisons with the earlier historic and cultural course. Is the current status of each group in any way tied to their historic view, treatment, or exchange with other groups? Have relations between groups changed substantially in any way for the better or worse over time? What can be learned about American society in the past and present from the point of view and experiences of each group?

The development of such courses and perspectives on knowledge is a challenge to the faculty. It would require team teaching, team courses, and material development as well as developing competence to teach across disciplines. It would require substantial new research on the histories, cultures, oral traditions, and literatures of virtually every cultural and historic group known. Such research is needed in order to reconstruct as best we can how each group perceived itself in the past and present. This has not been a focus of Eurocentric scholarship. But more importantly, it would require faculty to understand and develop a feel for the peoples, periods, cultures, and ideas they are teaching. Within the multicultural framework suggested by the authors of this book, faculty should first have experience and contact with the people they are teaching about. This will require some sort of orientation, training, and teaching in the nations and cultures they will teach about. It will require periodic overseas experience and, equally as important, it will require periodic experience in domestic ethnic and racial communities as well.

To make it possible for faculty to undertake such training, orientation, and research, there will have to be financial and professional support to do so. Our overseas study programs will have to be expanded, but equivalent domestic programs in various racial and ethnic communities will have to be developed as well. Faculty will have to be encouraged to devote sabbatical leaves to obtaining such training and retraining. Government and foundation grants should be made available to support such an extensive multicultural faculty development. Finally, such domestic and overseas exposure should become a required part of graduate training. The end result would be faculty able to organize challenging and high-quality courses that will be multicultural and will provide students with multiple perspectives on themselves, their histories, and current circumstances. Students will also have many opportunities to see themselves through the eyes of others and to see others as they see themselves. In doing so, they might arrive at a better understanding of themselves and others than is achieved in the current fragmentary and monocultural offerings.

Courses

Multiculturalism calls for a broadening of pedagogy as well as course content and organization. In most selective to very selective colleges and universities, one objective of lower-division undergraduate courses is to select student majors for each discipline. Introductory courses are by intent and design meant to weed through the ranks of freshmen and sophomores for the brightest and best. In the Eurocentric university, faculty take great pride in the selectivity of their introductory courses. The more selective the process, the higher the quality of students selected as majors. Through introductory courses, faculty take what they believe are the best and discourage and leave the rest. The departments and faculty who get the best students are considered the better departments, while the departments and faculty who get the rest are devalued and are often viewed with contempt. This is not education.

Education from African and American Indian perspectives would suggest a different approach. When you admit students to a college or university, first find out what their strengths and weaknesses are. Accept them for where they are as students and for whom they are as persons. Then show them how to improve their weaknesses and demand that they work hard to turn their weaknesses into strengths and become the best students that they can be. Education is not measured by what students already have and can demonstrate, but rather by how rapidly they can grow and improve as students and persons. This is a student rather than a departmental- or disciplinary-centered education. Despite Eurocentric curricula, a number of elite small liberal arts colleges in the United States offer such an education. A student-centered education should be the national norm rather than the exception.

Given the diversity of backgrounds, talents, cultures, strengths, and weaknesses that multicultural students are bringing to college, the large introductory lecture class is an efficient way to weed and screen, but it is not an effective way to educate. As Harold Hodgkinson suggests, front load the curriculum. It is the freshmen and sophomores who need the smallest classes and seminars. Make these classes and seminars the centerpiece of lower-division education. These small classes and seminars will be the multicultural topical courses the faculty have developed rather than fragmented introductions to this or that field or "bonehead English."

These small courses or seminars should be designed to be intrinsically interesting to all students regardless of background. The course content and the faculty training and preparation to explore and deal with multicultural perspectives will enable students to formulate and ask the nontraditional questions and get answers grounded in their cultures as well as in scholarship. The nature of the course content and instruction will call for critical thinking and reading and will motivate improvements in writing and oral communications. Grading during the course should be based on individual student improvement and growth, and then the final grade can be based on demonstrating proficiency around a universal standard of excellence (such as a well done term paper). In this topical multicultural course, students who have difficulty for whatever reason will be identified early enough in the course for appropriate action and counsel.

As in any good strategic planning, there should be indicators in place to measure the extent to which this first level of multiculturalism has been attained. The most obvious indicators are whether or not faculty (1) have been trained across the disciplines and (2) have had domestic and foreign community based experiences. Additional measures would be whether or not topical-based courses are offered as required courses for all students in small classes or seminars, in which students are graded based on improvement in skill and performance. But there are less obvious measures which will show the extent to which genuine multiculturalism is not simply the form but the spirit of these courses as well: The dropout rate among U.S.-born domestic minorities should decline in the lower division, and incidences of racial conflict on campus should decline as more students have had these courses. Finally, minority students should no longer feel the necessity to become "white" in order to succeed academically and to get positive regard and attention from professors.

In this first level of implementing a multicultural curriculum, the basic Eurocentric structure of the university is still in place. Multiculturalism has become the centerpiece of lower-division undergraduate education—part of the general education requirement. If nothing else, multiculturalism will invigorate the lower division. It will provide students (regardless of cultural backgrounds) with perspectives and skills to be better students in disciplinary-focused upper-division courses. Students will begin to ask more pointed and focused questions in their other courses that will undoubtedly challenge their professors. Finally, this first level of multicultural education will give the colleges or universities that implement it an opportunity to gain trial-and-error experience, to derive benefits, and to decide their own approach to the further inclusion of multiculturalism.

LEVEL TWO

As has been the history of reform in higher education in the United States, each college and university will undoubtedly have to integrate multiculturalism into its educational plan and long-term mission. In doing so, they will devise numerous directions which might be taken to further reform the curriculum and manner of instruction. The prior chapters in this book have offered a series of additional prescriptions that, once implemented, would be indications of institutions moving to the next level.

Domestic and Foreign Community Experience

In level one, faculty should have both domestic and foreign community experiences. But in level two, a criterion for an educated person is first-hand experience in domestic communities of a different racial and social class background than one's own. In the same way, a student should also have first-hand experience living in a foreign country. None of the cultural ideals discussed in Part Two presume that education can be confined to classroom learning in one institutional setting. Involvement in one's own as well as other communities is essential to self and other understanding. This might begin as a required summer abroad and another summer working as an intern in a domestic community. The requirement might be expanded to a full year of instruction and/or internship overseas and in a domestic community.

Focus on Domestic and Foreign Languages

No one questions the need of native Spanish, Chinese, Arabic, Russian, and Vietnamese people to learn English as a practical requirement for living and improving their lives in the United States. There is the same practical necessity for Americans to learn foreign languages if we are to live and improve our lives in the next century. Even if English continues to be the common language of international commerce, we cannot expect respect or continued success as a political or economic player in the world community if we cannot understand the native languages and cultures of trading partners and competitors. Although a foreign language has been a general education requirement for most colleges and universities, it has been fulfilled by studying European languages. The range of languages available needs to be broadened to include those difficult non-European languages. There should be incentives for taking non-European languages and all students should be required to attain a higher level of proficiency than is now required. Part of being multiculturally educated is being able to read, write, and converse comfortably in at least one foreign language.

American attitudes toward non-English-speakers need to become the opposite of what they are. Native speakers of foreign languages are a national asset rather than a liability. These people should not only be encouraged to maintain their language, but their language skill should be improved and utilized. In no way does such an attitude and national policy forego the continued necessity for such people to learn English, but English acquisition should not be driven by making these people feel inferior and ignorant because English is their second language.

Multiculturalism in Science

The focus of multiculturalism as discussed in this book has been the social sciences and humanities. A similar revision of the curriculum and manner of instruction must take place in the sciences and in mathematics. In the second level of implementing a genuine multiculturalism, a critical assessment of Eurocentrism in science and mathematics is required, and plans for reform must be developed and implemented.

Multiculturalism in the Upper Division

The multicultural topical courses in the lower division will challenge disciplinary-specific upper-division courses. At some point, the challenge will result in topical and interdisciplinary upper-division courses. The benefits of multiculturalism by this point should be apparent in both student outcomes and the quality of education. Faculty will increasingly find that students will expect them to integrate into their courses domestic and foreign multicultural issues and concerns. Students will have questions, information, and perspectives that will call for continued study. A component in the measure of effective teaching will be the extent to which a faculty person can conduct a multicultural class and has a multicultural syllabus.

As with level one, there are a series of indicators to measure the extent to which a college or university has moved to level two in its multicultural development. Some possible measures are as follows:

1. Lower-division multicultural courses are accepted as introductions to and electives for regular disciplinary majors.
2. Faculty are required (as conditions for retention and promotion) to have overseas and domestic experiences with groups in communities other than their own.
3. A component of excellence in all course content and instruction are multicultural readings, illustrations, and skills in conducting discussions across domestic and foreign cultural groups.
4. Students are required to have direct experience overseas and in domestic communities other than their own.
5. Foreign (especially non-European) language instruction is extended and is required to be completed at a higher level of proficiency than currently required.
6. Multiculturalism in the sciences is underway in lower-division instruction.

Level two multiculturalism has been taken as far as it can go within the current disciplinary structure and organization of the university. The entire undergraduate curriculum has been touched by domestic and overseas multiculturalism. Faculty and students will be considerably more knowledgeable, experienced, and skilled in their relations with both domestic and overseas cultural groups. But, equally as important, each cultural group can maintain its integrity—and not feel that it is inferior, ignorant, and undesired. Each group can maintain and change its culture in whatever way it chooses. Groups can maintain their cultural integrity and be knowledgeable, skilled, experienced, and mutually empathetic toward one another. In addition, regardless of their cultural and academic backgrounds, the students that complete such an education will be better skilled to address our future domestic and international needs, will be literate across the disciplinary and cultural curricula, and will be better trained than prior generations of students. If level two of multiculturalism is achieved, Eurocentricity will no longer be the central ideology or the central purpose of the American university community. At the same time, it will be clear that the university can not only survive but thrive and improve in quality and outcome as a multicultural institution.

LEVEL THREE

There is a third level of implementing multiculturalism. First, the current division of knowledge grows out of the need of Europeans to understand the world through the humanities and social sciences and to dominate it through the sciences for their our purposes. Second, the organization of the university maintains hierarchical, caste-like division between students and faculty and between university and community. At this third level, the definition and organization of knowledge will give way to the needs of a new century, and the university for the first time in this nation's history will begin to reflect and respect the many cultures that constitute the American people. There will undoubtedly be more than one way to learn any subject as our sensitivity improves to many learning styles. Students and faculty alike (regardless of culture of origin) may know, respect, and be able to use Afrocentric perspectives and Indian ways of knowing as routine techniques for problem solving. The cultural perspectives of Africans, Indians, and Asians may provide the basis for new theories, applications, and combinations of technologies in the sciences.

In this third level of multiculturalism, the definitions and organization of graduate and professional level education will undergo revision. As the numbers of students and faculty increase who have intellectually and personally grown due to cultural inclusion, graduate programs will be changed. Again, there will be a great need for faculty who are multiculturally trained and educated. The same multicultural requirement will exist for graduate, professionally trained people in business and government as both domestic and international boundaries between groups and cultures are further reduced.

CONCLUSION

The plan outlined in this chapter is a strategic, multistage, and rational plan of transition from our current Eurocentric university to a multicultural one. It assumes that change will come in response to both external and internal changes in demographics and the relative political and strategic importance of people of color in the world community. Multiculturalism is not simply the ideological rhetoric of another interest group vying for political influence in education. It is a call for reform that is consistent with the movements of all people of color for self-determination and for participation as co-equals in what constitutes knowledge and how that knowledge will be taught. This plan also assumes that details in each stage of transition for each college and university will come out of debate, discussion, and intellectual persuasion over time. One might charge that these assumptions are ideal. They are as with any blueprint.

Certainly, there will be institutions that will successfully resist change in the short term. There will be many other institutions that will do only what they think others are doing. Then there will be leaders. Once it becomes clear that multiculturalism is the basis of maintaining and strengthening enrollments and is demanded by business and government as necessary for the nation's long-term interest, it will be accepted like all of the other reforms that were initially resisted in American university history.

One might argue that the predominantly white male and decisively Eurocentric professorate will resist such a change at all cost. To become multicultural is to share both their political control of the university and power to define knowledge and its organization. Such concessions will not happen voluntarily or through rational persuasion. This is a point well taken. But this point assumes that our present Eurocentric faculty will also be our future faculty and that what it means to be a faculty member as well as the composition of the faculty will be unchanged. At some institutions, upward to 70 percent of the current faculty will be retiring in the next fifteen years. We can anticipate that the next generation of faculty will be held much more accountable for what they do and how they do it. If there is any success in opening the educational pipeline from Kindergarten through twelfth grades, the next faculty generation will also be the last that will be predominantly white. It is already questionable that they will be predominantly male.

What is to prevent faculty from accommodating change by doing so in appearance but not in substance? Many can come to support multiculturalism as a form of political correctness but do nothing in their personal identity and professional approach to scholarship, research, or their discipline to transform their own work. In doing so, they can go on with business as usual and make no substantive change. This will undoubtedly be the most common form of resistance. But even this form of indirect resistance can be challenged by increasing faculty accountability and a principled implementation of multicultural reform out of dialogue, debate, and open discussion.

We prefer to state the ideal and to show how it can be achieved. Undoubtedly, the evolutionary change that we are calling for and mapping will come out of conflict in the nation and world community. While change will continue to be resisted, change is inevitable. But what form that change will take is not. We prefer to see change as a challenge and opportunity to shape a better university. The ideal can become the reality. But proaction requires vision and plans.

The following chapters attempt to take the information and perspectives presented in this book and to spell out the nut and bolts of a vision toward a genuinely inclusive multicultural university.

Chapter 8

Academic Grading and Assessment in a Culturally Diverse University

Etta R. Hollins

Academic grading is the sacred icon of the academy and a right belonging to university professors even more than to public school teachers. Students achieving the highest grades get their names posted, receive congratulatory letters from university administrators, and hear their names read with honor and reverence at banquets and ceremonies. Exactly what does it all mean? The quality value or letter grade given any completed assignment will vary from one instructor to another, in the same course, at the same college or university, and during the same academic year. The basis for determining a grade may be ambiguous or inconsistently applied from one assignment or individual project to another. Some factors considered in grading may have little or nothing to do with what has been taught in the course or described in the course syllabus.

Demographic shifts in the nation's population that increase cultural diversity have brought concerns and questions about the efficacy of the Eurocentric paradigm that presently exists in most universities. The content in the first two parts of this book focused on the history of the Eurocentric university and its organization and structure, curriculum content and perspective, demographic shifts in the nation's population that increase diversity, and brief descriptions of the history and culture of ethnic groups whose populations are likely to increase significantly over the next few decades. These issues have significant implications for universities interested in recruiting and retaining students from culturally diverse backgrounds. The mission of the university shapes admission and recruitment procedures, which in turn influence perceptions and practices associated with academic excellence and how it is demonstrated, assessed, and graded. This chapter extends the discussion to reexamine the values, perceptions, and practices involved in academic grading and assessment in a traditional university as compared to one committed to multiculturalism. The focus of this chapter is not to advocate lowering standards within the academy in order to improve the status and achievement of those ethnic minority students who are performing poorly; but rather to raise the quality standards for teaching and learning by replacing the present ambiguity in grading and assessment with clarity and specificity.

Many students have learned the culture of the academy and are able to decipher the cues of individual professors in ways that allow them to demonstrate competence by employing acceptable conventions for representing knowledge appropriately in a given context. The expected conventions are implicit rather than explicit. Policies and practices within the academy are based on the European American culture. Thus, students solidly grounded in this culture are more likely to succeed in the academy than the majority of those from other cultural and ethnic backgrounds.

Students enter the university from a variety of cultural and ethnic backgrounds and from different social class strata. These background experiences indicate more about the perception, knowledge, and skills students bring to the university than the grades they earned in high school or their scores on admission examinations. Students have acquired different learning strategies and approaches as well as different values placed on different types of knowledge. Although the majority of students in the United States attend public schools, the type and quality of schooling may vary widely. The nature of schooling students receive is influenced by geographical region, local politics, social class status, ethnicity, gender, teacher perception, parental guidance, and whether the location is urban, rural, or suburban. These and other factors influence the knowledge and skills students acquire in high school and the actual meaning of the grades they receive in terms of the expectations held by colleges and universities.

How a college or university responds to the diverse experiential backgrounds of the student population available for admission will depend on its mission. A central issue is whether the university should concern itself with talent development or talent identification. Elite universities are judged more often by their admission standards than by the quality of their program offerings. Astin (1991) states that

> rather than attempting to achieve common performance standards by differential treatment, we try to maintain standards through selective admissions. This is basically no different in principle from trying to achieve performance standards in a medical setting by refusing to admit the sickest patients. In American higher education we have developed a set of elite institutions that are so selective in their inputs that high performance standards are almost guaranteed, even if the institution contributes little to the educational process. (1991: 202)

In contrast, Astin also points out that the

> talent development approach to excellence creates a very different scenario. From this perspective, our excellence depends less on who we admit and more on what we do for the students once they are admitted. Thus our excellence is measured in terms of how effectively we develop the educational talents of our students rather

than in terms of the mere level of developed talent they exhibit when they enter. (1991: 199)

The increasing multiculturalism in the nation's population and in the pool of students from which the university must select makes talent development an imperative rather than an option. Talent development requires systematic changes from a Eurocentric paradigm of operation to one that is more responsive to the cultural diversity in the student population. In cases where talent development is embraced, admission is based less on ACT and SAT scores and more on other criteria believed to indicate potential for success given appropriate learning experiences and opportunities. For example, students may have creative or critical thinking talents not revealed in traditional classrooms or on standardized tests. In these institutions, excellence is determined by the ability to reveal and refine such hidden talents of the students admitted. Talent development relies on the innovative skills of faculty in reframing curriculum and developing more appropriate approaches to assessment, grading, and instruction which are central to the paradigm shift from the Eurocentric university to one that is more responsive to cultural diversity.

ADDRESSING THE TROJAN HORSE

The grading process at the academy is much like the Trojan horse for many students entering the university from diverse backgrounds. These students believe that they are prepared for advanced study at the academy, read the syllabi for their courses carefully, complete the recommended readings, complete the required assignments according to what is stated in each syllabus, attend classes regularly, prepare for the examinations as directed by the professor, and are greeted with an unexpected low grade for which the only explanation is that the quality of their work and performance on the examination was below average. In many cases, the professor is unable to show examples of high- quality work because either a file has not been developed or the quality standard changes with each course depending on the preparation and competence of the students enrolled. Examinations may be found to include (1) minor details not representative of any theories or principles studied in the course, (2) multiple-choice items that make detailed differentiations not emphasized in class discussions or readings, and (3) ambiguous essay questions for which the correct response is based on the subjective judgment of the professor.

Academic grading is a value judgment made by each professor separately and individually and based on often undisclosed criteria; yet the source and influence of grading extend beyond individual students and the boundaries of the university. Students from different cultural and ethnic backgrounds have acquired specific cultural norms, values, and ways of perceiving the world that are not necessarily consistent with those of the European American culture, although they are no less capable of complex thought and creative endeavors.

These students may not have acquired the academic discourse of the university. The academic discourse requires saying or writing the appropriate thing in the conventional way while playing the appropriate social role and appearing to hold the expected values, beliefs, and attitudes. James Gee describes academic discourse as "a sort of 'identity kit' which comes complete with the appropriate costume and instructions on how to act, talk, and often write, so as to take on a particular role that others will recognize" (1989: 7). Students who have not acquired the expected academic discourse are often viewed as inept and unsuited for study in the academy. Eliminating these students from the university maintains the status quo and reproduces the existing structure within the society.

CLARIFYING THE PURPOSE AND APPROACHES

Traditionally, university administrators and faculty have taken great pride in claiming those students whose academic accomplishments are exemplary; however, too few have accepted any responsibility for those who fail, drop out, or need special assistance and support. Those students who have not acquired the appropriate academic discourse are usually dismissed in shame and disgrace. Some will never again have the privilege of advanced academic study.

The purpose of grading and assessing student performance is closely related to the admission practices and ethos of the particular academy. It was pointed out earlier that some universities build a reputation for academic excellence by selecting the best and brightest students for admission. These institutions are more concerned with maintaining high and rigorous standards for assessing student performance than with the teaching performance of faculty or making curriculum content meaningful. Traditional approaches to instruction and curriculum are met with little criticism or resistance. The majority of students admitted to such institutions usually come from a similar mainstream, middle-class, European American orientation and share common expectations, perceptions, and values. The few students from different cultural and ethnic backgrounds admitted to these institutions are likely to be acculturated to the extent that they are representative of the status quo. Those who have obviously maintained aspects of their own culture are more likely to encounter problems than their more acculturated peers. These problems may result from the use of nonconventional approaches to the preparation and presentation of assignments, nonconventional ways of representing knowledge, and, at times, nonconventional general personal appearance. Nonconventional behavior may have a negative influence on grades whether or not it represents acquisition of the intended learning.

Traditional approaches to grading tend to be indirect and relative. Indirect grading occurs when the objectives on which the students will be evaluated are not made explicit. In this case, what the professor intends or hopes students will learn is not necessarily included in the course objectives listed in the syllabus; course assignments are not necessarily related to written or intended course objectives; and the grading is not necessarily based on concepts, generalizations, principles, or theories central to the discipline. Relative grading is based on a comparison of one student's performance to that of another or to an abstract standard known only to the professor. Relative grading is given the illusion of consistency when a letter grade is assigned to a specific range of points, percentage of correct responses on a test, or quality of performance on a written assignment or project. Where grading appears consistent, students may be able to predict accurately their final grade in the course after a few experiences. In extreme cases, grades are relative to the point that students are uncertain of their progress until all scores on tests and assignments have been evaluated and a final grade assigned by the professor at the end of the term. These characteristics of traditional grading are consistent with the practices of selecting, sorting, and maintaining standards.

Authentic grading is different from traditional grading. Authentic grading is explicit and absolute rather than indirect and relative. It is based on the stated objectives for the course as revealed in ideas central to the discipline. Course assignments are directly related to meeting the course objectives and applying concepts, generalizations, principles, and theories included in course content. Assessment or testing is performance based, requiring students to apply ideas and theories rather than the simple recall of facts. Authentic grading is based on an absolute or fixed standard. The specific tasks to be completed are clearly described, and critical aspects can be assigned a specific point value. When a student performs the described task, the designated points are awarded. Abstract judgments of quality are not appropriate at this point. Students are evaluated on the objectives of the course, and prior learning and incidental learning are not included in the evaluation. The attitudes of grading described as authentic are characteristic of multicultural colleges and universities that focus on talent development rather than talent identification. Success depends on an innovative faculty committed to redesigning instruction and reframing the curriculum to increase meaningfulness for a culturally diverse student population.

TECHNICAL ASPECTS OF PLANNING INSTRUCTION

Planning quality instruction that facilitates learning requires attention to the technical aspects of determining course objectives, designing learning experiences, assessing learner outcomes, and assessing the appropriateness of the objectives and the learning experiences. The objectives should state exactly what major understandings students are to gain from taking the course. The objectives should relate to (1) content knowledge, including principles, concepts, major ideas and arguments, and the organization or structure of knowledge within the discipline; and (2) procedural or process knowledge, including principles of inquiry and the representation of knowledge within the subject matter area.

Explaining the relationship between objectives, learning experiences, and assessment will help students focus their study efforts, decrease anxiety about examinations, and increase learning. Assignments, readings, guest speakers, and other learning experiences should be clearly linked to specific course objectives. The learning experiences should provide opportunities for students to examine the principles, concepts, major ideas and arguments, and organizational structure of knowledge within the subject matter area. Students should be provided with learning experiences that allow them to practice the application of related procedures, and processes including the principles of inquiry.

The assessment of learning outcomes should be tied directly to the course objectives. Two questions need to be answered by the assessment: (1) Did the students acquire the intended content and procedural knowledge identified in the course objectives? (2) Were the learning experiences adequate or appropriate for facilitating acquisition of the content and procedural knowledge identified in the course objectives? The assessment of students' acquisition of the content and procedural knowledge included in the course objectives may take the form of completing a project or producing a product of some type; making an oral presentation; or completing a written examination. In each type of assessment, the student should be required to demonstrate understanding of content and procedural knowledge at a level that permits recall and analysis or application in ways consistent with or that extend what has been presented in course content. Multiple-choice examinations should conform to this standard as well as other types of assessment. Assessing students' achievement of the course objectives brings clarity to the purpose of the learning experiences.

In analyzing the results of an assessment, it is important to determine the extent of students' learning and the validity and reliability of the assessment process and the learning experiences. It may be valuable to develop a frequency chart showing the type and quantity of errors students made during the assessment process. If there is a pattern, such as a high frequency of certain types of errors or students from a particular background making identifiable types of errors, it is important to reexamine the assessment process and the learning experiences. Check students' understanding of the language used in the directions or the questions asked in the assessment. Make sure students understood what they were instructed to do. If students understood what to do on the assessment, review their understanding and participation in the learning experiences. If a significant number of students understood what was to be done on the assessment and participated satisfactorily in the learning experiences and failed particular items on the assessment, the validity and reliability of the learning experiences are questionable. The learning experiences may need to be modified to increase validity and reliability.

STUDENT-CENTERED ASPECTS OF PLANNING INSTRUCTION

Engaging in talent development requires some knowledge of students beyond their high school grades and scores on admission examinations. Teaching and learning at the university level, like that in the elementary and secondary schools, requires making links between the students' background knowledge and the content being presented. One approach is to become familiar with the secondary school curriculum related to the content taught at the university and locate those areas most likely to cause students difficulty. University instruction can begin by reinforcing areas of weakness and building on strengths in the secondary school curriculum.

A second approach to improving instruction is the systematic study of one's own practice. In this case, the professor relies heavily on assessment and feedback from students. The objectives of the course are clearly tied to readings, written assignments, and other learning experiences provided for the students. Tests and examinations provide insight into the effectiveness of the learning experiences in facilitating attainment of the objectives of the course. The professor should note patterns of failure in attaining course objectives, such as a significant percentage of students not acquiring an adequate understanding of specific concepts or processes. In some cases, students with specific background experiences will need a particular type of learning experience.

A third approach to improving instruction at the university level is that of understanding and providing options for learning that allow students to make links between their own ethnic and cultural background, experiences or personal goals and course content. Students come from various ethnic and cultural backgrounds, with varying values attributed to some forms of knowledge and content and with a variety of approaches to knowledge acquisition, representation, and presentation. Some ways of knowing and presenting knowledge are more acceptable within the university than others; however, most can be used as bridges to learning new ways of acquiring knowledge and thinking about ideas. One way to think about providing options that allow students to make links with their own mode of learning is to use E. T. Hall's (1989) description of cultures as high context and low context. Hall describes low-context cultures as those that construct meaning from their experiences by using a building block approach. People functioning within high-context cultures employ a wholistic approach to extract meaning from common understandings of the interrelatedness of phenomena, situations, and people within their environment. Thus university professors should include both linear-sequential and wholistic-integrated learning experiences for their students. The learning experiences should encourage natural collaboration among and between different groups of students, and additional support should be provided for students who have difficulty getting through aspects of the learning experiences.

A fourth approach to improving instruction is to create a common experience that can serve as a reference point when students experience difficulty with technical content. A good example of this is that employed by Robert Moses et al. (1989), in which Moses initiated algebra instruction for sixth grade students by taking them for a ride on the Red Line commuter train in Boston. During the trip, the students developed a common language and reference points for understanding and communicating algebra concepts. This had a significantly positive effect on the students' progress in algebra. Although applied at a lower level, the principle seems to be applicable to university classrooms as well.

CONCLUSION

The success of students from culturally diverse backgrounds in an academic setting is influenced by curriculum content and how it is framed, clarity of course objectives and the learning experiences provided for their acquisition, and the extent to which assessment is explicit and directly related to the content, objectives, and learning experiences. In traditional universities, these relationships are not usually clarified. However, equitable access to knowledge in the multicultural university is more likely to be accomplished where faculty put forth the effort necessary to meet the conditions that support learning for students from culturally diverse backgrounds.

The approaches to assessment and planning instruction recommended in this chapter can occur in a Eurocentric university; however, this seems unlikely given the paradigm of operation. The proposed changes in assessment and instruction are likely to increase students' academic knowledge and competence whatever their background, the nature of curriculum content, or orientation of the university. It is important to acknowledge that there are students from non-European American groups who perform well in the university as it presently exists; however, it is likely that they too can benefit from the proposed changes.

REFERENCES

Astin, Alexander W. 1991. *Assessment for Excellence.* New York: American Council on Education, Macmillan Publishing Company.

Clark, Edward G. 1985. "Gading Seminar Performance." *College Teaching* 33(3): 129-133.

Cross, K. P. 1989. "Feedback in the Classroom: Making Assessment Matter." *In Proceedings of the Second Annual AAHE Assessment Forum.* Washington, DC: American Association for Higher Education.

Cross, K. P., and T. A. Angelo. 1988. *Classroom Assessment Techniques: A Handbook for Faculty.* Ann Arbor, MI: National Center for Research on the Improvement of Postsecondary Teaching and Learning.

Denton, Jon J. 1989. "Selecting an Appropriate Grading System." *The Clearinghouse* November, 107-110.

Gee, James. P. 1989. "Literacy, Discourse, and Linguistics: Introduction." *Journal of Education* 171(1): 5-25.

Gentile, J. Ronald, and N. Murnyak. 1989. "How Shall Students Be Graded in Discipline-Based Art Education?" *Art Education* 42(6): 33-41.

Hall, Edward T. 1989. "Unstated Features of Cultural Context of Learning." *Educational Forum* 54(1): 21-54.

Kraft, Robert G. 1985. "Group-Inquiry Turns Passive Students to Active." *College Teaching* 33(4): 149-154.

Lowman, Joseph. 1990. "Promoting Motivation and Learning." *College Teaching* 38(4): 136-139.

Milton, Ohmer, et al. 1986. *Making Sense of College Grades.* San Francisco: Jossey-Bass.

Moses, Robert, M. Kamii, S. Swap, and J. Howard. 1989. "The Algebra Project: Organizing in the Spirit of Ella." *Harvard Education Review* 59(4): 413-443.

Raths, James, et al. 1987. "Grading Problems: A Matter of Communication." *Journal of Educational Research* 80(3): 133-137.

Tracy, Saundra J., and E. Schuttenberg, 1986. "The Desirable and the Possible: Four Instructional Models." *College Teaching* 34(4): 155-160.

Wiggins, Grant. 1991. "Not Standardization: Evoking Quality Student Work." *Educational Leadership* 48(5): 18-25.

Wilson, Stephen J. 1991. "Teaching about Fractals." *College Mathematics Journal* 22(1): 56-59.

Chapter 9

Using Computers and Telecommunications to Advance Multicultural Education

Arthur E. Paris

Computing and telecommunications are transforming education at all levels and have as much potential to change higher education as the demographic revolution before us. In this chapter, I will give a brief outline of the technological background and history that have produced this potential to change education, and then I will show how this technical opportunity can be used to advance multicultural education.

BACKGROUND

Until recently, the initial and largest use for mainframe computing services was administrative (for financial and recordkeeping purposes). Educational institutions followed other large organizations, such as government agencies, corporations, and insurance companies, in using the processing power of mainframe computers to keep track of thousands of students, their courses, transcripts, payments, and other details that bursars, accounting offices, and registrars need to follow (McCredie 1983). Scientists began to use the computational power of this technology and were added to the roster of users. These scientists also pushed for direct communication links between their mainframe computers, which led to Vice President Gore's National Information Infrastructure (NII), also known as the Information Highway.

Two decades ago, the conventional view was that computers would get bigger and bigger and, ultimately, there would be a few giant computers to which all who needed access would be connected (Froehlich 1982). Just the opposite has happened. Giantism, centralized service, and centralized control are out. Instead, computers have gotten smaller, more powerful, and cheaper and are now virtually everywhere. With microcomputers, the price of entry into computer use has fallen below $1,000. Computers have now become commodity items, and computing is a mass market and mainstream activity. Millions of people have become users and have created a mass market for computer applications. Unlike other commodity markets that have reached their maximum, there are still millions of potential users and usages.

Relatively sophisticated use of computers is something that everyone can do. Any child can use powerful microcomputers for playing games. Other uses of computers include composing and playing music, monitoring control systems, keeping track of the stock exchange, tutoring languages, handling banking transactions, and paying bills. But the area in which computing has had its greatest impact has come as a surprise to everyone: its applications to communication.

Over a decade ago, "Ma Bell's" monopoly in telephone services was ended by a court decision. That decision opened telephone services to competition. Competition has led to dramatic rate reductions for long-distance services, rapid improvement in telephone technology, and a proliferation of new, low-cost services—call waiting, call forwarding, three-way calling, and answering services. Telephones themselves have been given computing power. By simply buying a better phone, one can get memory dialing, one-touch dialing, redial, speakerphone, and a fax function. Improvements in telephone technologies have included changes not visibly apparent to the user. There are new digital switching systems to transfer calls more rapidly, fiber optic cables to handle vastly larger call volumes in a noise-free manner, and satellite systems to connect telephones anywhere on earth. This increase in carrying capacity and call clarity makes it possible for the phone system to carry many more kinds of electronic signals than just voice.

As a result of the twin transformations in computing and telecommunications, it is possible to exchange voice, data, television, music, and text documents by telephone and television cable between anyone with access to a computer and telephone, anywhere on earth and at any time. Central computers serve as connection points worldwide on a vast system such as INTERNET and BITNET (Krol 1992; Quarterman 1990). The basic infrastructure is in place for information gathering and exchange through which we can search, gather, manipulate, and deliver information of different types in record time and at low cost.

APPLICATIONS TO EDUCATION

The new computer and telecommunications technologies have rendered obsolete the way in which educators maintain knowledge and teach it. The teacher and the classroom need no longer be separated from one another, the library, the video archives, the computer center, or any other place which contains information records and in which instruction occurs. The instructor can teach in one location, and the students can be in many other locations. It is now possible for a high school student or college freshman to do more comprehensive and larger bibliography searches than graduate students twenty years ago. They do it in a fraction of the time and from any location with a telephone line, computer, and modem. Information which we previously had to gather sitting in the library, using paper books, note cards, and pen or standing over the photocopier, now comes onscreen as we sit at our desks. We can also dial into other libraries near and far, scan online catalogs, census data, or other sources, download the information to our computer, and use it immediately.

Newer technological innovations within the computer and telecommunications revolution are pushing the possibilities even farther and bringing unimagined potential to us in short time periods (Strassman 1985). For example, innovations in computer storage technology have brought CD-ROM into widespread use. The result is that what took an entire library stack to store can now be placed on a small CD-ROM disk accessed by computer. The entire 1990 U.S. census of population and housing is on CD-ROM and is accessible to any individual who cares to review the menus of tables at a level of detail that only ten years ago required computer tapes and sophisticated programming. Not only are book and author searches possible, but one can search thousands of journal titles and subjects, develop specific bibliographies, and print out journal article abstracts. We are only at the beginning of using this technology. With the new storage capacities and faster processing speeds of new microcomputer systems multimedia communications and information dissemination are possible—image, text, and sound all at once. A Shakespeare play can be read, watched, heard, and replayed on computer or television. Soon the capability to interact creatively to alter the sound, image, script, and text will be possible.

The low cost of access and the mass audience needed to make these innovations profitable can enfranchise a broad swatch of users previously barred from access to places such as the library and databases such as the census. To take advantage of microcomputer-based software can bring entire subjects to any user who cares to turn on his or her computer and install the software. There are machine-based learning tools to help students practice the routine and repetitive work often necessary to master masses of material. More and more primary school students are enticed by math and language drills in the form of games, such as Coleco's Talking Teacher. Since 1992, K-12 students all across the country have been collaborating online, linked by INTERNET, to build a virtual city called CitySpace using sophisticated computer graphics (Salus 1994). Likewise, older students are benefiting from the enthusiasm of language teachers for such technology. Syracuse University students in Romance languages read texts onscreen and watch and listen to native speakers speak the same lines. They can then compare the native speaker's voice print with their own. Although this system is still new and will be developed further, it entices students not enamored with foreign languages. The same tools can be applied easily to non-Romance languages such as Arabic, Hindi, Mandarin, Xhosa, Navaho, or Wolof. With a multimedia window into the world of Swahili, Arabic, or some other language more students will attempt to learn about these worlds and languages. Such acquaintance is of self-evident value in our global village.

APPLICATION TO DOMESTIC MULTICULTURAL EDUCATION

Applications of the new computer and telecommunications technology can enhance multicultural reform of higher education. They are tools that can bridge the barriers between students and teachers, communities and universities, teaching and learning. This potential is evinced by looking at how telecommunications and computer technology can be used to advance some of the suggestions of previous chapters in this book.

In Chapter 1, Harold Hodgkinson pointed out that if we want to get more students of color into the sciences in college and graduate school, something will have to be done about the pipeline constriction between the sixth and ninth grades. The entire math and science curriculum for these grades (as well as the grades before and after) could be put into attractive multimedia software packages and used as supplements to classroom instruction. Computer-based tutorials could accompany each package. These software packages could be customized to reflect different domestic cultural experiences. A host of telecommunications distant experience laboratories and presentations could be developed for each class and year. In addition, testing and assessment could be developed around the subject matter and specific intellectual skills that students are expected to learn in each subject at each grade level. The assessment system would be able to identify a student's strengths and weaknesses and then suggest what tutorial and level instructional package needs to be worked on. Students, teachers, and parents could access the entire curriculum (with supplements, tutorials, and assessments) from the classroom or at home and at any time.

At the end of a class period or grading period, computerized test results and assessment information could be automatically reported to parents by voice mail, electronic mail, or cable television. Absences from school could also be automatically reported to all concerned. The new technology could help achieve the goals Hodgkinson articulated, such as to allow parents to be part of the team; expect achievement and reward it; and link schools to other youth resources and programs.

In Chapter 5, Milga Morales-Nadal discussed the need for others to see the world though the eyes of a Puerto Rican Latino. Visual images through technology could be useful in this transcultural learning. Morales-Nadal also discussed the need for a university without walls where internships, activities, and experiences in one's own and in other communities are important parts of the education. Technology lifts the time and space limitations that have traditionally separated the academy from the community. The potential to produce culturally sensitive and specific multimedia presentations exists. Students will soon be able to experience these other-cultural presentations through virtual reality systems that will provide interactive possibilities. Imagine a student being able to specify a common issue, such as approaching a person from a Puerto Rican cultural background and asking him or her to converse with the student about some topic. A student could choose particular options and get responses that give some insight into the cultural script and expectations that they may encounter in a real experience. Of course, nothing substitutes for real, face-to-face experience. Telecommunications makes it possible to maintain a central university in fact and identity, but the university's functions can be so decentralized that it is a university without walls. Students in distant communities and distant countries can not only stay in touch through electronic mail, but they can take courses via satellite link and/or CD-ROM sent through the mail.

In Chapter 6, Donald Fixico outlined the desperate need to preserve the rapidly disappearing American Indian languages; the need for community-based experience; and the need to learn how different ethnic and racial cultures arrive at answers to problems and use nonlinear analytic thinking. Once linguists codify a language, its potential to be preserved, disseminated, and learned is enhanced by the new technologies. It can be preserved on CD disk, and a native speaker, linguists, and computer applications specialists could develop multimedia tutorials that can use music, images, and immediate feedback on correct pronunciation. Games, tutorials, and presentation can be developed using alternative and nonlinear analytic thinking.

In Chapter 7, Benjamin Bowser and Octave Baker suggested using year-long interdisciplinary courses to provide students with the kind of whole-world views needed to learn and appreciate cultural and historic differences. Current information search and retrieval systems make finding the content for such a course possible. But, in addition, there is the potential to utilize hundreds of illustrations from art collections, geography, and the scripts and translations of local literature. Virtual reality could be used to reconstruct city designs and evolution, everyday housing, migration patterns, economic growth, trade routes, etc. Telecommunications could bring experts and people who experienced some event into the classroom. The present technology makes it possible for learning to be more than cognitive. All of the senses, as well as imagination and visualization could be used to make learning more interesting and engaging. Advance versions of the assessment systems used in K-12 could be used to identify a freshman's strengths, weaknesses, cultural orientations, and specific interests and then indicate where tutoring is needed and what initial courses are appropriate.

In Chapter 8, Etta Hollins pointed out that what faculty generally expect of students is implicit rather than explicit and that students have different learning strategies and approaches that may not match the implicit expectations of a faculty person. More often, these differences have cultural and social class origins. In a multicultural university, faculty must reach across cultural and social class boundaries. Their implicit expectations will have to become explicit to themselves and to their students. Expert systems could be developed to help faculty make their biases and implicit expectations known to them and to their students. Classroom instruction and interaction with students could be periodically videotaped and carefully reviewed by colleagues and experts. This would identify faculty strengths and weaknesses in combination with student assessments and would provide a measure of what student skills and learning abilities a faculty person favors and disfavors. This would give an instructor useful information

about his or her effectiveness with students from particular cultural backgrounds and with particular learning styles.

Regardless of an instructor's skills and biases, the new technology makes it
possible for each faculty member to develop tutorials for any recurring course.
These individual faculty tutorials could also include examples of what the instructor considers high quality work. They could drill students in the specific
skills that the instructor wants students to develop. They could test students simultaneously (as in an examination period or at any other time) and then report
the number of right or wrong questions on a rooster to the instructor's computer
account. This would, as Etta Hollins advocated, better link teaching and learning and bridge students' backgrounds with teaching and course content.

In Chapter 11, Terry Jones and Gale Auletta-Young discuss the information
imperative. The ease, convenience, and multimedia access to libraries and information for many disciplines will break down artificial and administrative
barriers. Academic departments and disciplines will have to become interdisciplinary to some extent. This means that the task of faculty will be to help students decide what kind of information to gather and investigate and how to
understand, question and explore that knowledge. Instruction will require team
collaboration at a minimum, because no single faculty member will be able to
teach across all the disciplines and perspectives. Jones and Auletta-Young provide an example of a music course taught by possibly a physicist, mathematician, sociologist, musician, musicologist, and historian. The entire potential
richness of the experience would be lost in a series of lecture-only presentations. This kind of necessarily multicultural and multidisciplinary course is a
natural for multimedia, virtual reality, a music library on CD-ROM, and distant
presentations by experts and artists alike.

APPLICATIONS TO INTERNATIONAL MULTICULTURAL EDUCATION

The new computer and telecommunications technology can enhance international multicultural contact in much the same way that it can enhance domestic
multiculturalism. The idea that the thousands of miles between any two or more
locations are a communications barrier is obsolete. Time differences are now
the only obstacle. Communications between locations in China and New York
are no more difficult than communications between offices in the same building. North American students doing overseas community internships can be
connected to their home and university or college with voice mail, electronic
mail, and eventually video mail via satellite. But equally as important, students
and faculty in North American and foreign universities and communities can be
directly in contact with each other and exchange multimedia information.
Classes could be conducted in different parts of the world and linked so that
students and faculty could ask each other questions, share information and per-

spectives, and do joint projects. Students in all subjects could benefit from such experiences, not just those in foreign language instruction.

If we simply look at what is going on now without multimedia, virtual reality, and CD-ROM, much can be done with existing computer networks. When the Berlin Wall came down in 1991, a BITNET list was started to discuss German-related issues. American participants in the discussion were able to read what Germans and others had to say about the events and their meaning, and were not restricted to the image and meaning management of the broadcast networks. Even more to the point, after Tiananmen Square, Chinese students in America used these same computer networks to communicate with and inform one another in considerably more detail than was otherwise publicly available about events in Asia (Keefe 1989). They were then able to feed world reactions back into the People's Republic. So access to these networks facilitated the linking of student populations that were spread across the country and world. It provided a platform for the growth of a public discourse and enabled this otherwise dispersed and economically disadvantaged group to affect the course of both domestic U.S. policy and political activity in China. These networks were so effective that the Chinese government sought to cut off all telecommunications links to the outside world.

East Indian students have made similar (though less dramatic) use of computer networks, sharing and spreading information about events and matters of concern to Indians at home and abroad (Malamud 1992). African students likewise have networked lists for the same purpose, as have Arab students and doubtless other regional and national groups. As non-Eurocentered faculty and students increase in number within domestic higher education, they provide a ready constituency for creating and expanding international electronic publics and networks.

THE QUESTION OF WILL AND LEADERSHIP

All these technologic developments and possibilities raise critical issues for software developers and college and university administrators, especially those charged more specifically with computing. When systems user demographics are examined, those who could most benefit from this technology are underrepresented. Although financing software and computer purchases is an issue, money is not the major impediment. Administrative inertia and lack of knowledge and awareness of the uses, advantages, and actual options are larger impediments.

For students and faculty of color who are unaware of the options, administrative leadership is vital for stimulating such use. Few will discover the realm of BITNET list serves and USENET news groups on their own. Most will not unless deliberately encouraged. Specifically, administrators have to make computers and their networks readily accessible to students and faculty. Simple availability is not enough. Use must be encouraged. Support and encouragement must accompany availability. If putting a computer on everyone's desk is not a high priority, then present and future technologies will not be utilized. If the administration makes the technology accessible and then uses it for faster, more efficient communication, faculty and student users will come along. Further, faculty need encouragement and support to integrate this technology into their work and classrooms. Students who complain that they cannot catch up with busy faculty are more likely to reach them via electronic mail and get prompt response to their queries.

The possibilities and potential to use present and future computer and communications technology outlined in this chapter are valid only if we are willing to take a new look at education. The status quo will bring more of the same, and these marvelous potentials will not be actualized. When the educational perspectives of African Americans, Puerto Ricans, and Native Americans are integrated into the mission and organization of the university, education will have to change. Multicultural reform will move education from a process that primarily rewards and certifies existing advantage to one that includes those who are different and without advantage. Multicultural educators will look at education as a developmental process. Then there will be a need, willingness, and exciting market for the computer and telecommunications applications outlined in this chapter.

REFERENCES

Froehlich, Allan. 1982. *Managing the Data Center.* Belmont, CA: Lifetime Learning Publications.

Keefe, Patricia. 1989. "High-Tech Gets Word to China." *Computer World* 23(24): 1, 6.

Krol, Ed. 1992. *The Whole Internet User's Guide and Catalog.* Sebastopol, CA: O'Reilly and Associates.

Malamud, Carl. 1992. *Exploring the Internet: A Technical Travelogue.* Englewood Cliffs: NJ-Prentice Hall.

McCredie, John, ed. 1983. *Campus Computing Strategies.* Bedford, MA: Digital Press.

Quarterman, John. 1990. *The Matrix.* Bedford, MA: Digital Press.

Salus, Peter. 1994. "Interactive Internet Game Shows Grow-ups." *Open System Today.* January 10: 30, 32.

Strassman, Paul. 1985. *Transformation of Work in the Electronic Age.* New York: The Free Press.

Chapter 10

The Organization of a Multicultural University

Benjamin P. Bowser

In Chapter 7, a strategic plan framework was presented for how we might transform the university into a multicultural institution. In this chapter, the issue of organization is addressed. As the university becomes more inclusive in its base of knowledge and of human concerns, its organization will be called on to change as well. If we use a planned evolutionary approach and take to heart the cultural advisement of the chapters in Part Two, then changing the lower-division undergraduate curriculum will be our first objective. The second objective will be the transformation of the upper division and the sciences. Finally, graduate and professional education would be reformed. Each of these levels of implementation will require some rethinking of department organization and ultimately the relations between sectors—department, administration, student life, and the communities beyond the university.

Figure 10.1 illustrates current university organization from the viewpoint of the curriculum. There is a central administration (Admin.), and there are autonomous departments (Dept.) each with its own introductory, upper-division, and possibly graduate courses. As William King pointed out in Chapter 2, this is the organization that ended the classicists' presumption that every-

FIGURE 10.1

**Traditional Organization
with Ethnic Studies**

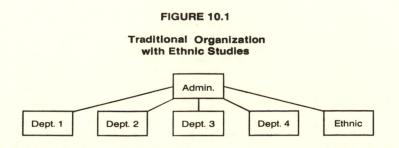

one had to be educated in exactly the same subjects—Greek and Roman philosophy, literature, music, logic, and mathematics. With independent departments and electives, the range of subject matter that can be offered has increased, specializations have proliferated, and what unifies the curriculum is that all students are required to take some variable list of department courses as a general education requirement (once these courses were considered remedial). Virtually all of these courses grow out of and reflect the experiences of the trade and merchant class of Europeans (European Americans) and implicitly require commitment to the world view, perspectives, and concerns of this limited class of people.

The way that demands for a culturally more inclusive education have been met is to add a course or two in ethnic studies (Ethnic). But adding one or two ethnic studies courses does not make a Eurocentric education multicultural. Even if most faculty incorporated multicultural readings into their course materials and suddenly became willing to address issues pertaining to African, Asian, and American Indian peoples, the curriculum would still not be multicultural. This alternative is expressed in Figure 10.2.

Note that each department has integrated multicultural material and perspectives into its courses. All of the department boxes are now a combination of traditional disciplinary offerings, with ethnic studies integrated into each department's offerings. One could argue that this model is superior to the model shown in Figure 10.1 because ethnic studies is vertically integrated throughout the curriculum and across all disciplines. If such vertical integration occurs, then one could argue that Ethnic studies as a stand-alone department or program may no longer be necessary. But this is not the case. The integrated framework for presentation is still based on the European presumption that knowledge can be found by fragmenting reality, and the single point of reference for discussion and comparison will continue to be primarily and centrally that of European peoples.

What is not apparent to many faculty members is that Ethnic studies involve a lot more than each major discipline using ethnic and racial groups as subjects of study. Maulana Karenga asserted in Chapter 3 that Afrocentricity is as much an African and African American vehicle of exploration, a world view and a potential series of methodologies as is the Eurocentric perspective. Afrocentric-

FIGURE 10.2

**Integration of Traditional
and Ethnic Studies**

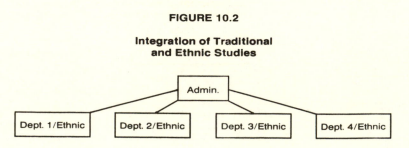

ity, like Eurocentricity, is open to anyone to use and learn from but not as the only basis by which one can be educated. Milga Morales-Nadal and Donald Fixico both showed (in Chapters 5 and 6) that to be Puerto Rican and a Muscogee Creek are much more than being the object of European's study. Like African Americans, these people have cultures, histories, and potentially much more to contribute to human knowledge than being simply the object of another's study.

An organizational framework is needed that will allow and advance wholistic world views as suggested in the African and American Indian perspectives. Within such a framework other cultural perspectives will be intrinsic to the course and its purpose rather than just add-ons or interesting digressions from the main point. Figure 10.3 shows an alternative to the Eurocentric segmented model of Figures 10.1 and 10.2. Students would enroll in at least two year-long courses that would be team taught and organized around themes rather than disciplines. The purposes of the course are to excite students about knowledge, to help them see themselves and their communities in history, and to allow personalized exploration regardless of ethnic and social class background.

A theme such as social justice or economic prosperity could be the basis of reading a period's history along with its literature, languages, philosophy, and anthropology. This would allow more wholistic comparisons and contrasts between historical developments in Europe, Africa, and Asia. This first set of year long comprehensive courses could be introductory, in which students' potential long term interests could be identified. Their academic strengths and weaknesses could also be identified early and worked on during this year within the context of the comprehensive courses. A minimum proficiency in library research, writing and critical thinking could be the basis for advancement to the next level. The second and any subsequent level of proficiency could also be based on new and more specific themes, the study of contemporary times, the introduction of new disciplines, and a focus on specific nationalities and cultures. Subsequent levels could require attaining additional and higher proficiencies.

The model shown in Figure 10.3 would require extensive departmental cooperation and collaboration. In this model it is not Ethnic studies that might

FIGURE 10.3

**Interdisciplinary
Competency Levels**

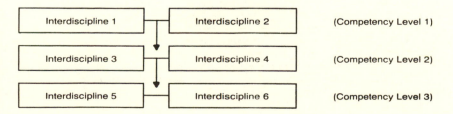

FIGURE 10.4

**Integrated Model with
Domestic and Foreign
Community Experiences**

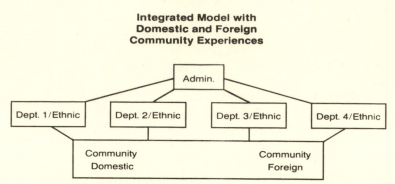

disappear, but rather the departmental structure as we know it. The new division might emerge based on interdisciplinary faculty interests and the ability to work together. If such a change is too drastic, there is another alternative. A corrective for seeing other peoples and cultures as objects would be to have students and faculty live and work in foreign cultures and domestic co-cultures. We could take the current model (Figure 10.1 and 10.2) and add to it the experiential components, as shown in Figure 10.4.

What distinguishes the model shown in Figure 10.4 from those of Figures 10.1 and 10.2 is that students and faculty are required to have spent some specific period of time (such as a summer, semester, or year) overseas and in domestic ethnic and social class communities other than their own. While the domestic and overseas exposures will invigorate discussion and provide the basis for alternative perspectives, the structure and context of discourse will continue to be segmented and Eurocentric in focus. Again this brings us back to the comprehensive multilevel model of Figure 10.3. But this time, the domestic and overseas experiences can be added to further enrich classroom discourse from

FIGURE 10.5

**Interdisciplinary Competency Levels
with Domestic and Foreign
Community Experiences**

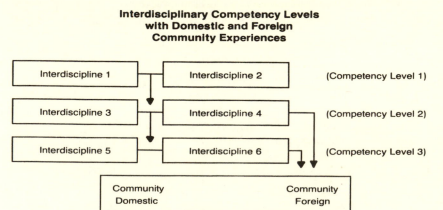

student experience. What the African, American Indian, and Puerto Rican experiences have to bring to education must be conveyed as not simply theory and abstraction, but through experience as well. The comprehensive, wholistic approach with domestic and overseas community experiences is shown in Figure 10.5.

But segmentation of knowledge, as in the Eurocentric approaches, has advantages. For one thing, a student can learn a discipline more thoroughly and in depth. Students with different talents, experiences, and backgrounds are attracted to majors and approaches that they are more comfortable with. An organizational structure that has the potential to be inclusive and takes advantage of the strengths of the current model (Figures 10.1 and 10.2) and the proposed model (Figures 10.3 and 10.5) is illustrated in Figure 10.6.

There is a comprehensive thematic introduction to knowledge that is also used as a diagnostic and training opportunity. These baseline courses cannot work if they are not small, exciting, and personalized. To reiterate Harold Hodgkinson's advice, we need to front load the curriculum. If we are serious about education and want to retain students who are not European in background and/or middle class, and improve education for all, we have to provide direct instruction so students can see the importance of ideas in their and other worlds. This is very different from using the introduction as a way to screen students and to obtain only the top students as majors. Note that levels 2 and 3 organize knowledge as a series of courses much as they are now. In these courses, students can study for majors and focus more specifically on subject matter that interested them in the comprehensive and topical level 1. Domestic and overseas community exposures can be added to this model and should be taken in the second and third years. In the fourth and final year, students would come together again in a more specific comprehensive and thematic final set of courses.

FIGURE 10.6

**Combination of Interdisciplinary
Competency Levels with Integrated
Departments and Community Experiences**

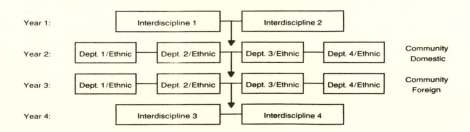

INTEGRATION BETWEEN UNIVERSITY AND COMMUNITIES

One of the great disappointments in higher education is that diverse groups of students who sit together in the classroom form distinct and often antagonistic cultural (race) and social class worlds outside of class. Campus life replicates the separate communities they come from. But not all communities are equally distant or positioned apart from the university's academic and social lives. The senior faculty and administrators are more often a part of the European American upper middle and upper class communities, even if many had roots in the working class. In this case, they have much in common with students from the same social class and cultural background. This closeness carries over to student life—on and off campus living, cultural activities and athletics. What is taken for granted as student life is in fact middle-class European American student life. The sports, social clubs (fraternities and sororities), etc. come out of the history and experiences of one social group, as does the curriculum.

The presumption on the part of many European American faculty members and students is that faculty and students of color should be part of their social world, since they take for granted that they are the university. But students from other cultural and social class backgrounds come from communities with interests and concerns foreign to European American middle-class faculty and students. These nontraditional students do not have the same informal and community connections to the academic life of the university, even in large public urban and state universities and colleges. The only place that students from other class and cultural communities can acknowledge their specific interests and concerns is in multicultural student organizations and alternative cultural events, much like foreign students. Ethnic studies is the only academic unit in which students of color are likely to encounter faculty familiar with their backgrounds.

The social class and cultural segregation in student life is most common at large impersonal universities. Students of color at smaller and more personable universities and colleges are better integrated into the social life of the university. But more often cultural integration in these settings has a distinct context. Students (faculty) of color must not only be prepared and willing to learn (teach) a Eurocentric academic curriculum, but they must also be willing to be a part of the middle-class European American social life of their university or college. They must be willing to conform and be just like other (white) students. It is presumed that this is why a student of color comes to such a college. One's culture, community concerns and interests, and possible connection to the larger world community are rejected and are literally to be left at the gates. Figure 10.7 illustrates the relation between communities and the academic and social life of the university.

This separation between communities and the academic world is certainly not the Eurocentric ideal. There should be a close relation between student life and the academic side of the university. But this ideal is seriously compromised when there is one dominant cultural focus in the curriculum and a diverse stu-

FIGURE 10.7

**Intersection of Academic,
Student, and Community Life**

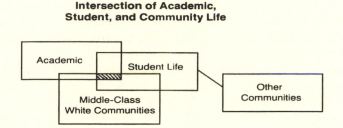

dent body. Would a multicultural curriculum make a difference in student life? If students have structured opportunities to learn about one another's culture, histories, and contemporary circumstances, campus social life should be affected positively. In addition, if they also have domestic and overseas cross-cultural and social class work and study experiences, there should be a difference in campus life as well.

A multicultural curriculum will make a difference in student life in the following way. The membership and purpose of these nontraditional student groups will change. There will be a continuing need for student organizations to represent and reflect the diversity of domestic and foreign cultural groups that make up the student body. There will be more European American students willing to and interested in joining the clubs of foreign and domestic cultural students. Foreign and domestic students of color will be more open to having knowledgeable and experienced European American students as club members. In turn foreign and domestic students of color will be more welcomed and interested in traditional campus organizations. Knowledge about one another and experiences across communities will progressively, for each class year, break down the barriers that students brought to the university from their parent communities. The multicultural alternative is illustrated in Figure 10.8.

The academic sector, student life, and foreign and domestic community sectors are all closely connected. Instead of being isolated from all but the upper-middle class European American community, the university becomes a bridge between potentially all foreign and domestic communities. Students learn

FIGURE 10.8

**Realignment of Academic,
Student, and Community Life**

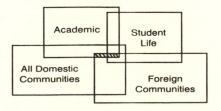

across the disciplines. All of human history, culture, failures, and successes become subject matter, not just that of Europe and Europeans. History is connected to the present. Ideas are connected to experience, and there is ample opportunity to learn a specific discipline in depth. It is in this organizational framework that ideas, people, and things that are middle class and European can become part of a larger educational mission that can also include (as central to its mission) ideas, people, and things African, Latin, American Indian, and Asian.

Chapter 11

Beyond Disciplinary Borders: Creating a Genuine Multicultural Curriculum

Terry Jones
Gale Auletta Young

Chogyam Trungpa, a Tibetan Buddhist teacher, escaped the Chinese invasion by hiking across the snow-bound Himalayas (1987). He did not escape by pretending he was in Hawaii. He and his colleagues had no other choice but to deal with the present situation and each of the obstacles. However obvious this may seem, as educators we deny the present much of the time by designing the "perfect" curriculum and forgetting to consult with our students, the members of their communities, and their future employers. The society in which our students live, work, and confront their particular challenges often becomes peripheral or even irrelevant to our curricular considerations. Whether through omission or commission, when we ignore their world and how they perceive us and the purpose of education, we assume to know what our students need although we know so little about them. We assume that our current knowledge base is the best for them. In other words, we often map out educational plans for our students that place knowledge in Hawaii, when they are scaling the Himalayas. Instead, we envision a curriculum that both grows out of the life experiences of the students being educated as W. E. B. Du Bois (1973: 92) states, and also prepares them for the life they will experience in the future.

As educators, we learn to connect, synthesize and interpret our own ideas with other people's scholarship, usually within a European and European American framework. Moreover we learn to do this within a particular disciplinary structure and usually we are encouraged to keep our expertise within that discipline. These boundaries can severely limit our ability to integrate our knowledge creatively and productively with other disciplines and with other cultural knowledge bases. The Association of American Colleges report went so far as to argue that discipline loyalty was one of "the chief causes for the disarray of the curriculum and the demise of good teaching" (1991: 20). In this chapter we propose that the faculty's skills in connecting, synthesizing, and interpreting knowledge be applied within a much wider interdisciplinary structure while at the same time reconstituting the knowledge base to focus on the past, present, and future lives of our students, including their experiences with their culture(s), communities, gender, sexual orientation, and class.

Implementing the kinds of changes suggested by all the authors in this book will require a massive political power struggle whether we want to admit it or not. Many people with power will attempt to maintain, expand, and refine that which they control (Bourdieu and Passeron 1990) despite the demographic and educational imperatives to change. We will suggest some strategies for ensuring that the change process is both inclusive and substantive.

THE IMPERATIVES TO CHANGE

All of the authors in this book argue persuasively that change is imperative, that the current Eurocentrically laden version of college curriculum is miseducating our diverse student body, and that uncovering and developing the rich resources embedded in the multicultural perspective is the greatest intellectual challenge of the twenty-first century. Our proposals for curricular transformation incorporate what we see as the five imperatives for change presented by the other authors. We also draw upon the scholarship of the many excellent writers who have contributed to the area of multicultural curriculum (Banks 1975, 1988, 1991; Banks and Lynch 1986; Bennett 1990; Gollnick and Chinn 1990; Pai 1990; Sleeter 1991) as well as those in the area of interdisciplinary or learning communities (Bricker 1989; Gabelnick et al. 1990; Kuh et al. 1991; Smith and MacGregor 1993).

1. *The demographic imperative*: If change in higher education is a matter of self-preservation (Hodgkinson) and if new environments have a way of modifying old cultures (King), then the inevitable changes in demographics make a multicultural curriculum imperative.
2. *The personal imperative*: If the "objectification of knowledge has become a matter of power and privilege" (King) and if curriculum, to be relevant to an increasing multicultural population, must be intensely personal (King, Karenga, and Morales-Nadal), then curriculum must focus on the human experiences with culture, gender, class, and sexual orientation. In addition, faculty need to be held both personally and professionally accountable for relating to their students' experiences and for their students learning a multicultural curriculum. This imperative implies as well that faculty need to be held accountable for honestly knowing their own experiences and biases.
3. *The reality imperative*: If we can no longer afford to study a desired reality (King), then curriculum must examine what is. If education can no longer become the tool for creating certainty and simplicity, then it should increase (not decrease) the uncertainties and complexities of the world (King). If we are to educate students to become effective and contributing members in our pluralistic society and the global village, then we need specifically to prepare them to deal with the world's problems, or at least the problems in their own communities.
4. *The information imperative*: Given the information explosion, educators can no

longer expect students to master certain subjects. We should be imparting critical frameworks that help students decide what kind of information to gather and investigate and how to understand, question, and explore that knowledge, particularly as it relates to and impacts on other known information. These critical frameworks need to inform students about the self, other, community, and the universe (King and Karenga).

5. *The interdisciplinary imperative*: In an increasingly complex world, rigid departmental borders may be obstructing the students' pursuit of knowledge. Students may need educational structures which represent their educational purpose, which is creatively to connect and construct knowledge across disciplines. We need to consider interdisciplinary structures that transcend traditional boundaries (King and Bowser).

A MULTICULTURAL INTERDISCIPLINARY APPROACH TO CURRICULUM

The Multicultural Curriculum Lenses

We believe in a college curriculum that is not a pre-packaged knowledge base to be deterministically handed over to the students. Rather, education necessitates the process of questioning what all cultural frameworks bring to our understanding and experiences with the world. We cannot be steeped in one culture and claim to have a universal education (Banks 1975, 1988, 1991; Banks and Lynch 1986). This is exactly what the Eurocentric model does, as illustrated by Banks (1975). It views mostly European and European American knowledge, both present and past, as the universal standard and then critiques and understands all other cultures by that standard. With this critical lens the knowledge by and about Europeans and European Americans (especially upperclass, heterosexual Northern Europeans and Northern European American males) is viewed as superior and acceptable while all other perspectives for understanding knowledge are most often considered spurious, insignificant, wrong, or are self-righteously ignored or avoided. [1]

Banks' original conception of this model (see Figure 11.1) works well to present the basic vision of multicultural education, but it leaves out some necessary components. One might assume that there is only one Eurocentric, Afrocentric, etc. perspective and it either excludes or is all inclusive of gender, class, and sexual orientation. While Banks' other models support a more inclusive framework, the model shown in Figure 11.1 does little to discourage a reductionist view. Moreover, by placing the social or historical event in the center, departments of physics, biology, chemistry, music, mathematics, etc. are visually excluded. Just as the Eurocentric male perspective is rich with variety, contradictions, and multiple interpretations and arguments over minute details in the arts, letters, and social sciences, so too are other perspectives. They have just not received the support and attention of the Eurocentric male perspective. We have revised and added to the Banks' model to represent these intersections and

Figure 11.1
Four Models of Teaching Ethnic Studies

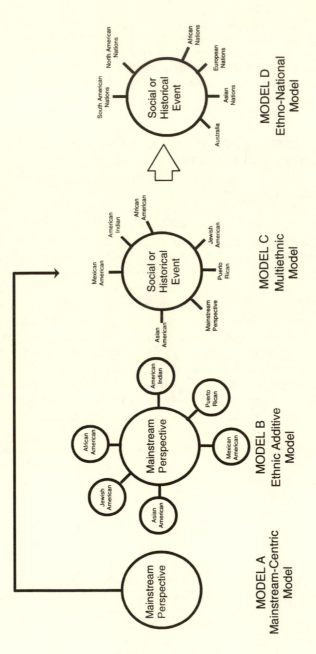

Source: James Banks, *Teaching Strategies for Ethnic Studies*, (Boston: Allyn and Bacon, 1991) p. 17. Reprinted with permission of the author.

complexities. The model shown in Figure 11.2 makes explicit what may be implicit in the Banks model.

The multicultural model (see Figure 11.2), again based on our revision of James Banks' model (1975), places the event in the center and then sees that event or phenomenon through the various cultural lenses. Any event, object, or phenomenon, whether it be physical, mathematical, social, historical, emotional, psychological, communication etc., becomes the central focus. From this position the various cultural, gender, class and sexual orientation perspectives are overlaid and intersected. Culture, gender, class, and sexual orientation become critical theoretical lenses that invite analysis and explanation. More questions than answers will be raised. If technology, for example, is placed in the center, then we can ask, what do we know, what can we learn about how the women in specific indigenous Native American tribes view technology? What do they see as the possible rewards, uses, drawbacks? How are their views similar and different from the males in the various tribes? What happens when we intersect class issues with tribal and gender experiences?

The clusters of circles around each major culture group in Figure 11.2 represent not only the rich cultural differences between each major group but also the myriad of perspectives that can exist within one group. The Asian American lens, for example, necessitates particularizing which Asian American cultural perspective is being used. We have been studying the fine distinctions between European American male paradigms for centuries. This model visually represents the need to explore and understand the many distinctions and variations which exist within each group of intersections. By intersecting the various cultural perspectives with class, gender, and sexual orientation perspectives, we can study and see (even if we don't yet understand) the many-faceted complexities within each of the communities.

Honestly seeking and struggling with this "new" knowledge can become part of the public discourse and thus available as the focus of study for faculty, students and community members. The growing debate between the conservatives and the liberals in the African American community, for example, would surface on such issues as educational philosophy, immigration, civil rights, homosexuality, and the growing AIDS crises. Additionally, we would be able to see the Latino communities' differences on such issues as bilingual education, assimilation, immigration, and gender roles. Moreover, when Asian Americans become the critical lens, we can understand in a far more sophisticated way the controversies over the shaping of a shared political identity as opposed to the diverse ethnic identities and divisions. Such an understanding will necessarily include the class differences between the Vietnamese, Laotian, and Cambodian refugees, well-financed immigrants, and the second through fourth generation Chinese and Japanese Americans who have experienced ongoing oppression in the United States.[2] These are just a smattering of the kaleidoscopic possibilities for studying and teaching the controversies and challenges within ethnic groups, including the myriad of legacies, intricacies, and current experiences of each group.

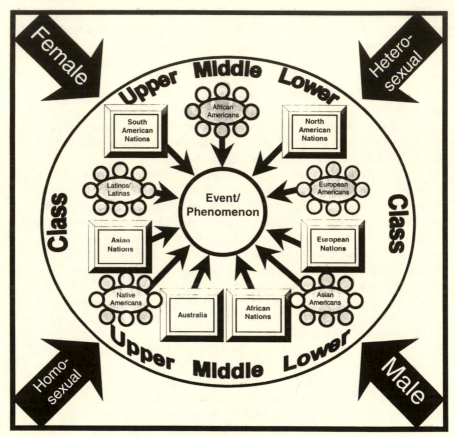

Figure 11.2
Teaching by Using Event/Phenomenon

Clearly, a curriculum founded on this type of model will increase the quantity and quality of knowledge that we expect students to acquire and faculty first to learn and then impart. This framework draws different issues to the foreground. It not only offers other lenses in which to understand our existing knowledge base, but also it serves as a general guide for where to explore, expand, deepen, and reconstitute the knowledge base that qualifies as a university education.

An Interdisciplinary Structure for Multicultural Curriculum

We assume that education must prepare our students for effective participation in an ever-changing multicultural and multiracial society. This means that students need the tools to investigate and contribute to solving society's most pressing problems. For us, such a goal must involve implementing an interdisciplinary team teaching approach. The interdisciplinary structure has strong and articulate support (ACC 1991; Banks 1991; Gabelnick et al. 1990; Giroux 1991; Schmitz 1992), many structural variations, and is currently being practiced in different forms across the country (Gabelnick et al. 1990). By *interdisciplinary* we mean that learning is "organized around specific intellectual themes or tasks" (National Institution of Education 1984).

We extend and revise James Banks' interdisciplinary model (1991) to propose what Gabelnick, et al. refer to as a "coordinated studies approach" (1990: 28-31). By placing the problem, issue, or theme in the center, the discipline knowledge base is treated as lenses with which to understand and work with the center problem (see Figure 11.3). For example, what would happen if we take freedom, which was a reoccurring theme throughout the previous chapters and represents one of humanity's most pressing issues, and examine it from the various disciplinary as well as cultural, gender, class, and sexual orientation lenses? Currently many nations are asking, what is freedom? How do we balance individual freedom with community and global responsibility? What is the relationship between personal and public freedom? By placing freedom in the center, one or a series of courses could be developed that looked at freedom from a variety of disciplines, such as the psychological, sociological, biological, artistic, and/or legal dimensions. No single course should be taught using only one disciplinary lens. In addition to these disciplinary lenses, freedom would be looked at in each case through the cultural, gender, class, and sexual orientation lenses as well. In other words, what does freedom mean to African American women, European American male homosexuals, etc.?

Let us place a traditional subject, such as "music" in the center. An interdisciplinary teaching team might include a physicist, a mathematician, a sociologist, a musician, and a historian. Together they would study and teach music and its impact on society and the individual while using the various disciplines and cultures as critical lenses. The relative importance of music to the different cul-

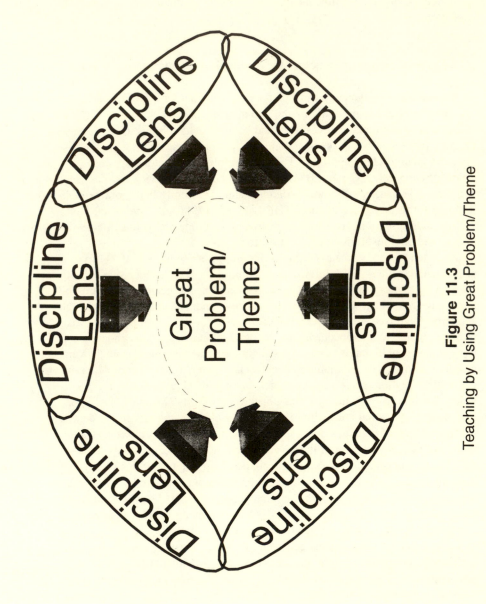

Figure 11.3
Teaching by Using Great Problem/Theme

tures, socioeconomic classes, genders, and sexual orientations could also be explored.

College committees would have the delicious task of deciding what constitutes society's most pressing problems, the most important controversies that divide our individual communities, and the greatest challenges humans face as we grow and change. These committees would have to decide which disciplinary lenses might be the most relevant for the student's knowledge base. One of the problems or issues, we would argue, that must be placed in the center is what constitutes a pluralistic society in a democratic nation. What should be the elements of a common core that holds a multicultural society together? What is equity and how do you distribute scarce resources?

A great problems/issues/themes approach naturally raises questions about an appropriate academic structure in which to contain such an approach. Are academic departments and majors really necessary? Perhaps not (at least not at the undergraduate level). More and more, business and industry and community agencies need people who are broadly educated and who can work collaboratively and creatively with others. To us, this means being able to study and draw upon many disciplinary and culturally based lenses. We are not ready to propose completely flattening out academic departments, but we are not alone in our concerns "that deep seated structural [traditional] factors weaken the quality of undergraduate learning and inhibit the development of community" (Smith and MacGregor 1993: 8).

Departmental and school structure and the vertical approval process for curriculum and budget appear to promote disciplinary defensiveness and hinder curricular coherence. A move away from the departmental structure toward one that reflects a great problems/themes approach might simplify efforts to bring various disciplines together to focus on particular problem areas. Smith and MacGregor argue that "learning communities directly confront multiple problems plaguing undergraduate education: fragmentation . . . , isolation of students . . . , lack of meaningful connection-building between classes; the need for greater intellectual interaction between students, faculty and lack of sustained opportunities for faculty development" (1993: 8). The purpose of a multicultural interdisciplinary approach to education is to create curriculum and intellectual coherence that is personally and socially relevant (Smith and MacGregor 1993). Faculty placed in interdisciplinary learning communities would be forced to approach their knowledge base as one critical lens with which to understand significant societal problems, phenomena, or issues. This approach necessitates team teaching in interdisciplinary, intergender, and intercultural teams. Faculty teams would model for students the importance of their personal and professional connections to the knowledge being taught as well as how the many critical lenses (cultural, gender, class, sexual orientation, and disciplinary) can be brought together to understand and creatively address the problem or issue under study.

If genuine (as in "really being what it is said to be," *New World Dictionary*, 1976: 583) educational synthesis will break down traditional departmental and school boundaries within the students' minds, then why not provide external structures that encourage the genuine synthesis of multiple perspectives? In addition, the multicultural and interdisciplinary focus we propose increases the possibility of involving members from the communities outside of the college in the curricular development process. Although academics know a lot, it would be foolhardy to attempt determine what the great problems or great events list should look like without extensive and ongoing consultation with various elements of the extended communities in which the college exists. No matter how many academic disciplines are brought to bear on a problem or event, an authentic (as in reliable and trustworthy) curriculum will only be achieved when knowledge has some use and validity for the communities in which our students live and work.

STRATEGIES FOR CHANGE

Community Involvement

When a university seriously values its community as a potential advisory body for assisting in the development of curriculum, there are any number of ways to constitute such a committee as long as the committee is truly multicultural. The criteria for a multicultural committee include equal representation for each of the communities of color, homosexuals, heterosexuals, males, females, and upper, middle, and lower classes in such a way that no single group dominates. Faculty and administrators need to recognize and honestly consult with representatives from the community, students, alumni, future employers, and even legislators. Each of these constituencies can inform us of their own experiences and needs. We are not suggesting that these folks design the actual curriculum. What we are suggesting is that they be honestly listened to and engaged in dialogue.

A Diverse Governing Board: People of color, women, gay/lesbians, and other diverse populations will have to be included as trustees, regents, and overseers on governing boards of colleges and universities if significant change is to occur. These are the people appointed by governors and recommended by the wealthy. They hire and fire presidents, formulate broad goals and objectives, approve budgets, and see to it that their constituencies are well represented. These boards obviously need to be genuinely diverse. We suggest exploring the idea of regionally elected boards of governors designed to ensure significant diversity, so much so that no single group has the majority.

A Diverse Community Advisory Board: A diverse community advisory board is needed to give input into the development of curriculum. This may sound revolutionary, but it is not. We only have to look to the extension division of most colleges to see one model for consideration. Most extension programs are cash-and-carry operations that live and die on the satisfaction of the consumer. Individuals and groups are continually making suggestions about courses and expressing their needs and even their dissatisfactions. To continue in existence, extension programs must pay close attention to the customer. Although our colleges cannot function totally like extension programs, we do believe that we can respond much better to community needs if we become more customer conscious (and it may even be financially more productive). Some version of the extension process, in which students, community representatives, businesses, and government agencies are given the opportunity to sit with faculty and offer input into the development of curriculum and programs, is necessary if we are to respond adequately to the needs of our increasingly diverse student populations.

Faculty Development

The multicultural interdisciplinary model for curricular transformation that we have proposed requires that faculty must change what, how, and when they teach and with whom they teach.

Rewards and Disincentives: Our experiences working with faculty have led us to believe, as one editor once told us, that getting faculty too change is like herding cats. For faculty to change, they need incentives, rewards, changed expectations, and even denials of scarce resources (i.e., promotion, tenure, grants, etc.). To make both rewards and punishments a reality, we suggest that the first area of focus should be the promotion, tenure, and retention document. If institutions of higher education are to be truly multicultural, then the value of diversity must be reflected not just in the missions and goals statement but in all policies, including the promotion, tenure, and retention document. While diversity and service to the community are showing up as a criterion in important faculty documents, they tend to be peripheral to the criteria considered most important when making determinations. The multicultural perspective should be core in all policies both in word and deed. If faculty are not demonstrating how they are addressing such issues in their classes, research, and publications, they should not be recruited, promoted, retained, or tenured. Perhaps this sounds harsh, but we don't know how else to measure success.

Service to the community, especially diverse communities, will have to be seen as exceptionally meritorious and should be a primary criterion for evaluation. Moreover, members of the community receiving the service will need to be a significant voice in determining what is considered meritorious service to the community.

To become a genuinely inclusive institution, we will need to develop strategies for confronting those who continue to perpetuate racism, sexism, homophobia, and classism in the academy. Presently, in all but the most egregious cases, faculty invoke the rule of silence. They ignore, rationalize away, or only mildly chastise those who act out their racism, sexism, classism, or homophobia against students and other faculty and staff.

We propose that a faculty fairness committee, balanced for culture, gender, sexual orientation, and class, be established to hear and study cases involving charges of exclusionary behavior. These committees should be empowered to make recommendations ranging from reprimands to specialized training to dismissal from the institution. Those eligible to serve on such committees should have a history and current practice for understanding and sensitivity to the issues of gender, culture, class, and sexual orientation. We are talking about a core committee that is well publicized and supported by the central administration and academic governance, not just another rubber stamp. The difference between most faculty fairness committees and the one we suggest is that this committee will gather and study the covert and civil forms of individual and institutional oppression and exclusion in the academy as well as the more formal and overt forms of exclusion.

Expanding the Knowledge Base: Once multicultural populations and equity are covalued in the university, then faculty need the means to become multiculturally literate and competitive. This, we believe, will require increased development opportunities for them. Faculty must be given the time and resources (including mentors and the best scholarship available) to explore, study, and develop new course materials. Colleges must make multicultural literacy their highest priority. Longterm faculty development programs will be needed so that faculty can develop new course materials, teaching strategies, assessment procedures, and classroom management techniques that reflect sensitivity to the multicultural perspective. Summer institutes are an excellent vehicle for providing faculty with a sustained period of time to develop curriculum and explore alternative teaching strategies.

Faculty need to begin by studying in multicultural, intergender, interdisciplinary teams if they are to teach in interdisciplinary, multicultural teams. We also recommend using Women's studies and Ethnic studies faculty as valuable resources. Faculty in these programs are interdisciplinary by nature and have developed expertise on ethnic-specific materials intersected with gender, class, and sexual orientation. They could share their materials, but their sharing needs to be valued by the institution. Mentor or master teacher programs could be developed with Women's and Ethnic studies faculty pairing up with other faculty.

Professors should be trained to use alternative delivery systems. Computer conferencing, two-way live distant education and video instruction are already breaking down traditional time/space boundaries for instruction. However, we need to learn to use these new technologies so that effective multicultural curriculum and interdisciplinary teaching and intercultural sensitivity will increase.

Reconstituting Faculty: Of course, colleges need to do everything possible to recruit and retain a diverse faculty with terminal degrees. But does it really take a Ph.D. to teach in an institution of higher education? We think not. In fact, a significant amount of the current teaching that does occur in the academy is already being done by graduate students or lecturers with Master's degrees.

A certain percentage of appointments to the faculty could be made based on criteria other than completion of the Ph.D. Actually, business and professional schools have led the way in this approach. Highly qualified practitioners in business, social work, science, criminal justice, art, communication, etc. are regularly sought after in prestigious colleges and universities. We believe that institutionalizing such a practice would improve both the quality of instruction and learning and the affirmative action records of many institutions of higher education. By using the team teaching approach, highly professional non-Ph.D.s teamed up with other interdisciplinary Ph.D.'s would enrich the learning and synthesis. While Ph.D.'s know a great deal and constitute the standard for higher education, we recognize that seasoned professionals, even wise community people, also have something to offer us in higher education. We are not talking about mere guest lecture or one-time appearances. Rather we want colleges to institutionalize the expertise of nonuniversity faculty into the team teaching and interdisciplinary structure. We recognize that such a policy runs the risk of institutionalizing a group of second-class faculty, but if the expertise of these new faculty is truly valued, then surely this concern can be overcome.

We are not recommending a move away from the use of Ph.D.s in teaching. Rather, we are saying that if we are to provide our students with a relevant education, we will have to rely on a more diverse teaching pool, which includes diversity of experiences. Since there are many ways of knowing, there are many ways of teaching and many ways of being qualified to teach. As college educators, we need to do a better job of recognizing that there are different ways to qualify as a teacher and that in order to select teachers with credentials outside of traditional academia, we will need input from the communities in which our institutions are located.

The changes needed to create an inclusive institution are everyone's responsibility, but being aware of the folk saying "everybody's business is nobody's business," we know that it will take both the formal and informal leadership of our institutions to step forward. Lone administrators and small groups of committed faculty have been and can be somewhat effective. But we assert that the necessary paradigmatic changes can only happen with a wide and deep collaboration among presidents, vice presidents, deans, department chairs, faculty leaders, and followers. We describe three paths for just such a collaboration.

Budget Priority

The budget is the "straw that stirs the drink" of education, to evoke a phrase from the legendary baseball star Reggie Jackson. While Jackson's analogy may say something about his sense of self-importance, it fits when applied to the role that budget priorities play in establishing educational policy. Policy is often discussed in isolation from the budgets, yet the truth is that budget allocations determine policy. Some policies are legally mandated, but most are established by (1), not touching sacred cows, and (2), those in power debating whose priority is more important and making allocations based on the stronger power and perhaps the stronger argument. Essential items receive full funding, while nonpriority items get less.

The budget is a highly political document in higher education. Of course, the bills must be paid, but what bills should be accumulated in the first place? You can tell an institution's values by its budget. While this notion may appear self evident, let us focus for a moment on affirmative action. College after college gives lip service with glowing pronouncements to being an affirmative action employer yet the budget tells another story. All too often, what we see is a lone affirmative action officer with little support and even less power or respect monitoring the affirmative action efforts of the academy. We see colleges claiming to be on the cutting edge of multicultural curriculum, yet their budgets are woefully inadequate to support such claims.

We believe that if institutions of higher education are to make significant gains in creating a truly inclusive and multicultural curriculum, faculty, staff, students, and campus climate, then colleges must (1) build such an intent into the mission and goals statement and, (2) link all budget decisions to the priorities established in the mission statement for the college. Until this linkage occurs, mission and goals statements will be little more than paper products gathering dust on vice presidents' and associate deans' book selves. The following guidelines are suggestions for how to link the budget to the missions and goals statement:

1. *Strategic planning.* Write the mission and goals statement to make educating diverse students in a multicultural and multiracial society a priority. This statement should include (1) a truly diverse faculty, administration, and student body in terms of race, gender, sexual orientation and class; (2) a multiculturally literate faculty who can teach their subject matter from a variety of cultural perspectives; and (3) a faculty that honors students' different learning styles by using a multitude of teaching and assessment strategies. If administrators and faculty are serious about this goal, they will link it directly to hiring practices and curriculum and then policy will stir the budget.
2. *Establish accountability.* The president should charge the vice presidents, deans and department chairs, and all budget committee members with developing a plan to link the budget to such a mission and goals statement. The relationship of the mission and goals statement to the budget should be demonstrated by attaching a budget amount to each goal. The budget officer needs to make available to all the exact dollar amounts being spent on each diversity, affirmative action, and multicultural curriculum effort. Such a report can be used as a barometer to monitor the progress of an institution in reaching its goals and objectives.
3. *Make every unit accountable.* Every interdisciplinary and disciplinary unit in the college should be required to develop and have approved goals for integrating race/culture, gender, class and sexual orientation diversity into every aspect of its domain, including staffing, policy, practices, curriculum, promotion, hiring, assessment, teaching, and managing styles. Even such aspects as holidays and schedules should be included.
4. *Link budget requests to mission and goals.* All budget requests should demonstrate how the money will directly relate to fulfilling both the mission and goals of

the colleges and the particular disciplinary and interdisciplinary unit's goals for interdisciplinary and multicultural integration. This recognition will necessitate individual and group sacrifice. What will the dominant group give up for an inclusive multicultural campus community?

Assessment

The massive changes we are suggesting are potentially volatile and politically risky. Prior to making these types of changes, a substantive needs assessment of the campus and community climate will have to be undertaken. All of the different cultural, gender, class, sexual orientation, disciplinary, and community-based concerns need to be surveyed, listened to, and assessed for the current level of inclusion and exclusion. Who is feeling the most protected by the current system and the most threatened by the proposed changes, and who is likely to cause the most trouble and be the strongest ally? How will the various communities perceive the proposed changes?

Any such assessment needs to be done by a multicultural, multiracial institutional team. No single major cultural group should dominate this team. The team should gather responses from the major cultural/racial, gender, class, and sexual orientation groups within the disciplines and support units in the university and the major communities of interest in the surrounding communities. In other words, the assessment questions need to be placed as the center focus, with significant numbers from each of the major groups (ethnic/racial, gender, class, sexual orientation, and discipline) questioned for their perceptions and experiences with the college, its curriculum, faculty, students, policies, etc. Whenever possible, we recommend strongly that the interviewers be members of the same ethnic/racial, gender, class, sexual orientation, discipline, and community group as the people being interviewed.

Such an assessment needs to focus on the contextual factors, the communicated messages (both public and private), and the internal responses and experiences of those being interviewed. If done in a comprehensive and sensitive manner, the outcome of this type of assessment will chart the health (cultural, gender, sexual orientation, discipline, and relationships with the community) of an institution. The perspectives and experiences that will be brought into the open will become the data collected. This information is likely to be complicated and messy with few easy solutions, but patterns of exclusion will become apparent. Moreover, an assessment by a multicultural team representing diverse constituencies within the academy can generate curiosity about the results while also building consensus for a change process.

Once the areas with the greatest potential for perpetuating the most exclusion are identified and analyzed, then problems need to be prioritized and both long and short range action plans developed, including proposed time lines, budget projections, structural and strategic changes, and assessment and accountability systems. While there are as many paths up the mountain as there are problems and people, common knowledge tells us that slippage back down is far easier, especially if there is no commitment to hold faculty and administrators accountable. Moreover, as the change process is occurring, regularly scheduled focus group assessments need to be done in order to make adjustments and model an inclusive process. To some extent, the process we've outlined is both a precursor to and an attendant part of the strategic planning process that has been so popular in higher education.

Pilot Programs

Pilot programs can serve as a bridge between the assessment process and a comprehensive innovative program. Presidents, vice presidents, deans, disciplinary and interdisciplinary coordinators can make funds available on a competitive basis for innovative programs that promote diversity and affirmative action and work with communities of color, women, and homosexuals. These programs can serve as the prototypes for the eventual comprehensive changes. We list a few examples.

1. Begin a master teacher program with Ethnic studies and Women's studies faculty team teaching courses for faculty who want to teach from a more multicultural perspective. Since these programs are already interdisciplinary in nature, faculty will be learning to study and teach from an interdisciplinary and multicultural perspective.
2. Establish a self-contained program for a special group of student (e.g., full time workers), whereby they can receive a bachelor's degree in four to five years. Their courses are predetermined and the students attend all the same classes. Such a program would require the teaching faculty to base curriculum around relevant societal issues and team teach by approaching those problems from a variety of disciplinary and multicultural perspectives.
3. Begin a partner's program with community agencies and businesses whereby chief executive officers or other designated representatives team teach with faculty in appropriate courses and students do work assignments in the community agency or business. Another variation is to have college faculty teach college courses in a community-based organization.
4. Develop a community-based program that involves student in-service learning with low-income communities of color. Students, faculty, and community agency personnel could develop a course that couples service with academic assignments.

Pilot programs such as these allow a group of innovative faculty to work through the major problems and make inroads into designing cooperative and comprehensive programs. While many such innovative programs are already in existence, what we propose requires the strong financial and political support of the faculty and administration and a serious commitment to integrating the successes into the mainstream educational package.

CONCLUSION

The suggestions we have made are not the end-all and be-all for higher education in a multicultural society. They're not even all that revolutionary. Rather they represent our reading of the state of education today and our hope for a more coherent multiculturally inclusive curriculum knowledge base and educational community. We put them forth as possible paths away from the narrow monocultural paradigms. We hope our suggestions will fuel your commitment to struggle with the issues and to genuinely educate yourself and your students for the multicultural twenty-first century.

The strategies we suggest will work. So will a hundred other ways, once the courage is mustered to struggle. To struggle in the spirit of Frederick Douglass, the great abolitionist, means being willing to agitate and be agitated, to plow up our personal and collective ground, to endure the thunder and lightning and the awful roar of the ocean's many waters (1857). Only then can we have progress and freedom and only then will the possibilities lay out before us "like the empty sky [with] no boundaries. Yet . . . right in this place, very profound and clear" (Cheng-tao Ke 1957: 145).

NOTES

1. James Banks (1975, 1988, 1991; Banks and Lynch 1986) present many models graphically representing how we should address multicultural curriculum reform. We share with you the one that we feel is the most visionary.

2. Kathleen Wong, personal communication, June 16, 1993. These ideas are being explored in a major research in progress by Wong, a doctoral student at Arizona State University, Tempe, Arizona. The personal communications took place in Berkeley, California.

REFERENCES

Association of American Colleges. 1991. *The Challenge of Connecting Learning: Project on Liberal Learning, Study-in-Depth, and the Arts and Sciences Major*. Vol. 1. Washington, DC: Association of American Colleges.

Banks, James. 1975. *Multiethnic Education: Practices and Promises*. Bloomington, IN: The Phi Delta Kappa Educational Foundation.

Banks, James. 1988. *Multiethnic Education: Theory and Practice*, 2nd ed. Boston: Allyn and Bacon.

Banks, James. 1991. *Teaching Strategies for Ethnic Studies*. 5th. ed. Boston: Allyn and Bacon.

Banks, James, and J. Lynch. eds. 1986. *Multicultural Education in Western Societies*. New York: Praeger.

Bell, Derrick. 1992. *Faces at the Bottom of the Well: The Permanence of Racism*. New York: Basic Books.

Bennett, C. I. 1990. *Comprehensive Multicultural Education: Theory and Practice.* 2nd ed. Boston: Allyn and Bacon.

Bourdieu, Pierre, and J. C. Passeron. 1990. *Reproduction in Education, Society and Culture,* 2nd ed. London: Sage Publications.

Cheng-tao Ke. 1957. *The Way of Zen.* New York: Vintage Books.

Douglass, Frederick. 1857. Speech at Canandaigua, New York, August 3, 1857. As quoted in John Bartlett, 1992, *Familiar Quotations,* 16th ed. Boston: Little, Brown and Company.

Du Bois, W. E. B. 1973. *The Education of Black People: Ten Critiques, 1906-1960.* H. Aptheker, ed. New York: Monthly Review Press.

Gabelnick, F., et al. 1990. *Learning Communities: Creating Connections Among Students, Faculty and Disciplines.* San Francisco: Jossey-Bass.

Giroux, H. A., ed. 1991. *Postmodernism, Feminism, and Cultural Politics: Redrawing Educational Boundaries.* Albany: State University of New York Press.

Harding, Vincent. 1991. *Hope and History: Why We Must Share the Story of the Movement.* Maryknoll, NY: Orbis Books.

Lenth, C. S. 1992. "Curriculum Contracts: Restructuring Public Policies to Meet Contemporary Educational Needs." *Liberal Education: Meeting the Needs of Diverse Adult Learners.* 78(4): 26-31.

Marden, Charles E., et al. 1992. *Minorities in American Society,* 6th ed. New York: HarperCollins.

Pai, Y. 1990. *Cultural Foundations of Education.* Columbus, OH: Merrill Publishing Co.

Schmitz, Betty. 1992. *Core Curriculum and Cultural Pluralism: A Guide for Campus Planners.* Washington, DC: Association of American Colleges.

Sleeter, C. E., ed. 1991. *Empowerment through Multicultural Education.* Albany: State University of New York Press.

Smith, B. L. and J. T. MacGregor. 1993. "What is Collaborative Learning?" *Washington Center News* 7(3): 3-11.

Takagi, Dana Y. 1992. *The Retreat from Race: Asian Americans and Racial Politics.* New Brunswick, NJ: Rutgers University Press.

Trungpa, Chogyam. 1987. *Born in Tibet.* London: Unwin Paperbacks.

Watzlawick, Paul, et al. 1967. *Pragmatics of Human Communication: A Study of Interactional Patterns, Pathologies, and Paradoxes.* New York: W. W. Norton and Company.

West, Cornell. 1993. *Beyond Eurocentrism and Multiculturalism: Prophetic Thought in Post-Modern Times.* Vols. 1 and 2. Monroe, ME: Common Courage Press.

Conclusion:
Toward the Multicultural University

Benjamin P. Bowser
Terry Jones
Gale Auletta Young

As we complete this book some education news is not encouraging: The numbers of African American and Native Americans attending colleges continue to
decline; the cost of a college education is going up while federal student support
is declining; highly talented senior faculty will soon retire and are not likely to
be replaced any time soon; and racial conflict is still all too common on American college campuses (Gilley 1991).

That middle-aged and middle-class white male instructor discussed in the
introduction to this book may see parallels to his classroom situation and the
collapse of the Greek or Roman civilization—the barbarians will no longer be
kept on the fringes of the empire. Of course, he is not alone. There are women,
African Americans, Latinos, Asians, and others who teach, are scholars, and are
also fearful of what the future may bring. All who are serious about the teaching
and scholarship that they are devoting their lives to wonder about their work's
effect, longitude, and accuracy. They are also worried about the future of the
university (Noley 1991). It really does not matter what college, university, or
institution you teach at or how well or poorly you are paid. Teaching and contributing to any body of knowledge is a highly personal, life-long, and all-con-
suming activity. What you teach and publish is a part of you and your making
sense of the world. So to have seemingly marginally qualified students or other
scholars challenge the relevance of your life's work, question its authenticity,
and suggest that you have missed points of importance strikes at the core of who
you are and what you do.

Most of us in the academy have responded to these challenges emotionally
and personally. Camps of the like-minded have circled their wagons around
their respective turfs and have fired acts of faith at those who challenge them—
Eurocentrists, Afrocentrists, multiculturalists, feminists and so on. To get along
from day to day in such a politically charged environment requires walking
away from any number of potential battles and learning what to and not to say

depending on the company—multiple versions of political correctness. This is not education. But we contend that this is no reason to look back at the good old days when students were better qualified (fewer and less diverse). Then virtually no one in the academy challenged relevance, questioned authenticity, and had other perspectives from which to challenge what everyone knew and agreed to. In either case, then and now, real learning is the exception rather than the rule. There were then and are today few students making discoveries about themselves and the world, and there are still a lot of sacred cows walking around—old ones and new ones. Students are receiving degrees, but it is questionable how much better they are made from the experience.

Fortunately, there is another view and a bigger picture. We are in the midst of a period of rapid social change, both here and overseas. Norms, values, customs, and social contracts that have sustained us in a multitude of communities, including the university, are in transition. These changes are not due to one or the other point of view winning any ideological struggle. The changes that are happening are due largely to historic accidents of population growth, of the emergence of a world economy, and of decline in the effectiveness of national states. While conservatives may see the optimal world in the past and view change as social decry, those who attended our two multicultural conferences saw otherwise. Change is an opportunity to broaden the mission of the university to address more effectively the national and international challenges of the twenty-first century and to improve the quality of instruction and outcomes. We want a university or college education to mean all that it can, to be an essential rite of passage into many worlds and to improve students as a rule rather than as an exception.

MULTICULTURAL EDUCATION

What the authors and editors of this book point out is that the university cannot continue to be simply a reflection of the European experience and interpretations of the world. We propose a process by which the university can transform from an essentially Eurocentric institution to one that is multicultural. No one in this collection suggested that knowledge from and about Europe and European peoples is not important. What everyone agreed to was that it is not sufficient. It is possible for well-run, effective educational institutions with quality programs to exist and to make major contributions to the human community without European studies as the central and core curriculum. As Jones and Auletta-Young suggested, the university can have a series of area and cultural foci. Students are to master their own as well as one or two other social cultures. There might even be common themes across areas and cultures at different points in a student's program (See Chapter 10).

But you protest: It would be impossible to have enough trained faculty to staff such an organization; the knowledge is not sufficiently broad enough or developed for most groups, and it would be administratively impossible to run such a university—what would hold it together? Our proposals in Part Three suggested an evolutionary transition. If it became the mission and intent of enough institutions to train a domestically and internationally expert cross-cultural faculty, eventually such faculty would exist. And once they completed their training, they would be in great demand. Again, as Donald Fixico proposed, if it became the mission and intent of enough institutions to explore, reconstruct, codify, and disseminate knowledge about Native Americans or any other groups of people, this too could become real. Finally, administration of such an institution is possible because there will be a basis of unity for the university community other than the budget or a common core Eurocentric curriculum. We propose that a new and more appropriate common core will become the advancement of multicultural knowledge and communities.

Advancing domestic and international multiculturalism within the university will not be celebrating an endless series of ethnic holidays, food samplings, and recitations of oppressive histories. It will be as it should, teachers and scholars from many different backgrounds coming together as communities of teachers, scientists, and scholars. While each may come from a different place and social context, they will be united around not only their disciplinary lines but their cross-cultural and cross-community training and experiences as well. The search for the human spirit, for ways to improve society and the quality of life will not come from one culture, one regional history, or one social class. Working in collaboration across disciplines and cultures will be essential to address common problems that affect everyone. For example, conditions for African Americans in the United States cannot improve or further deteriorate and not also affect every other American ethnic group. In the same way, improvement or deterioration in the life conditions for South American peasants or Muslim women in the Middle East cannot happen without affecting life in U.S. cities and urban service industries. While we are different, we are all now interdependent. No single national or international community can stand alone and affect no one else.

So we will have to come together across disciplines, national boundaries, languages, histories, and cultures. This will call for a new dialogue, new regard for each other, and new involvement in each other's worlds as students, teachers, and invited visitors rather than as colonialists, apologists, or one of many centrists out to make the world according to only one's own historic image and likeness. In this sort of dialogue, it will no longer be necessary to view other cultures from a standpoint of neutrality or to see them as all relative. Any belief, attitude, practice or tradition that cannot be questioned violates the essential spirit of inquiry that is the university community. Nor will a cultural practice be an excuse for intragroup exploitation or oppression. We will be able to question each other as never before because the study and knowledge of any one culture group will not be left up to those native to the group, and educated discourse on all group practices and circumstances will come from comparative knowledge and first-hand experience. What makes today's commentary on race in the United States and on national cultures in the world community problematic is that the vast majority of the present commentators have little knowledge of and no direct experience with the people and conditions they are writing about.

It should be apparent by now that the kind of mutual exchange and dialogue that will have to become the central ethic and value of the university community is not a tolerance of mutual political correctness. It will require confronting oneself and one's cultural community and having outsiders ask questions as well. We must realize that what people have produced as culture, as ways of surviving and of bringing quality to their lives, is not theirs alone. It is for all to see, study, and appreciate for its strengths and weaknesses. Anyone who has even been immersed alone or as a minority in a foreign world, whether that world is foreign or domestic, knows that this is very hard work. The person who entered that community and became part of it long enough to learn its social reality is not the same person when he or she walks out. It is much harder to be a supremist of any sort after you have encountered other people as peers and have been a part of their world.

What we propose is not only hard work, but it adds a social and interpersonal rigor to the college experience and opens additional and important areas of excellence. It means that students will have to mature interpersonally, learn to communicate with others, and step outside of their social class, ethnic, and national worlds. The European wealthy have always known that it is better to study European history in Europe and art in Paris. Reading the novelist James Joyce made greater sense while in Dublin, as does listening to the recordings of the jazz bassist Charlie Mingus in New York. How did we ever come to think that people of many different backgrounds could study and appreciate Joyce or Mingus without any sense of Dublin or New York?

Students of all backgrounds can become good at computing if they have access to computers because computing skills are experiential. The more you work with a system or software, the more skillful you become in using it. Donald Fixico and Milga Morales-Nadal, in sharing with us their cultural views of education, questioned the wisdom of the walled campus. They spoke for the power of apprenticeships, direct experience, and being in the community as alternative and effective ways of educating.

We need to reduce the walls, not eliminate them. There are benefits and advantages to spending periods of time on a college or university campus. Students who go from walled residential communities to walled campuses do not appreciate the opportunity to reflect as do students who come from the work world or a period of immersion in domestic or overseas communities other than their own. Students who have no experience in the world really need to go into that world before they come to the university. Those of us who have taught more experienced "reentry" students can see the difference. They have experiences to draw on, they will aggressively question what is taught, they will challenge you with other perspectives, they will read everything and work very hard. They are the ideal student, yet their grades from twenty years ago are often very poor and their academic records right out of high school may have showed little promise. Clearly, we are not advocating that students wait twenty years before beginning college. But it is clear that not everyone is ready at the same time and that experience in the world is essential for an optimal educational experience.

For many, broadening the curriculum and decentering the Eurocentric core poses other problems. First, most faculty cannot imagine what there is to study outside of the core curriculum and specialties. These are the majority of faculty, who may have studied others from a Eurocentric perspective and have no first-hand experience as peers with people of color and even Europeans of other social classes. Their greatest fear is that the other foci of the curriculum will be a glorification of what they know about others, which are essentially stereotypes of the other ethnic and national worlds. When African American studies began, there was laughter that it would be "chicken eating 101" or that Indian studies would be "peyote smoking" and Mexican American studies would be "siesta time." For those who have bothered to look, where sufficient resources have been provided, ethnic studies courses have evolved into solid academic offerings with a few exceptions (as is the case in any other area or discipline). As has been the case among European scholars, other domestic and national group scholars are going to want to bring their best ideas and most difficult problems to the forum, just as occurs today in ethnic studies.

A second problem with decentering the European emphasis will involve determining what will constitute new measures of intelligence. We now make decisions about all students based on their standard English-only test performance. If these students are bicultural, tricultural, bilingual, and trilingual (as are most students of color), they often have lower standard English verbal test scores than their monocultural European American peers. Within a multicultural educational context, the absurdity of such a conclusion is immediately apparent. The English-based standard should not be the only standard and the only measure. In fact, who is more knowledgeable and who has had to learn more? Clearly, the answer is the student who has learned more than one language and can conduct himself or herself in more than one community. How can a bicultural and bilingual person be less intelligent than someone who has never stepped outside of his or her own culture and community? Regardless of what might be a student's native intelligence, a multiculturalist would view a student who is either domestically and/or internationally bicultural and bilingual as more accomplished.

A third problem posed by decentering the European world view is that of merit. Who will deserve to be in the university and how will different grades of achievement and merit be determined? The kind of multicultural university proposed here calls for a more demanding basis of excellence rather than less. It should no longer be sufficient to have high grades and test scores through one cultural focus. Students should have higher grades and test scores if they come into a university instructed by their own ethnic, language, and social class faculty. For these students, the university is an extension of their homes and communities. But excellence in a multicultural university will require superior grades across several cultural foci and at least one domestic and foreign community experience. This is a higher definition of excellence and one that students from all backgrounds can strive toward.

The multiculturalism we pose here does not directly answer the question of who deserves to be in the university. But there is a surprise. We have as a nation already answered this question. Carefully study any guide to American colleges and universities, such as Cass and Birnbaum's *Comparative Guide to American Colleges* (1989). What you will find are a few very selective universities and colleges, a few more selective ones, and then the vast majority that are nonselective. Fewer than 10 percent of all the four-year senior colleges and universities in the United States are elite or near elite. But you would never know this from the self-declarations of many colleges and universities in the United States. There are many self-proclaimed elite private schools whose faculty cannot match department by department the range of skill, publications records, and breadth of coverage of their local state university faculty. Yet to many middle-class consumers, the private school is by definition better. This is not educational excellence. It is social class arrogance and an attempt to use the university as a way to maintain class privilege regardless of native talent.

The point is that this nation has achieved because, in comparison to most other countries, it has a broad base of college- and university-trained citizens. Only the students who complete degrees at our most select institutions may compare to British or French university graduates, but the fact that we have so many more people who are better educated than their overseas non-college-trained counterparts has given this nation a competitive edge. This could not happen without the large number of virtually open enrollment private and public colleges and universities in the United States. So we do not see the multicultural university as the exclusive province of either elite or nonelite schools. Whoever is going to be a competitive player in the next century will have to be multicultural. We may see a new configuration of very selective colleges and universities developing in the next century depending upon whom can adapt and refine such a curriculum and faculty first. Such a development will not be an exception to the history of university reforms in the United States. As William King pointed out, this is exactly how change and reassignments of institutional prestige have occurred.

Finally, multiculturalism is likely to achieve something that the Eurocentric university was not able to do: Enable students to rise above their native cultures, to look squarely at the myths of their elders. If you know only one world view, you cannot rise above it. All you can do is defend it. To know other views and to be in community with others who know your view and other views makes it possible to see yourself within your own culture and to not reflect on the possibilities. As in the case of having domestic and overseas community experiences, students who reach this level of reflection will no longer be the same. They will still be members of their own communities, but it will not be by default but rather by choice. Those who return to their native communities will then be grounded in their culture in a reflective and knowledgeable way that will not require denying a place in their world for others or other cultural communities.

A NEW UNIVERSALISM

As long as having a Eurocentric education is considered the universal measure of what an educated man or woman is, then all Europeans and all things European must be central to the university curriculum. Everything else is secondary. By replacing the Eurocentric foci within a multicultural one, no single world experience is the one and only way. What will then become universal will be the search in all human experiences for meaning, peace, happiness, and the ideal community. A person who has knowledge and experience across communities can reflect upon the achievements and failures, strengths and weaknesses of several communities. Such people are closer to achieving individuality apart from community than those who have never ventured away from the taken-for-granted and familiar. They are also closer to the ancient ideal of the university and are better prepared to provide counsel and leadership in the next century. For real knowledge belongs to no one. It cannot be possessed, claimed, or controlled by any race, nationality, or culture. It belongs to all of us.

REFERENCES

Cass, James, and M. Birnbaum. 1989. *Comparative Guide to American Colleges*. New York: Harper and Row.

Gilley, J. Wade. 1991. *Thinking About American Higher Education: The 1990s and Beyond*. New York: Maxwell Macmillan International.

Noley, Grayson. 1991. "Fear, Higher Education and Change." *The NEA Higher Education Journal*. 7(2): 105-114.

Index

Academic community life, 159
Academic grading and assessment, 135-143
Acquired Immune Deficiency Syndrome (AIDS), 165
Afrocentricity and multicultural education: assumptions, 41; contribution, 46-53; definition, 45-46; ethical dimensions, 56-59; grounding, 42-43; historical perspective, 54-56; origin and development, 43-45
Aging population, 11-12
Alaska Urban Indians, 104
Alianza Federal de Mercedes, 79
American Association for Retired Persons (AARP), 12
American College Test (ACT), 137
American Indians. *See* Native Americans
American universities, origins, 26-31
Americans for Generational Equity, 11
Angel, Ronald, 81
Aptheker, Herbert, 69
Asante, Molefi, 43, 46-47
Assimilation: African-American, oppression to, 71-75; common characteristics of opposition, 81-83; cultural resistance, 68-71; Euro-Amercian dominance, 65-68, 83-84; Mexican-American, opposition to, 78-81; Native-American, opposition to, 67, 69, 75-78; opposition to assimilation, 65-86; opposition to racial-ethnic cultures, 65-86; pressures forbidding, 66, 83-84; tradition vs assimilation balance, 109-110
Association of American Colleges, 161, 162
Astin, Alexander W., 136-137

Banks, James, 97, 163, 165, 167
Bay, Mia, 32
Belpre, Pura, 94
Bilingualism, 10, 95-97; English-only policies, 80
Blauner, Bob, 66
Bobo, Juan, 93
Bracetti, Mariana, 94
Brown University, 28

Budgetary implications, 173-175
Bureau of Indian Affairs, 116
Buthaune, Mary McLeod, 52

Campos, Pedro Albizu, 97
Catholicism, 25, 67, 92
Cavers, Dean, 117
Cheikh Anta Dion, 54
Civil disobedience, 74
Clarke, John Henrik, 23-26
College entrance examinations:
    American College Test (ACT),
    137; Scholastic Aptitude Test
    (SAT), 15, 118, 137
Columbia University, 28
Community involvement, 170-171
Community experience, 156-157;
    academic, student, and
    community life, 159;
    combination of interdisciplinary
    competency levels with
    integrated departments of
    community experience, 157;
    integrated model with domestic
    and foreign community
    experience, 156;
    interdisciplinary competency
    levels with domestic and foreign
    community experience, 156
Competency levels, 155-157
Computers, 145-152
Congress of Racial Equality
    (CORE), 74
Cooper, Anna Julia, 43
Cordero, Juan, 93
Culturally-diverse university. *See*
    Multicultural university
Curriculum, 162-178

Dartmouth, 28
Darwin, Charles, 32
de Certeau, Michael, 69-70
de Gobineau, Joseph Arthur, 32

Demographics, 1-19; aging, 11-12;
    college, 17-18; education, 12-18;
    high school, 12-13; immigration,
    9-11; middle class, 8-9; states,
    7-8; world, 4-7
Dropouts, high school ranking by
    state, 12
Druker, Ernest, 17
DuBois, W.E.B., 43, 47, 52-53, 56,
    73, 161
Dunster, Henry, 26-27

Eco, Umberto, 69
English-only policies, 80
Ethnic studies, 41-61, 153-160;
    Afrocentricity, 41-61; teaching,
    164; transitional organization,
    153
Eurocentric culture, 21-39
European Common Market, 10
European universities, origins,
    24-26
Event/phenomenon, 166

Faculty development, 171-173
Finnestad, Ragnhild B., 48
Fiske, John, 69
Fixico, Donald, 149, 155, 181, 182

Garcia Marquez, Gabriel , 81
Gee, James P., 138
Gender, 170
Gonzalez, Corky, 79
Gordon, Milton, 66
Gore, Albert, 145
Great problem/theme, 168
Guthrie, Robert V., 33
Gutman, Herber G., 68, 72
Gwaltney, John Langston, 70, 73
Gyekye, Kwane, 45, 52

Hall, E.T., 141
Hammerschlag, Carl, 119
Hare, Nathan, 52
Harvard, 27-29
Head Start, 17
Hechter, Michael, 69-70
High school dropouts, ranking by
    state, 12
Hollinger, David A., 23
Howard, J., 141

Illich, Ivan, 23
Immigration, 9-11
Indians. *See* Native Americans
Institute of Puerto Rican Policy,
    Inc., 89
Integrated model, domestic-foreign
    community experience, 156
Integration of traditional ethnic
    studies, 154
Interdisciplinary competency
    levels, 155
Interdisciplinary competency levels
    with domestic and foreign
    community experience, 156-157
Ireland, 70
Italians, 66

Jackson, Jesse, 58, 74-75
Jackson, Reggie, 173
Jefferson, Thomas, 67
Jews, 66, 67, 74

Kamii, M.,141
Karenga, Maulana, 126, 154
Keefe, Susan, 80
King, Dr. Martin Luther, 74-75
Kuhn, Thomas, 27

Malcolm X, 50, 54
Marden, Charles F., 28

Mexican-Americans, opposition to
    assimilation, 78-81
Meyer, Gladys, 28
Middle class, 8-9
Ming, Tu Wei, 45
Minority middle class, 8
Mormon church, 76
Moses, Robert, 141
Multicultural university, 126-185;
    academic grading and
    assessment, 135-143;
    curriculum, 162-178;
    organization, 153-160; planning
    for change, 126-134
Muscogee Creeks, 103, 105-106,
    110, 112, 113, 155

National Association for
    Advancement of Colored People
    (NAACP), 73
National Science Foundation, 14
Native Americans: Alaska Urban
    Indians, 104; assimilation, 67,
    69, 75-78; Bureau of Indian
    Affairs, 116; concepts of oral
    and written word, 113-114;
    educational results, 117-118;
    government education and
    training, 115-117; higher
    education, 103-122;
    intellectualism, 110-111;
    Muscogee Creeks, 103, 105-106,
    110, 112, 113; native methods
    obtaining knowledge, 111-113;
    personal identity, 107-109;
    polarization within groups,
    104-105; racism, 110; relocation
    programs, 116; Seminoles, 103,
    110, 112, 113; substandard
    educational results, 117-118;
    thought and mainstream, 115;
    traditional life, 106-107;
    tradition vs assimilation balance,
    109-110

NATO, 4
Newton, Isaac, 27
Niangoran-Bouah, G., 54
Nieto, Sonia, 93
Nixon, Richard, 73, 76

Organizing multicultural university, 153-151

Padilla, A.M., 80
Pell Grants, 13
Pennsylvania, University of, 28
Population, countries ranked, 5
Population, 3-12; aging, 11; implications, 6-7; projections, 5
Preschools; Head Start, 17
Princeton University, 9, 28, 32
Puerto Rico and Puerto Ricans, 87-102, 155, 157; Bobo, Juan, 93; Bracetti, Mariana, 94; Campos, Pedro Albizu, 97; Cordero, Juan, 93; culture and education, 87-102; Institute of Puerto Rican Policy, Inc., 89; Nieto, Sonia, 93; Rodriguez de Tio, Lola, 94; Stevens-Arroyo, Antonio, 90; Vega, Marta Moreno, 91

Racial-ethnic cultures, opposition to, 65-86; African-American, 71-75; Mexican-American, opposition to assimilation, 78-81; Native-American, opposition to assimilation, 67, 69, 75-78
Reagan, Ronald, 73
Rodriguez de Tio, Lola, 94
Roman Catholicism, 25, 67, 92
Rush, Benjamin, 67
Rutgers University, 28

Scholastic Aptitude Test (SAT), 15, 118, 137
Seminoles, 103, 110, 112, 113
Sexual orientation, 170
Smith, Samuel Stanhope, 32
Spencer, Herbert, 115
Srole, L, 67
Stanford University, 120
Stevens-Arroyo, Antonio, 90
Strategic planning, 125-133
Stuckey, Sterling, 74
Student Nonviolent Corrodinating Committee (SNCC), 74

Taylor, Edward B., 115
Teaching by great problem/theme, 168
Teaching by using event/phenomenon, 166
Teaching ethnic studies, 164
Telecommunications, 145-152
Texas Christian University, 120
Tienda, M., 80
Tijerina, Reies, 79
Tradition vs. assimilation balance, 109-110
Transitional organization with ethnic studies, 153
Tribalism, 21-19
TRIO, 17
Trungpa, Chogyam, 161

UCLA, 9
UNESCO, 6
Universities, history of, 17-18, 21-39; *See* also Multicultural universities; American universities, origins, 26-31; European universities, origins, 24-26

Vega, Marta Moreno, 91

Virgina, University of, 28

Warner, W. Lloyd, 67
Washington, Booker T., 73
Washington, George, 67
Wells, H.G., 3

William and Mary College, 28
Wisconsin Plan, 120
Witt, Shirely Hill, 76
Woodson, Carter G. 43

Yale, 28

About the Contributors

GALE AULETTA YOUNG is Professor of Communications and Co-Director of the Center for the Study of Intercultural Relations at California State University at Hayward. Her publications and consulting focus on communications issues in multicultural settings. She is co-recipient of the Woman of the Year Award for contributing to diversity in the California State University, 1988.

OCTAVE BAKER is senior partner with Communications Training Consultants in Sunnyvale, California and a lecturer in the Engineering Management Department at Santa Clara University. As an organizational consultant and trainer, he specializes in helping organizations value and manage cultural diversity in the workplace.

BENJAMIN P. BOWSER is Associate Professor of Sociology and Social Services at California State University at Hayward, Associate Editor of Sage Race Relations Abstracts, and coeditor of *Impacts of Racism on White Americans* (1981). He has held administrative positions and consulted in student services, computer management, and graduate studies. His research and publications have focused on race relations and AIDS prevention.

JOE R. FEAGIN is Graduate Research Professor of Sociology at the University of Florida. His research interests are centrally in the area of racial and ethnic relations. His latest book is *Living with Racism* (1994).

DONALD L. FIXICO is Professor of History at Western Michigan University in Kalamazoo. His writings have been on American Indians in the twentieth century, and he is the author of *Termination and Relocation, 1945-1960* (1986) and editor of *Native Views of Indian-White Historical Relations* (1989). He has lectured and been a visiting professor at a number of universities in the United States and United Kingdom.

HAROLD L. HODGKINSON is the Director for Demographic Policy, Institute for Educational Leadership in Washington, D.C. He has directed major research projects for the Carnegie Commission, the U.S. Office of Education, the Exxon Foundation, the Ford Foundation, and the Atlantic Richfield Foundation. He is the author of twelve books and over 200 articles and lectures widely on educational policy issues.

ETTA R. HOLLINS is Professor of Education at California State University at Hayward. She has spoken on preparing teachers before the California State Curriculum Commission, the National Council of Chief State School Officers, and a number of state offices of education. She is editor of *Teaching Diverse Populations* (1993) and author of *Applying the Wisdom of Practice in Teaching Diverse Populations* (1994).

TERRY JONES is Professor of Sociology and Social Services at California State University at Hayward, Vice President of the California Faculty Association, and Co-Director of the Center for the Study of Intercultural Relations at CSU, Hayward. He has published and consulted in the areas of race and racism, criminal justice, and the sociology of sports. He was voted Outstanding Professor, 1990, and recipient of the Human Rights Award for the California Faculty Association, 1991.

MAULANA KARENGA is Professor and Chair of the Black Studies Department at California State University at Long Beach. He is also chairman of US Organization and Director of the African-African Cultural Center and The Institute of Pan-African Studies, Los Angeles. He is widely known as the creator of Kwanzaa and the Nguzo Saba. He is the author of numerous scholarly articles and eight books, including *Introduction to Black Studies* (1991).

WILLIAM M. KING is Professor and Coordinator of Afro-American Studies in the Center for Studies of Ethnicity and Race in America at the University of Colorado at Boulder. His specialties are science and society, the philosophy of science, and African American history in Colorado. His latest book is *Going to Meet the Man: The Last Public Execution* (1990).

BONNIE L. MITCHELL is a Ph.D. candidate in Sociology at the University on Texas at Austin. She has extensive community-based work experience with Native Americans and has held administrative posts and visiting lectureships at several colleges and universities.

MILGA MORALES-NADAL is Assistant Professor of Education at Brooklyn College of the City University of New York. Her doctoral study focused on bilingual education and developmental psychology. She is on the Board of ASPIRA of New York and is project director for the Bilingual Teacher Education Program at the School of Education.

ARTHUR E. PARIS is Associate Professor of Sociology in the Maxwell School at Syracuse University. He is author of *Black Pentecostalism: Southern Religion in an Urban World* (1982). His current work focuses on American urban policy and technology and computer issues.

CHARLES V. WILLIE is Professor of Education and Urban Studies, Graduate School of Education, Harvard University. He served on President Carter's Commission on Mental Health, was on the board of directors of the Social Science Research Council and the Council of the American Sociological Association, and is a former President of the Eastern Sociological Society. His more recent book is the coedited *The Education of African-Americans* (1990).

ISBN 0-275-94767-X

90000>

9 780275 947675

HARDCOVER BAR CODE

EAN